Departmental Leadership in Higher Education

SRHE and Open University Press Imprint
General Editor: Heather Eggins

Current titles include:

Cathering Bargh *et al.*: *University Leadership*
Ronald Barnett: *The Idea of Higher Education*
Ronald Barnett: *The Limits of Competence*
Ronald Barnett: *Higher Education*
Ronald Barnett: *Realizing the University in an age of supercomplexity*
Neville Bennett *et al.*: *Skills Development in Higher Education and Employment*
John Biggs: *Teaching for Quality Learning at University*
David Boud *et al.* (eds): *Using Experience for Learning*
David Boud and Nicky Solomon (eds): *Work-based Learning*
Etienne Bourgeois *et al.*: *The Adult University*
Tom Bourner *et al.* (eds): *New Directions in Professional Higher Education*
John Brennan *et al.* (eds): *What Kind of University?*
Anne Brockbank and Ian McGill: *Facilitating Reflective Learning in Higher Education*
Stephen Brookfield and Stephen Preskill: *Discussion as a Way of Teaching*
Ann Brooks: *Academic Women*
Sally Brown and Angela Glasner (eds): *Assessment Matters in Higher Education*
John Cowan: *On Becoming an Innovative University Teacher*
Gerard Delanty: *Challenging Knowledge*
Gillian Evans: *Calling Academia to Account*
Sinclair Goodlad: *The Quest for Quality*
Harry Gray (ed.): *Universities and the Creation of Wealth*
Andrew Hannan and Harold Silver: *Innovating in Higher Education*
Norman Jackson and Helen Lund (eds): *Benchmarking for Higher Education*
Merle Jacob and Tomas Hellström (eds): *The Future of Knowledge Production in the Academy*
Peter Knight and Paul Trowler: *Departmental Leadership in Higher Education*
Mary Lea and Barry Stierer (eds): *Student Writing in Higher Education*
Elaine Martin: *Changing Academic Work*
Ian McNay (ed.): *Higher Education and its Communities*
David Palfreyman and David Warner (eds): *Higher Education and the Law*
Craig Prichard: *Making Managers in Universities and Colleges*
Michael Prosser and Keith Trigwell: *Understanding Learning and Teaching*
John Richardson: *Researching Student Learning*
Stephen Rowland: *The Enquiring University Teacher*
Yoni Ryan and Ortrun Zuber-Skerritt (eds): *Supervising Postgraduates from Non-English Speaking Backgrounds*
Maggi Savin-Baden: *Problem-based Learning in Higher Education*
Peter Scott (ed.): *The Globalization of Higher Education*
Peter Scott: *The Meanings of Mass Higher Education*
Anthony Smith and Frank Webster (eds): *The Postmodern University?*
Colin Symes and John McIntyre (eds): *Working Knowledge*
Peter G. Taylor: *Making Sense of Academic Life*
Susan Toohey: *Designing Courses for Higher Education*
Paul R. Trowler: *Academics Responding to Change*
David Warner and David Palfreyman (eds): *Higher Education Management*
Diana Woodward and Karen Ross: *Managing Equal Opportunities in Higher Education*

Departmental Leadership in Higher Education

Peter T. Knight
Paul R. Trowler

The Society for Research into Higher Education
& Open University Press

Published by SRHE and
Open University Press
Celtic Court
22 Ballmoor
Buckingham
MK18 1XW

email: enquiries@openup.co.uk
world wide web: www.openup.co.uk

and
325 Chestnut Street
Philadelphia, PA 19106, USA

First published 2001

A catalogue record of this book is available from the British Library

ISBNs 0 335 206751 (pb)   0 335 20676 X (hb)

Library of Congress Cataloging-in-Publication Data
Departmental leadership in higher education/Peter T. Knight and Paul R.
   Trowler.
     p. cm.
   Includes bibliographical references and index.
   ISBN 0-335-20676-X — ISBN 0-335-20675-1 (pbk.)
     1. Education, Higher—Administration.   2. Universities and colleges—
Departments.   3. Departmental chairmen (Universities)   4. Educational
leadership.   I. Knight, Peter, 1950–   II. Trowler, Paul.
LB2341.D4143 2000
378.I′01—dc21   00-060676

Typeset by Graphicraft Limited, Hong Kong
Printed in Great Britain by St Edmundsbury Press, Bury St Edmunds, Suffolk

Contents

Preface

He [Peter Senge] challenges our traditional notion of leadership in traditional machine organisations where change is regarded as needing to be 'driven' and 'from the top'. His alternative is to explore the parallels between companies and living organisms. Growth is organic and comes in addition to what is already happening, not instead of existing structures. The role of the leader or change manager is thus one of preparing the ground, nurturing the growth and fostering creativity. Work with the organisation as if it is alive, and the growth, development and learning comes naturally.

(Training Zone 2000)

This book is primarily about leading subject departments in higher education, although we often write 'teams or departments' because our analysis is, we believe, broadly applicable to sub-sections of departments and to other functional groupings such as programme teams. So in large departments, especially in the natural sciences, people may identify with a sub-unit or team as much as they do with the department as a whole and, in many ways, these teams are departments in miniature. We also suggest that the teams responsible for teaching academic programmes leading to named awards (a BA in history, an MSc in information and communications technology, a doctoral programme in public administration) can be treated as equivalents to departments, although that position needs to be qualified. While some institutions have effectively devolved mid-level management to programme teams, and departments have become vestigial, in others programme teams struggle against departments for identity and authority. In these cases, leading a programme team may be a thankless administrative job and nothing more. Nevertheless we talk of teams and departments because most analyses of how programme leadership could be improved come up with suggestions that are tantamount to making the programme team more like a department, with their own budgets and spaces, specialist academic, technical and support staff, and research activities. So this is a book about communities of practice in HE, communities that usually take the form of departments but that may be sub-sections or programme teams.

In focusing on this meso-level between the individual and the organization, we find that we are in the company of increasing numbers of theorists, the crucial importance of workgroups or teams having become increasingly recognized in the later part of the 1990s (Northouse, 1997). Although much of what we say is applicable to leading faculties and schools – to the work of deans – this is not a book about that level, one reason being that many faculties cannot be described as communities of practice in the same way as departments, which means that any analysis would need to be somewhat different from the ones we offer here. At the 'local' level, as opposed to faculties, interactions involve a much closer relationship with individuals and there is more personal investment in those relationships and closer 'identity' links. The task at hand is usually more focused and clearer to all parties, and has often already been the subject of mutual 'constructive' work, which has happened within a network of ongoing relationships in a variety of contexts.

Another reason why we concentrate on the departmental level and below is because we argue that much of the work of leading is contingent, by which we mean that it involves dealing with the specifics of a time, a place and a set of people. Ours is more of a particularistic than a universalistic approach. If we agree with Hopkins (1992) that leading is more like sailing than driving then the significance of context is brought to the foreground: the wind, the tide, the currents, the characteristics of the boat and its crew. There are, of course, regularities, general patterns and recurrences in leading but an understanding of what is general about the work has to be combined with an appreciation of specifics. So although what deans do has much in common with what departmental chairs do, it is sufficiently different for it to be unwise to claim that what we say here is as useful for the dean-to-be as it is for the new departmental chair or head of department. Bolton's (2000) book is more obviously about managing faculties and schools. That said, it would be an odd book about mid-level academic leadership that had nothing to offer deans and we suggest that our view of what is involved in leadership (Chapters 1–3) and our suggestions for leading (especially Chapters 5–9) will be thought-provoking.

Our aim in this book is to provide some tools for reflection on the practice of leading at the departmental level and below in higher education. In particular we offer a conceptual torch to illuminate practice and highlight the possibilities for changed practice. If leading well is partly about thinking well, then (to change the metaphor) we present some food for thought. This is definitely *not* a book of axioms for leaders, a prefabricated pack of self-assembly 'tips and tricks': one of our key theses is that situational contingencies mean that such packs have strictly limited utility. We do, however, indicate a preferred *approach* to leading in higher education contexts, and a picture of what desirable communities of practice there might look like. We recognize though that how far and how frequently these ideas are realized is subject to the vagaries of task, context and what we call the 'rules of appropriateness' in particular settings.

In general we prefer to talk about leading rather than leadership because the verb avoids the noun's implication that a commodity called 'leadership' really exists and, presumably, might be acquired by anyone with the right sort of currency. The position that we develop in Chapters 1–3 is that there are problems with expecting 'leadership' to improve higher education *and* that thoughtful people (leaders) can improve it by repeatedly acting wisely in many different circumstances (leading). This emphasizes the situated, constructed, dynamic and human elements that can get reified into abstraction by talk of 'leadership'. Plainly – and not least in a book that must deal in generalities – it would be absurd to maintain that leading is only about specifics, which is why we insist that leading is about praxis, the interacting of thinking and doing, the blends of understanding of the general with understanding of the specific. Despite our unease with the term, 'leadership' is embedded in discourse to such a degree that it would sound too artificial if we always replaced the noun with the verb. We also prefer to talk of leading rather than managing (and of leadership rather than management) because we think that leading is 'managing plus', that is managing change with a fundamental concern for values and people that guides understandings of appropriateness and desirability.

So this is a book about the activity of leading departments and other teams that can be treated as communities of practice in higher education institutions. Organizationally, our interest is in activity systems and communities that are considerably smaller than the whole institution and more complex than the lone academic or faculty member. As the terminology suggests, our interest is also an international one and we indiscriminately use 'faculty' as a synonym for 'academic staff' and mean the same when we refer to 'chairs' as we do when writing of 'heads of departments'.

The book is organized in two parts: 'Contexts' and 'Issues'. In making this distinction we do not wish to separate theory from practice: we know that this is impossible and our aim is, as we say, to infuse improved practice with good theory. Rather, the distinction is there to help busy readers navigate the book more easily. The first part of the book (Chapters 1–4) sets out the context of the discussion, both in terms of the relevant theory and of the environment of higher education. In offering ways of thinking about leading in higher education it draws from work on higher education and on organizational management, and international research on school effectiveness and improvement. Chapter 4 indicates what these ideas can mean by assessing their usefulness in understanding complex educational organizations: in this case schools.

In Part 2 (Chapters 5–10) we offer a contribution to the ongoing dialogue about leading in six key areas of higher education. These chapters are based on review of a wide literature, our experience, data and careful thought founded in research as well as practical experience of leading at the departmental level in higher education, including (for one of us) as head of department. The book as a whole is informed by data from a number of studies with which we have been involved including research into the experiences of new academics (Knight and Trowler, 1999; Trowler and Knight, 1999). These have ranged across all educational sectors, as have our academic interests over some years. We conducted web and email enquiries with academic leaders specifically for this book and use a number of illustrative quotes from them throughout it. What each of our studies has had in common is an interest in facilitating appropriate change and professional learning in educational organizations.

Thanks go to the chairs and other leaders who responded to our international electronic enquiries about their work. Their words greatly enrich our writing. Thanks also to those individuals who helped spread the word about our enquiry and encouraged practising leaders in higher education to spend some valuable time reflecting on and writing about their experience.

Peter T. Knight and Paul R. Trowler

Part 1

Contexts

Part I

Contexts

1

Changing

A long-standing popular misconception places a Great Person with a Large Idea
at the front end of change . . . Ideas become realistic and capable of some steering
as they reflect organizational capability and tested environmental possibilities.
New organizational ideas are symbolic experiments in the art of the possible.

(Clark, 1998: 143)

Preview

Leading, as opposed to management, is intimately connected to change
interventions: leading involves attempting to bring about change that is
desired (at least by some) or challenging change that is undesired (at least
by some). Theories of leadership always involve theories of change. Implicitly or explicitly they try to tell us something about the mechanisms of
change. Theories of change, meanwhile, have implications for leadership
approaches; some suggest that leadership, as traditionally understood, is
inappropriate. While later chapters focus on leadership, this one concen-
trates on exploring how change happens and on what prevents it from
happening or subverts it. Rather than try to encapsulate theories of change
in one grand schema the chapter gives an overview of theories of change
and introduces social practice theory, which is discussed in more detail in
Chapter 3.

Perspectives on change and its
implementation: an overview

Borrowing from and expanding on Lindquist (1978) and Elmore (1978) we
can distinguish five perspectives on change: bureaucratic process; conflict
and bargaining; collegial; social practice; and technical-rational. Each of
these involves three dimensions in varying degrees of prominence: the descriptive, the explanatory and the normative. Some of the perspectives are
more concerned than the others to offer practical advice to managers and
leaders and so emphasize the normative dimension: they are what Alvesson
(1990: 39) calls 'pragmatic' theories. Others are more analytical and 'academic' in character and so give more emphasis to the explanatory dimension;
Alvesson describes them as 'pure'. All offer a description of reality, at least

implicitly, although some confuse the descriptive and the normative so it becomes unclear whether the reader is being offered a description of what is or what should be. We will briefly review them here.

Bureaucratic process theory and change

Descriptive and analytical rather than normative, this perspective focuses on the recurrent behaviours of those at the 'ground-level' of organizations and on the 'implementation' of policy and change there. The exercise of discretion in the following of routines is a key issue and so power is seen as fragmented and dispersed: the informal distribution of power may be quite different from that which appears on organizational charts. To borrow a metaphor from Brown and Duguid (1996a), the policy or vision of change developed by the 'top team' of an organization or by government provides a route map, but is not sensitive to local road conditions, which demand responsiveness and the exercise of discretion from road users. Staff at the local level need to take the complexity and unpredictability of 'real life' into account, interpreting government policy or management vision as they put it into action in often ambiguous situations. They often need to find 'work-arounds' to problems and issues unforeseen by policy makers or senior managers. The fact that this discretion is both necessary and inevitable is illustrated by the fact that the phrase 'work to rule' refers to a form of industrial action designed to inconvenience and delay normal processes.

Actors at the local level do not just find practical ways of implementing change, however. They have their own situated rationality, which can lead them to amend or ignore aspects of centrally derived policy. Staff working at the local level are perceived to be 'policy making' too in this perspective, rather than simply 'implementing' policy. Their situated rationality may partly be based on professional ethics, on cultural characteristics or a number of other locally relevant factors of a structural character. It may also be partly based on judgements about the profitability for them of behaving in one way rather than another (Levine, 1980). The New-Right notion of producer-capture emphasizes the need to counter that kind of self-interested behaviour within public organizations, replacing it with a market-driven ethos.

A theoretically developed account of the bureaucratic process model comes from Martin Lipsky (1980). Lipsky focuses on 'street-level bureaucrats' (SLBs): those who interact directly with citizens in the course of their job and have substantial discretion in the execution of their work. This definition would include most academics, even if many would balk at the designation 'bureaucrat' and not see the university as a bureaucracy, although higher education institutions (HEIs) arguably have many of the characteristics of bureaucracies (Stroup, 1966). SLBs have considerable power because of the discretion they must exercise in making decisions about the people they interact with, in the allocation of resources and in decisions about whether, and how, to apply rules. In addition they use their power in order to control clients as far as possible, sometimes in the interests of an easier life for themselves. They may also modify their conception of the job so that any dissonance between what they are supposed to do and what they actually do is minimized. In periods during which the provision of resources does not match the demand for them, SLBs may respond in terms of the way they conceptualize their clients, including stereotyping, so drawing distinctions between them to rationalize the exercise of discretion that favours one group over another.

Considering the implications of this perspective for educational change, Smyth *et al.* (2000) point out that a range of ethnographic studies of schools have shown that when teachers oppose or doubt the soundness of change proposals they can and do respond to them in a variety of ways (see also Wolcott, 1977; Apple, 1982, 1989; Broadfoot, 1988; Woods, 1995). They may ignore the innovation, reconstruct it, selectively apply aspects of it or just refuse to comply. Trowler's study of the English unchartered university 'NewU' (Trowler, 1998) found the same things happening among academics. The decision to adopt some or all of the components of the 'credit framework' (modularity, semesterization, franchising, etc.) elicited a wide variety of responses among the university's academic staff. These were articulated on multiple levels: front-stage, back-stage and under-the-stage (that is, respectively, in the official arena, where deals are done in private, and where gossip is purveyed among trusted colleagues). The attempt to implement the policy was met with compliance (both enthusiastic and reluctant), with resistance, with coping strategies, and with attempts to reconstruct the policy during the 'implementation phase'. The effects of these responses were largely unpredictable and involved outcomes not intended by any actor. In particular the cultural configuration of 'NewU' as an organization changed, but not in ways that were originally intended or that would be considered desirable by most observers.

This perspective suggests that Perrenoud's comment about teachers probably applies to academics just as much:

> Like soldiers in armies the world over . . . teachers make the best of a bad job, ride out the storm, laugh things off in self-defence, complain behind the scenes, wait for the minister of education to change or 'calm down', for the authorities to forge their own decision or for the experts to repudiate their idols; they are cunning, they conceal what they are doing by working alone behind closed doors, and those supposed to inspect their work may turn a blind eye. They do not ask to be entirely independent; it is enough to be able to bend the rules.
>
> (Perrenoud, 1996: 516, quoted by Smyth *et al.*, 2000: 51)

Problems with applying the bureaucratic process perspective on change in universities
The key problem with the application of this perspective in a university context lies in the word 'bureaucrat': although academics conform to the

definition of an SLB in formal terms, the thrust of Lipsky's argument and examples portrays SLBs as asocial agents making individualized decisions in a clear, rule-bound framework. This may or may not be an accurate description of the kind of welfare officials from whom his examples are largely derived, but it is certainly not an accurate depiction of academics. In particular, allegiance to an 'academic tribe' operating within disciplinary territories and the professional ethos and norms that are associated with them mean that academics are likely to respond to policy and change in ways that are more complex, and possibly less self-interested than Lipsky's perspective might suggest.

In addition there are areas of academic practice that do not involve a 'client' in the direct way Lipsky conceptualizes them. Funded research, for example, clearly has a client: the funder. But the nature of both the interaction and the relationship between the two parties is quite different from that of the SLB interacting with a member of the public. Interactions are spasmodic; they concern an area of common interest rather than the direct provision of a service from SLB to client. Moreover the academic's behaviour is at least as much constrained by a set of academic rules of appropriateness relating to research as by any other consideration. Applied wholeheartedly to this area of academic life, at least, the bureaucratic perspective becomes tenuous.

The conflict and bargaining perspective on change

Descriptive and analytical rather than normative, the conflict and bargaining perspective sees the outcomes of change as resulting from battles over scarce resources; battles that involve the mobilization of power and that are only ever temporarily resolved.

In his case study of New York University, Baldridge (1971: 15–16) presents the main ideas of the perspective:

• Conflict theorists emphasize the fragmentation of social systems into interest groups, each with its own particular goals.
• Conflict theorists study the interaction of these different interest groups and especially the conflict processes by which one group tries to gain advantage over another.
• Interest groups cluster around divergent values, and the study of conflicting interests is a key part of the analysis.
• The study of change is a central feature of the conflict approach, for change is to be expected if the social system is fragmented by divergent values and conflicting interest groups.

Staff, including academic staff, are often viewed as a monolithic group in leadership and management texts (Trowler, 1998), but this misses the differences between them in terms of educational ideologies, personal goals and values, and ideas of self-interest. These differences give rise to highly complex micropolitical situations at the local level. So, for example, Hannan (1980: 6) sees the process of policy formulation in schools as 'best understood in terms of the ideologies and conflicts located in the structure of the school'.

However, conflicts remain implicit and subterranean most of the time, only occasionally bursting through to the surface because 'negotiated orders' (Strauss, 1978) are usually constructed locally, which enables things to get done. Key differences in educational ideology, for example, are brought to the surface by the need to make decisions: for example whether, how and how much academic credit value should be assigned to prior experiential learning (Trowler, 1996). Such decisions both reflect and illustrate sets of values and attitudes, in this case about what counts, and does not count, as higher education.

Authors of the classic texts in this field include Bacharach and Lawler (1980) and Cyert and March (1963), although they were writing in the context of business rather than education. The distribution of power in an organization is a key factor in this literature. According to this view numerous centres of power are mobilized largely in the pursuit of self-interest, with key figures wielding power over the medium to long term but in the context of an unstable overall distribution of power. Power is understood in a number of ways, as Lukes (1974, 1979) describes. We return to Lukes's discussion of power in Chapter 3. Here it is sufficient to identify three of its manifestations. The first involves compulsion with the intention of securing behaviour that will lead to desired outcomes or inflicting sanctions for deviance: making others do what they would not otherwise do (Gerth and Mills, 1970: 180). The second involves agenda-setting and, importantly, exclusion from the agenda. Power is exercised through the creation, reinforcement, reproduction, exclusion and undermining of sets of values and practices in order to delimit the parameters of what is conceived of as sensible, normal, possible and desirable. The third involves the exercise of power through 'discursive capture' (Bowe *et al.*, 1994). In a much more fundamental and 'invisible' way, the socially constitutive power of discourse is used to shape not only what is, and is not, on the agenda but what can and cannot be thought about (Foucault, 1975). In this dimension knowledge and knowing, discourse and personal identity become intertwined in the fabric of social life, which is permeated with power relations. There is a 'network' or 'web' of power in operation, which is largely invisible to participants but 'woven into the activities, events and social relations of bureaucratic organizations' (Foucault, 1977: 13).

Decisions are made on the basis of bargaining and brokering, sometimes with unintended consequences, or consequences that are deleterious to some parties. Rein, for example, talks about decision making as involving the 'achievement of settlements in the face of dilemmas and trade-offs among values' (1983: 211). Similarly, Ball points out that in local situations where conflict and bargaining are taking place, decision making is described by participants in the language of confrontation. They speak of 'rows', 'battles' and 'challenges'. Ball takes:

> virtually all . . . social organizations to be *arenas of struggle*; to be riven with actual or potential conflict between members; to be poorly co-ordinated; to be ideologically diverse . . . Compromises, negotiations and trade-offs, as well as threats, pressure and underhand dealing, have their part to play in the achievement and maintenance of the head-teacher's powers [in schools]. Decision-making is not an abstract rational process which can be plotted on an organizational chart: it is a political process, it is the stuff of micro-political activity.
>
> (1987: 19 and 26, original emphasis)

In its worst case change can become a process of just 'muddling through' (Lindblom, 1959), a directionless process of small steps that are non-cumulative in effect. We describe below how the technical-rational model is predicated on a top-down approach to policy making and its implementation, with the idea that, given that all the prerequisites are in place, policy will be successful and there will be no 'implementation gap' between outcomes as originally envisaged and those that actually occur. The conflict and bargaining model, by contrast, is located in a bottom-up perspective and stresses the importance of conflict and negotiation, of alliances and enmities and of competing definitions of the situation and goals.

Problems with applying the conflict and bargaining perspective on change in universities

The extent to which change really does proceed on the basis of conflict and bargaining at the local level, at least in universities, appears to be quite limited. The negotiated order within most university departments is often quite strong and stable. In the 'NewU' research (Trowler, 1998), our study of new academics (Trowler and Knight, 1999) and our web and email based enquiries about leadership we were far more likely to find correspondents commenting on the consensual nature of daily life than on conflict and diversity.

Decision making by conflict and bargaining became more apparent when considering the situation beyond the departmental level, for example at faculty level where the situation resembled feudal barons fighting for their 'patch' in what they considered to be a zero-sum game. However, Blase and Anderson (1995) – unlike Ball – see this situation as neither inevitable nor, indeed, characteristic of most educational situations. For these authors, as for social practice theorists such as Brown and Duguid (1996a), the relational context within organizations is extremely important. Vicious circles *can* be set in motion in which an adversarial leadership style among formal leaders and a climate of conflict and bargaining reinforce each other. None the less it is equally possible to establish a virtuous circle that emphasizes the building of a climate of shared values together with the exercise of 'power *with*', rather than have formal leaders using 'power *through*' or 'power *over*'. Connectivity can lead to the empowerment of the individual and group and to successful change. This situation is close to the ideal expressed in the collegial perspective, which is discussed next.

The collegial approach to change

Sometimes called the 'developmental' approach, this perspective is normative rather than descriptive or analytical in character and is based more on assumptions about change than on close analysis, although an abundance of case study accounts is available. It assumes that a variety of the needs of individual staff should be met if organizational functioning is to take place and change is to be instituted effectively. It stresses the building of consensus where possible, or at least the sensitive accommodation of change to a variety of needs. Wherever possible, supportive collegial relationships should be built. Participation and control should be spread as widely as possible, for example in joint planning for change among the staff. Widespread ownership of change is considered a vital key to success. To quote Hargreaves:

> Collegiality is rapidly becoming one of the new orthodoxies of educational change and school improvement . . . There are . . . claims, as well as some research evidence, that suggest that the confidence that comes with collegial sharing and support leads to greater readiness to experiment and take risks, and with it a commitment to continuous improvement among teachers as a recognized part of their professional obligation . . . It is also widely viewed as a way of securing effective implementation of externally introduced changes.
>
> (1992: 80)

Thus, for example, Rudduck says of schools:

> If an initiative for change comes from outside the school, then the staff will need to give local meaning to the abstractions of national or regional policy. There must be opportunities for collaborative analysis of the need for change, of the strategies by which change is to be achieved, and of the criteria for judging what progress towards change teachers and their pupils are making. Teachers must feel as individuals and as members of a working group that they own and are in control of the problem of change. Dialogue within working groups is crucial, 'not as a matter of empty courtesy or ritualistic adherence to some vague democratic ethos' (Sarason, 1982: 217), but to bring people in on the logics of planned change.
>
> (1991: 31)

From the collegial perspective, then, the real involvement of everyone concerned in change is crucial to avoid the feeling (and its behavioural consequences) that change is something that happens *to* them, out of their control, rather than something that they actively embrace and feel in control of. In the university context in particular there is a long history of calls for a 'return' to academic community, to organizing the university as a collegium, a community of scholars, rather than, for example, a bureaucracy (Goodman, 1962; Millett, 1962).

Fullan, a thoughtful proponent of collegial ownership of change, identifies what he calls the 'eight basic lessons' of the 'new paradigm' of educational change:

- you can't mandate what matters
- change is a journey, not a blueprint
- problems are our friends (they are inevitable and you can't learn without them)
- vision and strategic planning come later (premature ones blind you)
- individualism and collectivism must have equal power
- neither centralization nor decentralization work (both top-down and bottom-up strategies are necessary)
- connection with the wider environment is critical for success (to enhance external as well as internal learning)
- every person is a change agent (change is too important to leave to the 'experts').

(Fullan, 1993: 21–2)

Problems with applying the collegial approach to change in universities
Hargreaves (1992) points out that criticisms of collegiality from a technical-rational perspective (see below) point to the time required for the development of collegiality and for joint decision making. Other writers have pointed to the catch-all character of the notion of 'collegiality', which is a term that is applied to a wide variety of quite different professional contexts and activities. Moreover, in a higher education context the relatively privatized nature of some university departments makes this kind of collegiality very difficult:

[In] the school of education here most people feel a part of this institution, but they don't really have much contact with people out there. They don't really go to staff house for lunch, they may go to the bookshop or library but they actually work and exist within this building. I guess that's true of other schools as well. So that's one feeling of isolation that's quite common, apart from when you get E-mails and stuff about university-wide issues. You are further isolated by being within the four walls of your office, the only connection you have with anyone else is the central heating system, the telephone and the computer . . . people very much do their own thing.
(New academics interview 10, male, education,
English chartered university)

Several writers have noticed that collegiality can mask inequality and exploitative power relations, and that the boundaries of the 'college' have, in the past, been drawn so as to exclude and include in structured ways. Drawing on a micropolitical perspective (Blase, 1988) situated in the conflict and bargaining perspective, Hargreaves notes that 'some individuals and groups can realize their values at the expense of others, or have the power and influence to shape others' values in the image of their own' (1992: 83). Collegiality and collaboration may involve an infringement of the individuality of lecturers and may move into co-option. In such situations of *contrived collegiality* the characteristics are:

- administrative regulation: academics are required to meet and work together
- compulsion: there is mandatory peer review, team teaching or collaborative planning
- implementation orientation: there is an inauthentic collaboration oriented to implementing the mandates of others
- fixed in time and place: contrived collegiality occurs in a planned way in particular times and places
- predictability: the control and regulation outlined above are designed to yield predictable outcomes.

There is, too, a potential problem concerning the notion of collegial planning for change. The assumption in this perspective is that planning by ground level actors is superior to planning by central leaders because those at ground level are more familiar with issues and problems that are likely to impede or derail change than those 'above'. Thus, for example, Dyer's (1999) case study of a change initiative in Indian schools shows the deleterious effects of ignorance of local conditions in planning 'Operation Blackboard', a child-centred system of education for primary schools. Dyer recommends a 'backward-mapping' approach (Elmore, 1982) to implementation, which begins at the local unit and takes into account (or 'makes room for') local knowledge and knowledgeability as well as skill at the delivery level. For Dyer what is needed is simply a more 'thoughtful' (Dyer, 1999: 45) approach to planning, which involves those at the ground level.

However, research by Reynolds and Saunders suggests that involving those at the delivery level in the planning of change does not necessarily enable them to apply their local knowledge and knowledgeability to the process:

> While working with a group of teachers who had been asked to prepare curriculum guidelines for colleagues, we had noticed how frequently but fleetingly individual teachers voiced doubts about the ways in which particular curriculum statements were likely to be regarded or disregarded by their fellows. Generally these interpolations were rapidly overridden and superseded by sustained argument amongst the whole group which shifted attention back to the form and wording of the guidelines themselves. The flow of discussion consistently moved away from the rehearsal of teachers' likely thinking to rehearsal of justifications of the curriculum text itself.
>
> (1987: 195)

One explanation for this dissociation between curriculum planning and professional thinking about everyday work practices lies in the situated character of professional practice; that is, the process of (curriculum) planning is cognitively different from that of actually 'delivering' a lesson, for example. Thus the supposed benefits of collegial planning or leadership are not, in practice, realized. Although writing before the wave of thinking and writing about situated cognition had reached its zenith in this field, Reynolds and Saunders came to just this conclusion:

> the conventions that underlie curriculum writing and debate . . . [are] segregated from the tacit norms that teachers draw upon in evolving working practices between themselves, administrators, their pupils, and the situations that they recurrently experience. This dissociation makes it difficult to articulate curriculum competence . . . We are not implying that the advisers, head teachers and co-ordinators who helped us in our research were 'trapped' in the complicitous conventions of curriculum and managerial discourse. As our material showed, they frequently moved in and out of these conventions via jokes, irony, and informal asides. But spasmodic movement between passing insight into one's total situation and discounting that insight by inserting one's thoughts into another frame of reference is no basis for articulating curriculum competence.
>
> (1987: 213)

More recently Gherardi *et al.* (1998) noted the same discursive situatedness in their case study of the situated curriculum in the construction industry. While professional practice was complex, tacit, subtle and largely effective, asked to describe that practice for the researchers, the construction site manager in the study switched to a form of discourse that lost the subtlety and complexity of practice. Instead he produced an 'impoverished' account based on the discourse of schooling and the formal curriculum. The perspective we examine next helps to account for these puzzling phenomena.

Social practice perspectives on change

Recent thinking about communities of practice and activity systems in organizations has emphasized the socially constructed character of reality and therefore of change. These approaches are more analytical and descriptive than normative and, in a sense, could be said to give a theoretical underpinning to the collegial perspective discussed above. We discuss these perspectives in more detail in Chapter 3, noting there how the label 'social practice' is used in this book to cover both phenomenological ('community of practice') and activity theory approaches. In brief there is seen to be an accommodation of competing identities, values and goals in social action. The theoretical account of power sees it as distributed dynamically, largely conditioned by the issue at hand, although certain types of power may be 'clumped'. Individuals who have or take leadership responsibility make decisions, but any form of social action involves important aspects of agency so in practice this decision making is widely distributed.

With regard to *change*, this perspective stresses a number of things:

- Learning, and learning to change, happen with engagement with a task in a social context.
- New mediating devices may precipitate learning and (often unexpected) change: the introduction of email communication within organizations is one example (Sproull and Kiesler, 1991).
- Inconsistencies, conflicts or ambiguities within workgroups can trigger learning and change (Lave and Wenger, 1991: 113; Blackler, 1993: 881). New members of communities of practice both absorb and change existing cultures there.
- Communities of practice are in a state of constant change, although much of this goes unnoticed. Even what is, on the face of it, 'the same practice', actually is constantly reinvented as details of the circumstances change (Wenger, 1998: 94). Change can *result* in discontinuities and conflict as well as be produced by them.
- Because communities of practice are highly situated, innovations that 'work' in one context may not work in another and what has been integrated into the practices and understandings of one community needs work for that to be achieved in another. There *is* a point in reinventing the wheel.

Here we will not elaborate on this perspective any further, leaving that to Chapter 3. However it is worth noting that prescriptions for organizational learning do surface from this work. Brown and Duguid, for example, recommend the development of an *enacting organization*, which preserves and enhances autonomy among its constituent communities of practice, Wenger's constellations of practice, but seeks to build interconnectedness through which ideas and results can be shared:

Within an organization perceived as a collection of communities, not simply of individuals, in which enacting experiments are legitimate, separate community perspectives can be amplified by interchanges among communities. Out of this friction of competing ideas can come the sort of improvisational sparks necessary for igniting organizational innovation. Thus large organizations, *reflectively structured*, are perhaps particularly well positioned to be highly innovative and to deal with discontinuities. If their internal communities have a reasonable degree of autonomy and independence from the dominant worldview, large organizations might actually accelerate innovation. An organization whose core is aware that it is the synergistic aggregate of agile, semiautonomous, self-constituting communities and not a brittle monolith is like to be capable of extensible 'frame bending' well beyond conventional breaking point.

(1996a: 77–8, original emphasis)

Social practice theory looks inside the black box of change giving explanatory power to more normative collegial approaches. As a theory it helps to explain why there is often a large implementation gap between the original recipe and the pudding actually eaten, as McPherson and Raab (1988) put it.

Problems with applying the social practice perspective in universities
The critique of this perspective comes largely from proponents of the conflict and bargaining approach. Although there is a rhetorical acknowledgement of diversity and conflict within communities of practice in social practice theory, this rarely translates in any meaningful way into the analytical accounts provided within this perspective, even, paradoxically, among those influenced by Marxist-inspired activity theory. Thus, while Wenger (1998: 77) acknowledges that there are 'disagreements, tensions, and conflicts' in communities of practice and that what appears stable is in fact dynamic, the emphasis analytically is on coherence, mutuality, complementarity and integration. We return to this issue, and to a fuller evaluation of social practice theory, in Chapter 3. In the context of this chapter it is appropriate to note the problem of accounting for change, which bedevils theories that stress the maintenance of community: where change comes from and how is it enacted is puzzling when, as in this account, the emphasis is on continuity and the socialization of new recruits into the already existent rather than on change. Although most university departments and teams do develop a negotiated order, this is inherently unstable: a point we return to in Chapter 3.

Technical-rational approaches to change

Largely normative in character, these emphasize efficient, goal- or vision-directed processes in organizations. Power is hierarchically distributed in this model, although it is sometimes devolved to local units, which are subject to 'steering at a distance' (Kickert, 1991). Roles and responsibilities within organizations are ideally seen as clearly delineated and assigned according to precisely defined and expressed tasks, the stages of accomplishment of which are regularly monitored. The organization as a whole is assumed to act as a coordinated unit with a common understanding of objectives, at least in the ideal situation. The assumption is that the outcomes of properly managed change processes are predictable.

At a national policy level in the UK this perspective is evident in the discourse and policy of the Quality Assurance Agency (QAA) in its subject review procedures:

> When the higher education system was small and largely uniform, and made a relatively small claim on public funds, reliance upon implicit, shared assumptions and informal networks and procedures [for quality assurance] may have been possible, and sufficient. But with the rapid expansion of numbers of students and institutions, the associated

broadening of the purposes of higher education, and the considerable increase in the amount of public money required, *more methodical
approaches* have had to be employed.

(QAA Special Review of Thames Valley University,
1998: 6–7, emphasis added)

These 'more methodical approaches' include centralized benchmarking
of degrees for the different disciplines, subject review procedures, institutional reviews and demands for more and more paperwork from universities, who increasingly complain that they are being distracted from the real
task at hand. Such quasi-state bodies represent not just Neave's 'evaluative
state' (1998) but a state attempting increasingly centralized control founded
on technical-rational thinking. The latter is evident in the benchmarking
standards, for example, which attempt to articulate the threshold, modal
and 'best' standards of knowledge, understanding, skills and abilities that
graduates in different disciplines will achieve: exactly the kind of approach
that led Jean Rudduck, Professor of Education at Sheffield University, to
hand out car stickers that said 'Help Stamp Out Behavioural Objectives'
when she was younger (Rudduck, 1991: 18).

In higher education top-down models of change based on technical-
rational thinking have prompted searches for the prerequisites of successful
change processes and have led to lists of them such as (adapted from
Cerych and Sabatier, 1986):

- creating and sustaining the commitment of those involved
- having clear and stable policy objectives
- ensuring that the policy innovation has priority over competing demands
- ensuring that there is a real expectation of solid outcomes inherent in
  policy, not just a symbolic one
- ensuring that the causal theory that underlies the policy reform is correct
  and adequate
- allocating sufficient financial resources
- creating, as far as possible, a stable environment within which policy is
  being implemented.

In terms of management at the institutional level a classic example of the
technical-rational perspective is provided by Beckhard and Pritchard (1992):

Leaders of the organization must have a clear vision of the desired end
state of the entire system . . . [and] a clear commitment . . . to making
significant personal investment in developing and building commitment [among staff] to an inspirational vision . . . All of this requires
conscious and explicit planning and managing . . . It cannot be left to chance
or good intentions.

(Beckhard and Pritchard, 1992: 4, 15, emphasis added)

For Beckhard and Pritchard the ideal process of leading change involves
a number of clear steps controlled from above:

- create a vision of the future
- communicate the vision to staff
- build commitment to the vision
- align people and what they do to the vision.

Leaders are advised to diagnose their current situation and to facilitate this diagnosis by switching into 'learning mode'. After 'unfreezing' themselves from 'currently held beliefs, knowledge or attitudes' (1992: 14) they should enable other staff to do the same. Beckhard and Pritchard advocate using a variety of levers to move staff in the direction of the vision. These levers include: changing one's own behaviour as a leader in the direction of the vision (thus acting as a model for others); cascading these changes down the management hierarchy and among 'key players'; rewarding desired behaviours; improving the flow of information within the organization so that feedback about behaviours improves; changing recruitment policies and orienting staff development in the direction of the vision. After the process of change is complete the organization may 'refreeze' into its new mode, the 'essence' of the organization having been changed.

Problems with applying the technical-rational approach to
change in universities
One key problem with this approach is that universities tend to be loosely coupled rather than tightly coupled institutions (March and Olsen, 1975). Cohen and March's well-known comment would probably still resonate strongly with many academics around the world: '[in universities] anything that requires the co-ordinated effort of the organization in order to start is unlikely to be started. Anything that requires a co-ordinated effort of the organization in order to be stopped is unlikely to be stopped' (1974: 206). Likening universities to 'organized anarchies', Cohen and March say they have the following characteristics:

- problematic goals – '[the university] discovers preferences through actions more often than it acts on the basis of preferences' (1974: 3)
- unclear technology – it operates on the basis of a set of trial-and-error procedures, the residue of learning from the accidents of past experiences, imitation, and the inventions born of necessity
- fluid participation – the boundaries of the organization appear to be uncertain and changing.

Decisions associated with change in a situation of organized anarchy closely approximate to a 'garbage can model' in which various problems and solutions are dumped by participants: 'The mix of garbage in a single can depends partly on the labels attached to the alternative cans; but it also depends on what garbage is being produced at the moment, on the mix of cans available and on the speed with which garbage is collected and removed from the scene' (1974: 81).

This description is close to the conflict and bargaining perspective outlined above. Here policy making and policy implementation are the result of negotiation, compromise and conflict. It is not surprising, then, that leaders continue to express frustration and bafflement at the unintended consequences of their actions and the breadth of the 'implementation gap' between their (technical-rational) intentions for change and actual outcomes on the ground.

How far the garbage can and conflict and bargaining models accurately describe decision making across the higher education system and in different countries is a matter for no-doubt contentious debate: Cohen and March's book was published in 1974 after all. Perhaps, given the changing nature of higher education systems, especially in terms of systems of audit and control founded on technical-rational principles, the technical-rational model more closely approximates 'reality' than was once the case.

However, from a social practice perspective what never changes is the *situated* character of cognition and rationality. A number of tenets of social practice perspectives undermine the hopes of innovators basing their ideas on technical-rational principles:

- The development of local meaning systems crucially affects how change proposals are understood and received at the ground level. Universities are dialogical. The contexted character of change means that policies are received and used in different ways: ideologies, definitions of profitability and other factors affect how 'vision' is interpreted and put into practice, if it is.
- The central role of identity and the emotions in professional practice can lead to unpredictable outcomes.
- The meaning and use ascribed to the tools and technology used in practice are socially constituted so the introduction of new tools can also have unexpected consequences.
- Workers necessarily engage in 'non-canonical' practices (see page 52) in order to do their job and these are invisible to leaders divorced from daily practice on the ground.
- Tacit knowing is central to professional practice and is largely not amenable to rationalistic practices.

From a bureaucratic process perspective the technical-rational attempt to drive academics' behaviour will almost inevitably have deleterious consequences. Downs (1966) refers to a 'law of organizational behaviour', which states that 'the greater the efforts made to control subordinated officials, the greater the efforts by those subordinates to evade or counteract such control'. Support for this comes from work by Buswell (1980, cited in Smyth *et al.*, 2000: 49), who found in a British study of 100 teachers that they were alienated by tight work controls and this resulted in low morale and a reduced commitment to their school and work. A vicious circle was put in place as management attempted to deal with this with still further controls that only served to exacerbate the situation. Fox (1974) and Hill and Bramley (1986) found similar situations in other educational contexts. For Lipsky (1980) the attempt to control the work of SLBs too closely could not succeed for similar reasons. As Hudson (1993: 393) notes, SLBs are liable to respond to performance and accountability measures (such as the assessment of teaching quality or of research excellence) in similar discretionary ways. Resulting low-trust relationships may set in train a spiral of attempts to assert control and avoidance behaviour, with a corresponding diminution in intrinsic motivation and hence in commitment.

Elmore sums this up: 'What grates most on the sensibilities of teachers, social workers, employment counselors and the like is the tacit assumption in most policy directives that they are incapable of making independent judgments and decisions – that their behavior must be programmed by someone else' (1978: 209–10). Moreover, 'vision' and its equivalents ('moral art', 'purposing', 'mission', etc.) derive from a fallible and personal theory of reality. Meanwhile formal leaders are in a position to exercise power over others because of their institutional position. As a result a number of ethical and other questions are raised (Willmott, 1993; Allix, 2000). How should 'followers' evaluate the vision? What right does a leader have to meddle in the value systems of 'followers'? What effect would uncritical acceptance of another's vision have on the individual (particularly in a university context)?

From a social practice perspective Wenger also points to the deficiencies of the technical-rational approach to change and calls for more organic organizational structures:

> if we believe that productive people in organizations are the diligent implementers of organizational processes and that the key to organizational performance is therefore the definition of increasingly more efficient and detailed processes by which people's actions are prescribed, then it makes sense to engineer and re-engineer these processes in abstract ways and then roll them out for implementation. But if we believe that people in organizations contribute to organizational goals by participating inventively in practices that can never be fully captured by institutionalized processes, then we will minimize prescription, suspecting that too much of it discourages the very inventiveness that makes practice effective. We will have to make sure that our organizations are contexts in which the communities that develop these practices may prosper. We will have to value the work of community building and make sure that participants have access to the resources necessary to learn what they need to learn in order to take actions and make decisions that fully engage their own knowledgeability.
>
> (Wenger, 1998: 10)

Despite such criticisms, many of the well-known textbook approaches to change are founded on technical-rational principles. They usually hold out the hope that, using the right principles and methods, change can be regularized and routinized with predictable outcomes. Sarason says, 'An understandable but unfortunate way of thinking confuses the power (in a legal or organizational chart sense) to effect change with the processes of change' (1982: 29).

Assessing the heuristic power of perspectives on change

In attempting to come to some overall assessment of the relative value of each of these perspectives it is useful to distinguish between the three sorts of question they each address to different degrees:

- How accurate a description does it offer (its descriptive power)?
- How powerful an analysis does it offer (the analytical question)?
- How valuable are its prescriptions for action (the normative question)?

As regards the *descriptive* question, any answer partly depends on one's ontological perspective. From a foundationalist perspective, which sees social science's role as developing progressively more accurate descriptive and theoretical approximations to a relatively unproblematic objective reality the question is capable of a relatively straightforward answer. However, from a more postmodern position the possibility of an answer becomes more complicated. For postmodernists any account of a professional situation will only distort what it seeks to represent, partly because it relies on language to construct a narrative. The people represented in the account may not, in fact, know what they think, and may hold alternative, even opposing, views on the same issue and so act in contradictory ways. Such an account will, in drawing on recall of and reflection on a situation, be accessing not the situation itself but the residue that remains from the multiple inscriptions that the person recalling and reflecting has made in rehearsing the situation in the past (Denzin, 1992: 124–5). Social 'reality' is, according to this view, intensely problematic and certainly not amenable to easy, filmic, 'capture'.

Our position is closer to the second, relativist position than to the first, foundationalist one. We argue that the models will be more, or less, descriptively 'accurate' in different situations and, more profoundly, that in each situation there is the potential for quite different 'takes' on the situation. Choosing between 'takes' will also involve choosing between models. No one perspective is 'accurate' for all situations, or all interpretations of any one situation. It is incumbent upon the reader, therefore, to consider the application of the models to their own situation. We argue in later chapters for an approach to leading that is distributed and collegial. We describe the characteristics of workgroups and teams that, we believe, are likely to make them particularly effective. But we recognize that one size does not fit all, and good leaders often have to behave in ways they would prefer not to. Making good judgements about appropriateness is one of the distinguishing characteristics of the good leader.

Turning to the *analytical* question, the issue for us in this book relates to the level of analysis at which the model is pitched. Our focus here is on change interventions at the level of the higher education department and team. The technical-rational model is usually applied at national or institutional level rather than at the microsocial level, and for good reason. It is a strategic planning perspective oriented to the road map rather than the road conditions. Such approaches have their place but there is a danger of ignoring the road conditions entirely. As we noted above, there are important social structural reasons why this is the case. The level of analysis, then, is one important factor in assessing the analytical power of a particular perspective.

Moving to the *normative* question, again we would argue that the wisdom of any particular set of prescriptions is heavily dependent on context. And we are in good company in this. Elmore notes that 'It is conceivable that in certain times and settings, the use of management control is clearly appropriate, while in other circumstances only bargaining is appropriate ... The problem is to understand when certain tools of analysis and strategies of action are likely to pay off and when not' (1978: 227–8). Following Berman (1980) we argue that there are situational parameters in which it is more, or less, appropriate to adopt either a technical-rational programmed approach to implementation or a more adaptive approach as suggested, for example, by collegial perspectives. The characteristics of the task and of the context condition degrees of appropriateness and it is for leaders to make careful judgements about this. Elsewhere we have depicted a similar situation in relation to approaches to quality, noting that even within the same institution and department, different approaches are appropriate to different tasks: procedural tasks for which technical-rational approaches may be appropriate versus those requiring creativity and insight to which other prescriptions are more applicable, for example (Knight and Trowler, 2000a).

Attempting to apply top-down, technical-rational approaches inappropriately is particularly dangerous in universities as part of their raison d'être involves independent critical thought on the part of both students and staff. As Willmott (1993) and others have noted, a university that established a corporate monoculture involving unalloyed top-down control would be a contradiction in terms. Again, leaders need to assess the characteristics of task and context and make appropriate decisions.

Conclusion: some principles of change in universities

We would, however, draw a number of principles from our discussion of change that are not situationally contingent. Drawing on the work of Fullan (1989, 1991, 1993), Senge (1990) and others we can identify the following principles for effective change in university departments.

Visions and hallucinations

Change involves uncertainty and learning. It is a journey that involves a process of progressive clarification. Well-formed visions developed early on can be an obstacle to learning and to change because they prevent learning and set limits on the ownership of change:

> In our view, ownership of a reform cannot be achieved in advance of learning something new. A sense of deep ownership comes only through learning. In this sense, ownership is stronger in the middle of a successful change process than at the beginning and stronger still at the end. Ownership is both a process and a state.
>
> (Fullan and Miles, 1992: 749)

Karl Weick makes a similar point in his book *Sensemaking in Organizations*: 'A crucial property of sensemaking is that human situations are progressively clarified. But this clarification often works in reverse. It is less often the case that an outcome fulfils some prior definition of the situation and more often the case that an outcome develops that prior definition' (1995: 11). For this reason there is a point in 'reinventing the wheel' each time it is used: attempts to import solutions that have worked elsewhere will lack both a sense of ownership as well as the contextually specific sets of meanings and practices associated with it that have evolved in that other context. This leads us to our second point.

Men and women make their own history

But 'they do not make it just as they please; they do not make it under circumstances chosen by themselves, but under circumstances directly encountered, given and transmitted from the past' (Marx, 1950: 225). Change, as Taylor notes (1999: 29) is always *from* something, and that something usually carries a considerable investment on the part of the people involved and the institutions in which they operate, creating a degree of inertia. In thinking about visions of 'e-universities' in the future, Brown and Duguid make the same point: 'It's probably less helpful to say simply that higher education will change because of changing technologies than to say the emerging computational infrastructure will be crucially important in shaping an already changing system' (1996b: 11). Bolton (2000) gives the example of different models of work allocation in university departments, citing some examples that have successfully evolved in the UK. He rightly cautions, though, that the key word is *evolved*. As in the natural world, this kind of evolution involves adaptation to particular environments: sudden changes in environmental conditions or transplantation of species to different environments can have unexpected and sometimes catastrophic effects.

Change is resource-intensive

Bringing about change effectively involves addressing problems and latent conflicts that may have lain dormant or been actively avoided, sometimes for years. Social dynamics in workgroups will almost inevitably involve power relations, differences in interpretation, vested interests in the status quo and identity incompatibilities. Significant change will usually bring these to the surface: it is the rock against which they are thrown and made palpable. Finding inventive ways of dealing with these, developing new skills, new identities and new ways of seeing, while at the same time moving change forwards takes a good deal of time and other resources. Fullan (1989) suggests that significant change can take a minimum of two or three years, depending on the complexity of the change and the size of the system. We regard this as a significant underestimate for university contexts.

Change requires distributed but well-coordinated leadership

As Ramsden (1998a) notes, leading is a dynamic that attempts to keep contradictory forces in balance. Achieving consensus on any important change is impossible in most university departments: waiting for it will stop change in its tracks. But at the same time imposing change in the face of opposition will bring resistance, delay, non-compliance and innovative responses with unintended consequences. Distributed leadership of change involves engaging the differing sets of interests, interpretations and identities in the change process, thereby allowing for mutual adaptation of both the change project and those sets of understandings and interests. Again, though, the tension in this is between the anarchy of competing positions and the exercise of excessive power by one grouping. All of those involved need assistance in going beyond their parochial interests and interpretations to see an outcome of the change process that all can regard as successful as the key goal. Fullan sums up this tension: 'Assume that people need pressure to change (even in directions which they desire), but it will only be effective under conditions which allow them to react, to form their own position, to interact with other implementers, to obtain technical assistance, etc.' (1989: 194).

Significant change is systemic

This is the case in the (trivial) sense that non-systemic change will be ad hoc and often transient. More importantly, significant change will lead to wider alterations in the system that implements it: identities and relationships will change, and so will the way technologies are understood and applied. Those involved in the change process should expect changes in areas that appear to be 'outside' the change-related area. However, this should not be interpreted to mean that the only important change is large-scale, 'big-bang' change: in fact the contrary is often the case. In later chapters we argue that most important changes happen when educational professionals reflect on practices and tinker with them in small but incremental ways. Changing practices can lead, though, to changed relationships, new discourses and new identities. Even large-scale systemic change is always interpreted and 'implemented' locally, and significant change at the local level will usually have systemic consequences. This brings us to our next point.

Change needs global thinking and local action

The 'think global, act local' ditty for managers also applies to change: as Fullan and Miles put it: 'All large-scale change is implemented locally' (1992: 752). There are two sides to this proposition. Firstly, all significant innovations, including those emanating from government policy or global trends, will be played out locally, and so will be variable in their outcomes. Secondly, to turn that round, while the focus of this book is on departmental and sub-departmental workgroups, it is important not to lose sight of the (increasingly turbulent) context in which they operate.

Avoid reductionism, reflect well

Change is complex and usually involves unforeseen and unintended consequences, often in domains not apparently related to the change area. Navigation through complexity and turbulence in social life requires good theory and a sound keel of good working practices. By 'theory' we mean a framework of concepts, propositions and understandings that helps explain an aspect of reality and leads to predictions. Theory helps fit reality together, organizing apparently isolated and unrelated features and episodes into a coherent form. It offers new insights and highlights unasked questions. Theory exposes gaps in our knowledge and knowledgeability that we, as social actors, may need to fill. In short, theory turns data into information and this can be used to form a plan for change (as distinct from a vision of the change). On-the-spot decisions, whose quality is influenced by the character of the knowledge-in-use and theories-in-action possessed by those involved, are both extremely pervasive and extremely important in education. It is important to stress the dynamic interrelationship between conceptual thinking and practice: theory needs to be both expressed in and refined by practice, as Schön suggests:

> The learning agent must be able to synthesize theory, to formulate new projective models out of his [or her] experience of the situation . . . And

as often as not, his [or her] projective methods come apart. He [or she] must be willing for them to come apart, and to synthesize new theory in process as the old explodes or decays.

(1971: 235–6)

Fullan and Miles illustrate the kind of reductionism that can occur without good theory:

Before a recent workshop, one of us asked a group of principals to list the problems they faced in a specific change project. More than half said 'resistance' – variously known as intransigence, entrenchment, fearfulness, reluctance to buy in, complacency, unwillingness to alter behaviors, and failure to recognize the need for change . . . But it is usually unproductive to label an attitude or action 'resistance'. It diverts attention from real problems of implementation, such as diffuse objectives, lack of technical skill, or insufficient resources for change. In effect, the label also individualizes issues of change and converts everything into a matter of 'attitude'. Because such labeling places the blame (and the responsibility for the solution) on others, it immobilizes people and leads to 'if only' thinking.

(1992: 748)

Going beyond this reductionist thinking and, instead, understanding the ways in which people have learned to 'go on' in workgroups offers not only a map with which to improve navigation and identify potential hazards but, more importantly, a meteorological theory to help explain the significance of events and their probable consequences. While the writing of Fullan and others on change and change management are insightful and helpful, they often lack the kind of theoretical insight that leaders need. Let us give an example. Fullan writes, 'There are many competing versions of what should be done, with each set of proponents equally convinced that their version is the right one. Forceful argument and even the power to make decisions do not at all address questions related to the process of implementation' (1989: 185). Although undoubtedly correct, what remains occluded here are why there are so many competing versions, where they come from and why they are clung to so tenaciously by their proponents. In Chapter 3 we provide some indications of where the answers to these questions might lie.

Good theory, along with the reflection that helps to convert personal and tacit knowledgeability into personal, explicit knowledge, are undeniably important but not all tacit knowing can be converted into explicit knowledge (Tomlinson, 1999). Assuming that tacit knowing does affect what we do, it follows that some of what we do will not be theory-governed and that there are limits to what reflection and theory can contribute to actions. The conclusion need not be drawn, though, that this tacit knowing, which is effectively beyond the reach of reflection, is also beyond influencing. If it grows as we act then the quality of actions – of social practices – helps to shape it. So people who have worked in flexible people-centred learning organizations will, in some measure, have different implicit knowing from those who have not, even if they are unable to use reflection to make all of that knowing explicit. Reflecting well and constructing good theory are important but so too are the social practices to which leaders are habituated. This identifies a theme pervading this book, namely that leading well is a personal and a social matter, to do with reflecting well in the context of apt social practices. This leads to a final brief point.

Understand alternative realities

Getting to grips with the multiple realities of the main participants is crucial in implementing change, as is remembering that no one responds to realities other than their own (Fullan, 1989: 184). Because any group of people have multiple realities, and cling to them, any change attempt will involve conflict.

2

Leadership Theory, Leadership Practice

The University has lacked any period of stability. Since 1992 it has twice been entirely restructured, first between 1992 and 1994 and more recently as a prelude to the introduction of the New Learning Environment. After developing further its modularised academic programme in 1994–95, the University in the following two years embarked on a further programme of massive change, driven by the Vice-Chancellor and intended better to support the University's mission and to address increasing financial constraints. The University chose to implement this vision of a New Learning Environment at the same time as it completely recast the underpinning academic-related administration. As we believe might have been anticipated, this subjected the institution, its staff and its systems, to stresses which it was not able to bear.

(QAA Special Review of Thames Valley University, 1998: para 73)

Preview

This chapter begins by setting out our understanding of some of the key terms to do with leading and leadership. It next provides an overview of some of the key changes that have been occurring over the past 20 years or so in higher education and its environment in the UK and globally. The intention here is to identify some of the recent and not-so-recent challenges to leaders in higher education. It then moves on to offer an overview of some of the important perspectives on leadership to be found in the literature in this area. After conducting a short critical evaluation of these approaches the chapter concludes with an outline of the approach to leading advocated in this book.

Introduction

In one sense a leader is simply someone who 'goes first' and who, by implication, others follow. Writers in the area have tried to draw distinctions between leaders, and managers, leadership and management. For Zaleznik while *managers* are concerned with the operational level, the here and now, leaders address broader issues of direction and purpose and, in the process, attempt to 'change the way people think about what is desirable, possible and necessary' (1977: 71). Handy picks up this idea: 'Managers do things right; leaders do the right thing. Managers accept the status quo, leaders challenge it. Leaders create and articulate vision, managers ensure it is put into practice' (1992: 7). Thus leadership as a process relates to 'mission, direction, inspiration' while management 'involves designing and carrying out plans, getting things done, working effectively with people' (Fullan, 1991: 157–8). Another way of putting this is that leading involves the pursuit of *effectiveness* while management aims for improved *efficiency* (Bennis and Nanus, 1985). Here, however, we characterize the difference at a related but more general level as being between management's aim of the efficient maintenance of the status quo and leadership's concern with *change*. In the academic world it is possible to distinguish different domains of leadership, particularly between organizational leadership and intellectual leadership (Griffith and Mullins, 1972: 961), but we follow Clark (1983: 4–5) in advocating a more 'relaxed' approach to definitional questions than this because of the usually fuzzy borders between them in that context. *Administration*, finally, is here distinguished from both in that it is concerned with the detailed fulfilment of management actions: the operational nuts and bolts at a day-to-day level. It is worth noting, however, that the term administration is used in quite different ways in some of the literature, particularly from the USA and Canada: for Hodgkinson, for example, it refers to human behaviour that seeks to achieve ends through organizational means. Used in this way the term subsumes management and includes important aspects of leadership (Hodgkinson, 1991).

Although this book concerns leaders and leadership, a moment's reflection on the apparent distinctions between leadership, management and administration will reveal that in practice they represent overlapping activities and functions. The difference between them is often more symbolic than actual: 'leaders' usually report spending a very large proportion of their time on management and administration. The words 'leadership', 'management' and 'administration' themselves evoke images that are less than helpful and are sometimes problematic when translated into higher education contexts. As one of our respondents said, 'I am very ambivalent about the word "leader" (it's a cliche, like "excellence"), and really don't see myself in those terms. It's redolent of business and management' (Male, experienced leader, Canada). In particular the connotations of the term 'leader' need challenging: the solitary (male) hero inspired by a vision of the future and in turn inspiring, or forcing, others to follow. However, because we lack better terms we offer the definitions outlined in Box 2.1.

Challenges to leading in higher education: the changing context

Higher education in the UK and around the world has been undergoing rapid and remarkable changes over the past 20 years. These new challenges

---

Box 2.1   Some terms defined

- **Leading** involves social actions intended to identify and facilitate the fulfilment of the perceived goals of a workgroup or organization. These actions go beyond the management function outlined below.

  Leading is thus defined phenomenologically and teleologically: in terms of actors' understandings of and intents about the aims of action.

- **Leadership** is here used in two senses: as the skilled or artistic performance of leading (similar to the notion of 'connoisseurship') and as the enactment of a formal or informal leading role. Leadership in the first sense suggests actions that are based on conceptually and theoretically informed sensitivity to context and that are effective in achieving their intended purpose.

- **Management** is the performance or delegation of operational tasks to accomplish predesignated goals of a grouping.

---

and the changing environment have put the spotlight on leadership in higher education. With Cameron and Tschirhart (1992) we view these changes as symptomatic of a shift to a postindustrial environment. This involves turbulent change, information overload, competitiveness, uncertainty and an increased danger of organizational decline. For HEIs almost everywhere this environment has meant high levels of competition, scarce resources, a changing role and new relationships as well as unpredictable fluctuations in enrolments and revenues. Elsewhere (Becher and Trowler, 2001) one of us has elaborated in detail on the changing characteristics of higher education associated with postindustrialism. Here we are concerned primarily with those that impact on leadership in higher education. These are summarized below.

- Higher education is becoming increasingly globalized: that is information and resources increasingly flow along physical, social and economic networks that transcend nation states' influence. Higher education is increasingly 'borderless' in character (CVCP/HEFCE, 2000). This often results in turbulence for *nationally* organized systems and practices. For higher education the globalized landscape has fundamental consequences. It is creating new patterns of incentives and disincentives, new opportunities and dangers, and new structures and constraints (Slaughter and Leslie, 1997). For those involved in leading in higher education some important characteristics of globalization include: enhanced competition from other universities (including 'mega-universities'; Daniel, 1996); new challenges and opportunities in teaching and learning and the challenges and opportunities of new types of students and activities; the acceleration of technology transfer between the public and private sectors; downward pressure on funding; and increased accountability, perhaps via the marketplace.

• The higher education system is developing the characteristics of a quasi-market (Gewirtz *et al.*, 1995). The new system within which it operates is more deregulated than in the past and the once-monopolistic position of universities is being threatened by new rivals, including private industry and information technology on a global scale. 'Customers' of various sorts are gaining new power from the liberalized system. These include students, employers and the government acting as a core buyer (Dill and Sporn, 1995). British students have arguably moved from being 'consumers in waiting' to being fully fledged consumers since the introduction of student fees in 1998. There has been a discernible movement almost everywhere towards 'academic capitalism' (Slaughter and Leslie, 1997) in which market-like behaviours become common both at the institutional and at the academic staff level. In Australia, for example, the competitive environment has meant a new drive to initiate research, recruit fee-paying students and attract consultancies (McInnis, 2000). Turpin and Garrett-Jones (1997) show that universities are tending to develop formal commercial arms, which are increasingly likely to evolve into loose-knit organizational networks largely unbound from their university and industrial antecedents.

• Higher education is becoming increasingly a 'mass' enterprise throughout the world. The UK passed Martin Trow's (1970) benchmark for a 'mass' system of higher education in 1988 when its age participation index (API) surpassed 15 per cent. In the USA the system became a 'universal' one in the mid-1960s when its API went beyond 40 per cent, at least according to Trow's (1972) rather odd use of the word 'universal'. At the beginning of the new millennium the API in the UK stood in the mid 30 per cent area. Mass higher education does not just involve a rise in the total number of students (to 1.8 million in total in the UK in 1998: HESA, 1999) but involves changes in their composition. Compared to even ten years ago, students in higher education are more likely to be: female (53 per cent in 1998 in the UK); from minority ethnic groups (10 per cent classified as black or Asian in 1998 in the UK) and older (59 per cent over 21 in the UK in 1998). In the USA the student body became increasingly heterogeneous since the mid-1970s. The percentage of minority students for instance increased from 15 per cent of all students in late 1976 to 25 per cent in late 1996. This increase was due primarily to the growth in the enrolment of Hispanic and Asian/Pacific islander students. By late 1996, minority students at public two-year institutions made up a greater proportion of the student body than at all four-year institutions: 30 per cent versus 22 per cent, respectively (NCES, 2000). Students are accordingly likely to be less well prepared for higher education than was the case, and this has meant adaptation of the curriculum and the provision of more and better support services for them.

- While public funding for higher education may be increasing in real terms over the years this has not kept up with the expansion in student numbers. Hence there is a relative decline in income from the state (a 40 per cent reduction in expenditure per student over the 20-year period 1976–96 in the UK, according to Dearing (1997)). HEIs have needed to reduce their level of expenditure and/or diversify their income streams. Between 1980 and 1991 in the UK the percentage of university funding from private sources increased from 10 per cent to 20 per cent in 1991 (Williams, 1995: Table 9.2, 181). Increasingly, too, there has been an emphasis on a 'bid and deliver' system of public funding in the UK, which has seen financial allocations tied to tightly specified performance (Martin and Irvine, 1992). The same picture applies in the USA, with government intervention increasing and per capita funding declining. McGuinness (1995) has shown how the fiscal crisis that began in the USA in 1990 set the scene for the decade. Demand began seriously to outstrip resources, the state withdrawal from providing the major part of higher education funding accelerated, and a variety of constraints began to affect universities. Virtually all universities are becoming highly entrepreneurial and less and less reliant on state grants. 'Chasing the dollar' (or the Euro) has become an increasingly important part of the academic's role in such institutions, at least in some disciplinary contexts and at some professional levels. The search for new income has itself needed considerable effort and resources. Meanwhile there has been a simultaneous 'snake-like procession' of lower status HEIs with aspirations to emulate the research function of the higher status ones. These multiple ambitions have led to role ambiguity, stress and overwork for many academic staff (McInnis, 2000).
- With the gross increase in state expenditure on higher education (45 per cent increase in the UK in the 20 years to 1996, according to Dearing (1997)) has come increasing state concern with 'quality' and a consequent intervention in the affairs of universities. As a result there has been an increase in accountability and an emphasis on efficiency and economy with, at the same time, an erosion of the exceptional status and individual autonomy of HEIs. The research transparency exercise in the UK entails a further extension of surveillance and accountability, requiring universities to quantify the amount of time their staff spend on different types of activity. At the state level in the USA there has been increasing intervention, with numerous states implementing policies designed to regulate academic quality. In Federal government there have been debates leading to the creation of State Postsecondary Review Entities (SPRES), characterized as inaugurating a new era of governmental control (Dill and Sporn, 1995: 6). Similar processes have been occurring around the world, as accounts from Hong Kong, Germany, South Africa, Spain and Sri Lanka report (Massy, 1997; El-Hage, 1997; Strydom and Lategan, 1998; De Miguel *et al.*, 1998; Munasinghe and Jayawardena, 1999). It is not surprising then that higher education researchers have begun to refer to the 'evaluative'

or 'supervisory' state (Neave, 1997), one which presents new leadership challenges at both the departmental and institutional levels.

- In each country the higher education curriculum is becoming more vocationally oriented, while at the same time an expanded higher education system means there are more opportunities for access for lower status groups. 'Performativity', knowing *how* rather than knowing *that*, has become a key characteristic of the official goals of higher education, as is clear in White Papers such as *Learning to Succeed* (DfEE, 1999), just as was the case in the Conservative White Papers of the 1980s, for example *Higher Education: Facing the Challenge* (DES, 1987). Inside universities this has meant increasing debate over the basic purposes and nature of higher education.
- In parallel with the state–higher education developments there have been important changes involving the incursion of industry into state–university relations. Gibbons (1997) and his collaborators (Gibbons *et al.*, 1994) argue that private industry has been gaining the advantage over universities in technological development and exploitation, not only because of its ability to invest but because it is not restrained by now-outdated disciplinary structures, which make up 'mode 1' knowledge. Increasingly the technological application of science involves 'mode 2', transdisciplinary, problem-oriented knowledge. In mode 2, knowledge is produced in the context of application, transdisciplinarity is the norm, heterogeneity and diversity within the organization are common, there is enhanced social accountability and there is a more broadly based system of quality control. This second knowledge mode is considered extremely important for local communities of academics who must quickly establish integration of the different skills within a framework of action and a consensus about appropriate cognitive and social practice for the task at hand (Gibbons, 1997: 94).

HEIs around the world, then, are expected to do more with less and to meet successfully challenges, not only from organizations like themselves on the global stage, but from sectors of the society and economy that were previously separate from them. There is also growing pressure for better quality teaching and support services for students. In the face of these pressures universities are having to 'develop more creative, adaptable, and efficient means of organizing academic work' (Dill and Sporn, 1995: 16). Examples include the push to develop more sophisticated and well-managed organizations for the procurement, support and administration of contract research. Like it or not, and agree with it or not, in the face of well-financed, technologically capable organizations with a global reach, higher education is in danger of being viewed as 'a low-tech cottage industry managed by amateurs' (Michael Thorne, Vice-Principal of Napier University, quoted in MacLeod, 2000: 1). While there are many well-managed HEIs and departments around the world, and many examples of successful institutions that offer a very focused and specialized curriculum mainly to students from their region, Thorne's comment captures the currently dominant discourse about borderless higher education and its challenges.

Far more than previously, academics are likely to find themselves 'overextended, underfocused, overstressed, underfunded' in the words of one US university Principal (Vest (1995) quoted in Clark (1998: 146)). Academics are expected to work longer, on a greater variety of tasks, with fewer resources. There has, in short, been work intensification and degradation of academic work. Rhoades reports that between 1987 and 1992 contact hours increased in every category of institution except liberal arts colleges (Rhoades, 1997: 267). McInnis (1996), reporting Australian data, notes that academics are now working two to three hours longer per week on average than they did 15–20 years ago, and the longer hours are accounted for by non-core activities. These often involve searching for financial resources no longer provided by the state but achieved instead through consultancies, teaching on fee-paying summer schools, engaging in marketing activities and so on. Indeed, the search for resources is one of the most important contributing factors to their work intensification (McInnis, 1996; Slaughter and Leslie, 1997).

In developing adaptive strategies to address these trends the focus has tended to be on individual academics. A key concern has been helping them to find ways to manage their time better, teach larger classes with fewer resources and to make themselves and their colleagues more productive. There is in this an implicit attribution of blame to the victims of change based on a deficiency model. In addition this reification of the individual misses the crucially important locus of the collectivity in the local workgroup. In the next section we examine the theory and practice of leadership in higher education and then turn to think about the nature and role of workgroups in more detail.

Leadership theory, leadership practices

To what extent has academic thinking about leadership offered useful theoretical models for understanding, and perhaps improving, leadership in universities? In this section we will review some of the most important ones.

Trait and behavioural approaches

'Trait' and 'behavioural' approaches to leadership try to answer the questions 'what are leaders like?' and 'what do leaders do?', respectively. They were dominant in the first half of the twentieth century but frequently reappear. They are essentialist in character (Popper, 1945): that is they attempt to tease out the basic characteristics of the leadership concept that are assumed to exist regardless of context. In trait theory leadership is seen as a set of personal qualities that an individual either does or does not have, such as intelligence or self-confidence. This is a 'great man' theory of leadership, both in the sense that it stresses the individual leader and in the sense that the 'traits' identified are usually associated with men rather than women (Southworth, 1995: 147). Some variants stress that 'good leaders' (as understood from this perspective) are born, not made and some of our respondents agreed:

> You . . . presume that leadership can be taught. I'm sure management can and I believe some parts of leadership are learned. I think, however, that some of the foundational qualities must be either born or nurtured from a young age. Adulthood and learning experiences can then fulfill that promise. Formal training may refine it, but it can't create what isn't there. The seed of leadership is in passion. It may be nurtured by these other elements. It may be destroyed. Passion grows in a manner different from understanding. If it can be imbued by something external to the individual then by default it isn't leadership. A leader hears an inside voice and combines that with the outside cries. How to combine that inner voice with the outside can be helped along with educational experiences but it is a very individual experience.
>
> (Female, experienced leader, USA)

This innate trait theory has now largely been replaced in the academic literature by an understanding of traits as *acquired*:

> whereas in the past managerial competence went hand in hand with the possession of specific skills and abilities, it now seems to involve much more. Increasingly it rests on the development of attitudes, values, and 'mindsets' that allow managers to confront, understand and deal with a wide range of forces within and outside their organization.
>
> (Morgan, 1997: 11)

So nowadays a range of skills and characteristics capable of acquisition are usually identified as being important in good leadership. Leadership is seen as a set of behaviours that can be learned rather than a set of personal characteristics that are largely innate. Here *behaviour* – what leaders *do*, their style as Bryman (1999) calls it – is at least as important as their characteristics as people (Spencer and Spencer, 1993). Examples found in the literature include the idea that the best leaders behave to enhance followers' sense of worth; build close, satisfying group relationships; work to emphasize goal achievement; help others to achieve goals through removing obstacles; and so on.

This perspective is associated with the competence approach – 'the ability to do a particular task' – whereas trait theory is associated with competency – 'the underlying characteristics which allow a person to perform well in a variety of situations' (Trotter and Ellison, 1997: 36). The problem with focusing on behaviour is that it omits the key, but necessarily somewhat tacit, characteristics of professionals: their ability to engage in reflection-in-action and mobilize knowledge-in-action (Schön, 1987). Individuals involved in leading also rely on accumulated but tacit knowledgeability from experience when they encounter novel situations, making judgements that are more notable for the options that are unconsciously excluded for their 'obvious' (to the experienced leader) unworkability than for the conscious choices that are made. These exclusions represent leaders applying 'theories-in-use', which again are usually tacit (Argyris and Schön, 1974), and often built up from and applied on the basis of images and impressions held in memory but not represented in propositional form (Eraut, 1993).

Underlying the stress on leaders' behavioural competence is the view that individual organizational leaders are centrally important to educational effectiveness, which is a view prevalent both in official policy and discourse and in much research on the issue. This can be clearly seen in school sector policy: 'The quality of the headteacher is a crucial factor in the success of a school' (DfEE, 1997: 29). This attribution of central importance is founded on, or at least looks for support from, the school effectiveness literature. The key characteristic of effective schools identified by virtually all studies in this tradition is the quality of the leadership of the school, and most specifically its head teacher. In their summary of the research, Sammons *et al.* identify 'professional leadership' as the first of 11 key factors for effective schools, and say of it, 'Leadership is not simply about the quality of individual leaders, although this is, of course, important. It is also about the role that leaders play, their style of management, their relationship to the vision, values and goals of the school, and their approach to change' (Sammons *et al.*, 1995: 8). Important, then, is a combination of 'what the leader is like' and 'what the leader does'. However, as Southworth points out:

> school effectiveness research embodies formal models of management theorising. If the outer layers of policy makers' assumptions are peeled away, what can be seen at their core is a set of beliefs that sustain the idea that bureaucratic managers impose order, clarity and certainty on disorderly organizations.
>
> (1999: 54)

Greenfield spent most of his professional life arguing against the notion that it is possible to isolate the scientific laws of good leadership. He sought to replace the positive science of educational administration as he called it with 'humane science' (Greenfield and Ribbins, 1993). Most academic opinion has been swayed in his direction over the years. Yet government and its agencies continue to portray the heroic manager as the knight in armour, armed with an all-purpose set of managerial competences and precepts, doing battle with an initially recalcitrant group of staff, many of whom need to be shown the error of their ways. In this vision any perspectives other than the leader's are marginalized and diminished.

'The vision thing': utopia or hallucination?

At about the same time, the University . . . began a further re-structuring exercise of a more fundamental and radical nature, styled the 'New Learning Environment' (NLE). The NLE was, in the first instance, the Vice-Chancellor's concept and he has led its development . . . In the University's case, implementation proved a particularly challenging and demanding project . . . For its success it needed very careful and comprehensive planning, effective leadership, prior infrastructural development, good communications, fail-safe contingency plans, fully tested information systems, a realistic timetable and goodwill on the part of all staff. We believe that these were all pre-requisites, not merely desirable options, the absence or failure of any one of which would be likely to jeopardise seriously a successful outcome.

> (QAA Special Review of Thames Valley University,
> 1998: paras 16–18)

Exactly *how* leaders should go about using their hard-won competences is the subject of another set of theories. Now rather fashionable in educational circles, although already beyond its sell-by date in generic management thinking, are ideas of leadership associated with what Willmott calls 'cultural corporatism' (Willmott, 1993), or what Bryman terms 'the new leadership approach' (Bryman, 1992, 1999). In generic management texts on leadership in the 1980s there was a fashion for seeing leadership behaviour as best oriented to cultural manipulation (e.g. Deal and Kennedy, 1982). Here the leader's role is to change values, meanings, assumptions, discourse and recurrent practices in organizations: in short to 'manage meaning'. Symbols, stories, rituals, myths and the organizational saga are particularly useful means of cultural change. For Schein, 'the only thing of real importance that leaders do is to create and manage culture and . . . the unique talent of leaders is their ability to work with culture' (1985: 5).

More recently the much-cited 'how to' text by Beckhard and Pritchard (1992), discussed in Chapter 1, focuses on the leader as the central agent in the implementation of change in private and public organizations, particularly in terms of his or her role in shaping the culture. Their approach attempts to answer the question 'how can leaders manage meaning?' As we saw, these authors believe they have a fairly simple answer to this question that involves vision-driven leaders consciously shaping organizational practices, values, assumptions and artefacts through judicious use of various levers. The emphasis is on the top of the organization throughout. The need for leaders creatively to destroy and remake the organization around new visions, to change their essence, is the heart of Beckhard and Pritchard's message about bringing about change. This message is now being picked up by educational writers. Robertson (1994), Weil (1994) and Slowey (1995) all cite this text as an important influence on their thinking about change in higher education. Professor Robertson is particularly enamoured with their work:

Much of the contemporary material emphasises the need to produce *cultural change* rather than merely structural change (Beckhard and Pritchard, 1992, for example). This involves committing the organization to attitudinal readjustment . . . institutional leaders are encouraged to 'lead by example' in order *to commit others to their vision* . . . [O]ur investigation has convinced us that strategic change is cultural change, and cultural change is related to institutional mission.

(Robertson, 1994: 314–15, emphasis added)

Embedded within this 'new leadership' approach are two further prescriptive models of leadership behaviour for goal achievement. The first, *transactional leadership*, is close to 'scientific management' in that it adopts traditional Taylorist assumptions that the primary motivating factor in employee behaviour is individual benefit, often interpreted in narrow economic terms. It attempts to answer the question 'how can leaders strike bargains to achieve their goals?' It suggests that follower compliance is 'bought' by the leader in exchange for other benefits and we see this in Beckhard and Pritchard's (and their followers') talk of 'rewarding' compliance. Follower behaviour is envisaged as largely dependent on its 'profitability' (Levine, 1980) as they, the followers, determine it.

However, as a 'stand-alone' theory transactional leadership is now generally recognized to be inappropriate, at least in educational contexts, and has largely been replaced in both academic and demotic thinking by *transformational leadership*. This approach asks the question 'how do leaders inspire the group?' It suggests that leaders act to inspire followers to change their practices and attitudes for the better. Ramsden (1998a: 66) argues for this type of leadership, identifying it as 'value-driven [and engaging] followers through inspiration, exemplary practice, collaboration, spontaneity, and trust'. The leader sets high aims and purposes for followers: inspirational charismatic leadership is the key together with intellectual stimulation and individualized consideration for followers (Bass and Avolio, 1990), and again we can see it reflected in the proposals from Beckhard and Pritchard. There are much earlier resonances too: 'Behaviour that's admired is the path to power among people everywhere' (Heaney, 1999: 3).

However, for some writers at least the focus is much less on the leader as an individual than is the case in the perspectives discussed above. For these writers the leader is conceived as *first among equals* and the characteristics of the group being led need careful consideration by both leader and analyst. These models of *dispersed leadership* move beyond the focus of 'new leadership' theories by taking the spotlight off the heroic leader and focusing instead on *teams*, which could be described as 'leaderful' rather than leaderless (Vanderslice, 1988: 677). The stress here is on 'leading others to lead themselves' (Sims and Lorenzi, 1992: 295), either through dispersal of power or through liberating team members so that their abilities can be fully utilized (Kouzes and Posner, 1993). The argument is that leaders should seek to develop teams with complementary skills and shared goals,

Figure 2.1 Towards a dispersal model of leadership

Management	───────────►	Leadership
Vertical	───────────►	Sideways
Fixed roles	───────────►	Flexible roles
Individual responsibility	───────────►	Shared responsibility
Autocratic	───────────►	Collaborative
Delivering expertise	───────────►	Developing expertise
Status	───────────►	Stature
Efficiency	───────────►	Effectiveness
Control	───────────►	Release
Power	───────────►	Empowerment

(from Whitaker, 1993: 87)

the members of which hold each other mutually accountable (Katzenbach and Smith, 1993). Such an approach seems particularly compatible with university contexts in which the generation of mode 2 knowledge is supplanting mode 1. Summing up the differences between this dispersed approach to leadership and earlier approaches Whitaker writes:

> what is it that enables successful organizations to succeed and thrive? What emerges is a more productive answer than simply good leadership from the top. It seems that leadership is an altogether more diffuse concept than we have traditionally come to believe, that it can be exercised at all levels within organizations and that all participants are capable of practising it in some way. By focusing only on the behaviour of senior people we run the risk of losing sight of those aspects of human behaviour in organizations that lead to effectiveness and consistently high quality.
> (1993: 70–71)

The shift from earlier leadership approaches to this dispersed model is summarized in Figure 2.1.

A useful set of distinctions in thinking about this is provided by Blase and Anderson (1995), who identify: authoritarian leadership, based on 'power over'; adversarial leadership, which appears more open but which is essentially based on the leader's aggressively promoted vision; facilitative leadership, which devolves power but still involves power over; and democratic, empowering leadership, which involves 'power-with' rather than power over, in which an empowered community and teams within it become leaders themselves. An emphasis on groups (or 'teams') rather than on individuals became extremely popular in leadership theory in the latter part of the 1990s (Northouse, 1997). Although the positivist approach directed at solving management-defined problems adopted by much of the earlier literature on teams (e.g. Hackman and Walton, 1986) has been retained, there is now a shift from universalistic to particularistic approaches to leadership, that is to say the ones that emphasize the unique characteristics of particular groups. The increasingly diverse character of work groups, culturally and in other ways, as more 'non-traditional employees' have joined the workforce has presented an important challenge to theorists in this regard.

In related socially situated models the spotlight shifts to the context in which change is occurring. *Situational theories of leading*, as the name implies, ask the question 'where are leaders located?' Originally developed by Hersey and Blanchard, situational theory focuses on the characteristics of 'subordinates', especially their competence and commitment. The closely linked *contingency theory*, originally associated with the work of Fiedler (1967; Fiedler *et al.*, 1976), also emphasizes the importance of context on the effectiveness of leadership, particularly (for Fiedler) in terms of the character of leader–member relations, task structure and position power or, (for path–goal theory) appropriate motivators for 'subordinates'. The assumption is that different circumstances require different patterns of behaviour because they offer different constraints and choices. As Leithwood *et al.* put it, 'Times change, and productive leadership depends heavily on its fit with the social and organizational context in which it is exercised. So as times change, what works for leaders changes also . . . [O]utstanding leadership is exquisitely sensitive to the context in which it is exercised' (1999: 3–4).

Contingency theory emphasizes the large number of variables that can shape or constrain leadership. Fiedler *et al.* (1976), for example, identify the quality of relationships between leader and others, the degree of task structure and the position of the leader within the organization as important contingent factors. Studies of educational policy by Woods *et al.* (1996) and Arnot *et al.* (1996) on educational policy implementation have confirmed the importance of context in conditioning outcomes. Gewirtz *et al.* (1995: 88) also show the different contextual factors operating to condition the outcome of marketization of education locally: 'there is no one general market in operation in England. Education markets are localized and need to be analyzed and understood in terms of a set of complex dynamics which mediate and contextualize the impact and effects of the Government's policy' (1995: 3).

In the case studies of schools analysed by Gewirtz *et al.* some of the important contingent factors included: environmental factors such as the level of funding, policies on pupil recruitment and the management of schools; regional factors such as transport systems, demography and local education authority (LEA) policies; and institutional factors such as the nature of the management team and the governors, the school culture and the size of the school roll.

As we saw above, such an approach problematizes those analyses of leadership that seek to establish law-like characteristics of good behaviour in leaders. Many (but not all) of our respondents agreed on the situated character of leadership:

I was discussing this issue with a colleague recently. He was proposing the view that managing expansion is much easier than managing contraction since the tensions that exist in all departments will come to the fore a great deal more readily during periods of contraction.

(Male, new leader, Scotland)

Table 2.1 Common themes in theories of change and leadership

Theory of change	Theory of leadership	Ideas in common
Technical-rational	Trait Behavioural Transformational	Charisma Vision Goals Evaluation
Conflict and bargaining	Transactional	Exchange Brokering
Bureaucratic process	New leadership	Cultural change Appropriate practices Compatible values
Social practice	Dispersed or distributed leadership Situational and contingency models Collegial	Power through empowerment Collaboration Community of practice Collegiality

Some things are applicable to all settings such as interpersonal skills (tact, diplomacy, firmness(!), etc.). Different styles might be called upon in different settings but mostly, I think, success as a leader comes from valuing others, enabling them, giving responsibility and providing help and encouragement.

(Male, experienced leader, England)

Academics are intelligent, independent people. There is no set pattern to leading or managing such a group. At best, I believe one must strive to keep people informed and react to individual situations individually, but with as much consistency as is possible.

(Male, new leader, Canada)

Leadership is highly contextual, but basic strategies and value systems remain the same. Treating others with dignity and respect, honoring what they value, providing opportunity for growth and additional responsibility as appropriate . . . these translate across contexts. Individual tactics change, but strategies and values do not.

(Female, new leader, Canada)

In concluding this section we note that there is a certain degree of compatibility between some of the leadership theories examined here and the theories of change outlined in Chapter 1. This is summarized in Table 2.1.

Evaluating leadership theories and perspectives in higher education contexts

In considering the applicability of these approaches to leadership in a higher education context it becomes apparent that in different ways they could benefit from greater sociological sophistication. This relates both to their conceptualization of the social contexts, especially those of universities, and in their theorization (or lack of it) of 'follower' reception of, and responses to, the leading behaviours that the approaches advocate.

Let us consider these two dimensions in turn, taking first the conceptualization of a higher education context. Apart from those discussed latterly, most of these perspectives assume that a single approach to leadership is appropriate regardless of context and, in the case of 'new leadership' approaches, that context can be manipulated to suit the aims of the leader: his or her 'vision'. The notion that leaders do particular sorts of things regardless of context pervades much of the literature in this area. For Smircich and Morgan (1982), for example, leadership concerns the 'management of meaning', while for the Teacher Training Agency (TTA) in the UK school leadership involves particular ways of behaving, articulated in its National Professional Qualifications for Headship (NPQH). For example leaders 'create and secure commitment to a clear vision for an effective institution' (TTA, 1998: 7). The danger of the generic noun, *leadership*, then, is that it tends to move us from considering an individual leader (who may have a particular way of leading, different from another person) to attempting to conceptualize the essential characteristics of what it means to be a leader (Warren, 1998). These may be understood as: context-free ways of acting that require particular personal characteristics or traits in the leader (confidence, assertiveness, vision, etc.); and/or a set of generic practices that leaders can acquire (communicative competence, time management skills and so on). Theories that incorporate this approach, such as the trait and behavioural theories are *essentialist* in character, stressing a basic driving factor regardless of context. They encourage normative accounts of how leaders should behave: highly marketable commodities that are very attractive to management gurus keen to publish such works as *The Seven Habits of Highly Effective People* (Covey, 1992) ('over 10 million copies sold worldwide').

However, generalizing accounts of university organizational cultures, which attempt to categorize them into one of a few types, miss the complexity and diversity of cultures at the local (usually departmental) level. Universities have not one but many cultures: they are characterized by a shifting multiple cultural configuration so that norms, values and taken-for-granted practices and attitudes may be as different from department to department, or building to building, as they are between one university and the next. These ideas are discussed in more detail in Chapter 3.

Moreover, any attempt to manipulate culture or manage meaning is going to meet a different reception in the different locales, as was found at Thames Valley University:

> The consequences of the lack of comprehensive, accurate and reliable information were severe, and the fact that the whole system did not grind to a total halt was largely the result of extensive improvisation on

the part of the administrative staff in the colleges and schools. Manual systems were resorted to, ad hoc 'workarounds' devised, and a great amount of time and effort expended in trying to make sure that a basic record existed. But where goodwill on the part of academic or administrative staff was not forthcoming, little could be done to keep the system functioning. The existence of long-running and unresolved industrial relations disputes involving some of the academic staff meant that the necessary extra effort was not fully available in some schools . . . The Wolfson Institute seems in practice to pay little more than formal regard to many of the features of the new structures, and there was frequent emphasis, during the course of our visits, on the differences between the Institute and the rest of the University.

> (QAA Special Review of Thames Valley University,
> 1998: paras 42 and 34)

Many of the experienced leaders who responded to our web enquiries had also become conscious of the danger of transferring learning from one context directly to another:

At one university I seemed to have the Midas touch. I was unschooled in leadership but it didn't seem to matter. That university was much more informal than the one I presently work in and creativity in administration was admired and encouraged. There were very few of the structures there are here – no annual individual faculty reports (no merit pay neither! [*sic*]). Teaching evaluation was not required – you did it if you wanted to find out how things were going. Thus students were far more charitable – they were not being asked five times a semester to fill in reports on teaching – when they were asked they tended to take it seriously. Since I came here I find creative administration is inhibited by structure, frequent lengthy reporting, budgeting, etc. You could say the atmosphere is much more business-like here. It is. But the flare and chaos of real academic creativity is missing. I don't really wonder why. I am not as good at leadership here, partly I think because I am not the world's most meticulous administrator, but this system selects and promotes that type of personality for positions such as Chair. At the same time, this university has far less deadwood and probably provides a better-structured and thought-out education for students.

> (Male, experienced leader, Canada)

Situational and contingency theories, while taking context into account, are usually pitched at a level of analysis that misses important social processes. The identification of the nature of the task, the relationship with members of the team and the maturity of its members ignores the team's cultural context entirely. Fiedler's (1967) contingency theory, like several others, also focuses on the leader, ignoring the perceptions and responses of those being led.

We move on now, then, to 'follower' reception of and responses to lead-ing behaviours. Organizational theorists in the 'new leadership' tradition have tended to treat leadership behaviours and the symbols leaders used unproblematically. However, these are effectively 'texts' that can be read in a number of ways. As Tierney points out:

A manager who walks around a building, casually talking with subor-dinates, for example, may be considered a symbol of management's respect for everyone in the organization. Conversely, organizational participants may feel that the leader is 'checking up' on everyone and that such symbolic behaviour is intrusive . . . Indeed a manager's informal style can symbolize any number of messages to different con-stituencies – friendship, accessibility, intrusiveness, or harassment, to name but a few possible interpretations.

(Tierney, 1989: 155)

Thus the display of 'leadership traits' or behaviours, of interventions that attempt to manage culture or manage meaning will be interpreted and responded to in many different ways by the participants involved. Such characteristics do not have the kind of objective existence their supporters imagine they have: their sociological dimension is more important and palpable than their ontological dimension, although postmodernist think-ing might see no distinction between them.

It is clear that formal attempts to *disperse* leadership will be 'read' and responded to as symbolic actions. It is quite likely that they will be seen as managerialist in intent: part of a now familiar pattern of centralist steering at a distance (Kickert, 1991), of appearing to devolve responsibility but maintaining control from the centre while making the periphery account-able. For these kinds of reasons Gee *et al.* (1996) are sceptical of the enthu-siastic adoption by management gurus such as Tom Peters (1994b) of reworked versions of recent thinking about learning, meaning and work revolving around communities of practice (Lave and Wenger, 1991). We explore this strand of theory in detail in Chapter 3, along with Gee's criti-cisms of Peters' appropriation of them.

We concur with Wenger (1998) on the importance of distinguishing between *dispersed* leadership and *distributed* leadership. The former implies a conscious delegation of leadership roles by 'the' leader. Examples of the-orizing the latter include Manz and Sims' (1991) and Sims and Lorenzi's (1992) idea of 'superleadership', in which the role of the leader is to assist others in leading themselves. Katzenbach and Smith develop this idea in the context of small teams with complementary skills in which the leader helps empower and unite the team as a whole so that they become 'commit-ted to a common performance purpose, performance goals, and approach for which they hold themselves mutually accountable' (1993: 45). Likewise Vanderslice's critique of heroic, personal, notions of leadership, stresses the counterproductive effects of hierarchies and labels: 'the very existence of leader–follower distinctions may have the effect of limiting motivation or directing motivation towards resistance of effort' (1988: 683). One of our respondents notes that 'Trying very hard to be a good follower has been one of the most important factors in being a leader' (Male, new leader, Canada). However the alternative Vanderslice examines, in her case study of the Moosewood cooperative (a New York restaurant), involves a consciously dispersed model of leadership. In distinction from such notions of dispersed leadership we argue that in universities leadership at the level of the 'community of practice' (discussed in more detail in Chapter 3) is naturally distributed in character.

Tierney (1989) offers three pieces of advice to university leaders, and they are worth reiterating here in paraphrased form:

* *Symbols demand corroboration*: leaders should be aware of how symbolic forms, their words and their deeds, or different deeds, may contradict one another.
* *Use symbols consistent with the local culture*: rather than assume a functional view of symbols and a passive view of individuals, we need to reconceptualize culture as an interpretive dynamic whereby the leader's symbols may or may not be interpreted the way he or she intended. The challenge is to understand how these symbolic forms exist within particular cultural contexts.
* *Use all symbolic forms*: we tend to compartmentalize activities to simplify them, yet that is not how organizational participants experience reality. Virtually everything a leader does or says (or does not do or say) is capable of symbolic intent or interpretation.

Blumberg makes the same point rather nicely: 'it is the basic rhythm that the principal communicates through his or her use of strategies that is really important. The words are of little value without the music . . . Be careful, though, because in another [context] . . . the words and music may be different – but have the same effect' (1992: xiii).

Being able to do this calls for cultural awareness and sensemaking in organizations (Weick, 1995). Good leading involves reflection-for-action (Cowan, 1998) and reflection-in-action, as well as the application of theories-in-use oriented to present and future action. Such processes are largely tacit and their development comes from experience. Good leading, therefore, does not only involve explicit knowledge, abilities or traits as managerialist or technicist theories, policies and procedures assume. Leading well has ineffable as well as tangible characteristics and is therefore difficult to capture in the analytical hand. Fundamental to evolving theories-in-use from practice is reflection-*on*-action (Eraut, 1995b), particularly in cases where there are anomalies between expectations and outcomes (Landau and Stout (1979: 153) quoted in Vaughan (1996)). These guide future action. But, as Chapter 1 mentioned and Chapter 10 will argue, it also depends on having rich experiences before becoming a leader.

We argue that appropriate 'leading' behaviour is always context-specific: what counts as 'good leadership' in one context can be interpreted as abdication of responsibility in another, or as a potentially obstructive irrelevance to the important activities of a group in a third. Ours, then, is a situated approach. While we agree with Turner and Bolam (1998) (discussed in Chapter 4), that local leaders need certain forms of knowledge, knowledgeability and abilities, we very much endorse their proviso that what these actually mean and the form they take is contextually contingent. We argue too that important aspects of context vary in significant ways at the intra-organizational level: in universities at the department level or even more locally. For this reason we argue that an analytical focus on leading should use a microscope as well as a telescope: be locally oriented as well as fixed at the organizational, societal and global levels.

Summary and implications

Box 2.2 summarizes a set of axioms that derive from the discussion in this chapter and which presage the argument and conclusions of Chapter 3. The approach adopted towards leading and leadership set out here emphasizes the need for analysts to give more attention than they have hitherto to the local, departmental level in universities. It stresses the notion that cultural competence on the part of leaders and their ability to predict the reception and response to change are likely to enhance leadership in HEIs. Policy needs to be formulated with implementation in mind: policy formulation and implementation are not separate things but are inextricably linked, although they are rarely perceived in this way. Our approach emphasizes the *distributed* character of leading. However, and finally, it is worth noting that the logic of the argument about the importance of context means that in some instances approaches to leading that we have criticized here may in fact be the most appropriate ones to adopt.

Box 2.2   **Eight common features of good departmental and team leading in higher education**

- The particular characteristics of HEIs as knowledge-intensive organizations mean that good leading at departmental level is naturally distributed across the workgroup (although there are many examples where this good practice is not the case). Changes in the nature and environment of higher education have made this more so in recent times.
- Conscious attempts to *disperse* leadership across the workgroup by its formal leader (or someone else) should not be confused with *distributed* leadership. The former is often read locally as inauthentic or contrived, and can be associated with the now-familiar managerialist techniques of 'steering at a distance' (Kickert, 1991). There is a parallel here with communitarian notions of collegiality and 'contrived' collegiality (Hargreaves, 1992).
- Good leading involves reflection-in-action and the application of theories-in-use and knowledge-in-action oriented to present and future action. These are largely tacit and require experience to be developed. Good leading therefore does not only involve explicit knowledge, abilities or traits, as managerialist or technicist theories, policies and procedures assume. Leading well has ineffable as well as tangible characteristics and is therefore difficult to capture in the analytical hand.
- Reflection-on-action is fundamental to evolving theories-in-use from practice (Eraut, 1995b), particularly in cases where there are anomalies between expectations and outcomes. These guide future action and therefore represent reflection for action too.
- Workgroups in universities operate within a reality that is partly microsocially constructed. It involves tacit and explicit rules and conventions, taken-for-granted sets of recurrent practices, rules of appropriateness and sets of values. Behaviours will be interpreted in terms of these and 'read' differently in different workgroups. Hence the characteristics of good leading, and what counts as leading, is always contextually situated.
- But workgroups are not 'communities' in a functionalist sense. They are fractured by: a network of power that does not reside only in the formal leader; contest; struggles to create and defend identities; and harmony and cooperation. 'Meaning' is located in both the workgroup and the individual: 'any action or incident has many truths, one for each participant . . . social location determines one's access to information about the event, ability to interpret it, and frame of reference in which it is observed' (Vaughan, 1996: 282). Behaviours, including actions associated with leading (Tierney, 1987) within the workgroup, are capable of multiple interpretation: they

are polysemic. Awareness of this is a practical and professional issue as well as a research issue. Good leading involves good sensemaking; that is developing and redeveloping frameworks into which experience can be ordered and interpreted. As Weick (1995: 7) notes, sensemaking is about authoring as well as reading.

• In some cases, though, it is appropriate for formal leaders or others actively to disperse leadership across the workgroup and to use transactional or transformational leadership techniques. For example, where an issue needs to be tackled, which is defined by all members of the workgroup as onerous or in some other way negatively (as is often the case with preparation for external audit or review), then dissonance with the naturally distributed character of the workgroup will necessitate such inauthentic interventions. In these cases cultural sensitivity and an understanding of how their actions will be read is essential in the person/s involved in the dispersal process. In short, characteristics of task, context and the rules of appropriateness in particular workgroups should guide choices made.

• Workgroups are not isolated from their environment. Both the 'new institutionalism' (Powell and DiMaggio, 1991) and chaos theory (Baumard, 1999) rightly stress linkages between environment, organization and workgroup in daily work life. Awareness of this is a practical and professional issue as well as a research issue. Again, leading well involves sensemaking, in this case understanding the way the organizational and external environment impinges on the local microsocial context.

3

Leading in Higher
Education Departments

Accumulating history intertwines with structural and cultural factors to affect
decision in organizations . . . Culture is created as people interact in work
groups . . . and it shapes future decisions . . . Signals of potential danger can be
normalized [and] the incrementalism of organizational life . . . can contribute to
extraordinary events that happen.

(Vaughan, 1996: xiv)

Preview

This chapter begins with an overview of social practice theory, setting the
theoretical scene for the discussion that follows. Associated with the
Vygotskian activity theory, developed by Engestrom and others and further
elaborated in discussions of communities of practice from Chaiklin, Wenger,
Lave and others, social practice theory has much of value for understanding
leadership in university departments. The second section of the chapter
explores some of these. However, we do not suggest that social practice
theory should be adopted root and branch in thinking about local leadership, and in the third section we explore some lacunae and difficulties
connected with the theory. We conclude by returning to and elaborating
further the set of principles established at the end of Chapters 1 and 2.

Introduction

Clegg *et al.* (1999: 5) note that for many years those studying organizations
divided the field of study into two categories: the micro, which focused on
the individual; and the macro, which focused on the organization. This
brought a number of problems. It ignored the meso-level, which is the
primary territory of this chapter and the book as a whole. Also, it occluded
the linkages between the different levels: the fact that the individual and
their context, organizationally, nationally and now globally, cannot be mean-
ingfully separated. What we here call *social practice theory* has developed
more recently and addresses these issues to an impressive degree. In using

this term we are conflating two traditions: activity theory, which has a Marxist heritage; and communities of practice theory, which has roots in a variety of literature from the phenomenology of Berger and Luckmann and the constructivism of Dewey to the anthropological structural functionalism of Levi-Strauss. While these very different roots might suggest that an elision of differences would do serious damage to both perspectives, we would argue that the distance between the two perspectives is, in practice, not so great. Lave (1993: 21) argues that activity theory asks 'how it is that people live in *history*', while from the phenomenological perspective the important question is 'how it is that people *live* in history?' Both questions are important: one stressing structure, and the other agency.

To date, though, there has been only a limited application to the field of higher education of the set of tools that social practice theory provides, and then they are usually applied to pedagogical issues, particularly in relation to technological applications to teaching and learning (e.g. Brown and Duguid, 1993; Goodyear, 1995). Case studies tend to be drawn from anthropology (Lave and Wenger, 1991) and organization studies (Blackler, 1995), or to be concerned with health and other welfare services (Engestrom, 1990). The theoretical antecedents go back to Dewey (Palincsar, 1989), Oakeshott (Tripp, 1996) and Berger and Luckmann (1966). The account below, then, is constructed with the practical implications of social practice theory for leadership in higher education at the forefront of attention.

An overview of social practice theory

Individuals' professional engagement with the world is largely social. Extended joint engagement on a project involves the development of recurrent practices and sets of meaning that are localized, and endogenous in character. This 'social construction of reality' also involves the development of rules, including rules of appropriateness, conventions, taken-for-granted understandings, connotative codes, and so on. At the same time particular ways of interacting with the technologies employed to achieve tasks also evolve and become taken for granted. In their teaching practices, for example, university departments develop ways of thinking about and involving their students, approaches to course design and implementation, assessment practices, and so on, that become invisible to the members of those departments but that can seem odd, novel, exciting or just plain wrong to others. Underpinning these practices are values, attitudes and ideologies that are partly developed and communicated locally.

Meanwhile, as well as developing *shared* characteristics, the process of identity construction and development is going on at the individual level through interaction processes that occur as individual participants engage with each other and their work projects. At one and the same time a 'community of practice' and the public identities of the participants involved are developing. Committee meetings, staff meetings and informal interactions in corridors or over coffee, as well as email messages and memos, inevitably involve identity 'work' and interpretation. As Eraut (1993) notes, a great deal of information in education is acquired piecemeal: images and impressions are built up on the basis of comments, overheard remarks and fleeting incidents rather than only from more systematic and formalized sources.

At the same time the members of the group draw on and enact behaviours, meanings and values from the wider environment, but they do so in somewhat different ways, depending partly on their age, gender, ethnicity, professional experience, and so on. For example, men and women bring their particular experience of sex-role socialization with them and meet expectations associated with gender roles from others in their daily practice. This 'sex-role spillover' (Nieva and Gutek, 1981) can have important implications for the experience and effectiveness of practice (Trowler, 1998). So, too, with age, 'race', and so on.

Meanwhile, group members operate within a common organizational environment that has its own sets of rules (professional codes or course validation procedures, for example), taken-for-granted attitudes and conventions. Professional identities are constructed within a 'given' (or structural) framework, which involves, for example, formal roles such as head of department or course coordinator, which themselves often have exogenous connotative codes associated with them. These will be different for different institutions: the role of the head of department and dean are quite different, for example, in British 'new' (unchartered) universities compared to 'old' (pre-1992) ones, and in most countries these roles have distinctive institutional features.

Some key concepts within this strand of thinking, then, include:

- *Activity (or practice)*: particularly as derived from Vygotsky, this concept implies social engagement with the world. The important characteristic is that the nature of the activity is not objectively discernible but is defined by the participants. Engagement on a research project is one example. The character of what the project means may appear to be objectively 'given' but is actually socially constructed in the process of doing it. 'Activity systems' consist of groups of individuals in distinct roles engaged in a common activity using mediating artefacts and operating on the basis of largely shared rules and conventions. There are clear links in this with the work of Dewey and G.H. Mead in the USA.
- *Community of practice*: a closely interacting group of practitioners within which contextualized, situated learning is always happening and is legitimized (Lave and Wenger, 1991). The research project team or teaching team may form a community of practice within a research centre or department. A single community of practice may incorporate a number of activity systems, depending on the number of distinct projects or activities they are engaged in, and a person may belong to a number of communities of practice.

- *Identity*: is not a fixed entity but a relational process and for this reason is sometimes referred to in terms of 'subjectivity' (Prichard, 1999) or the self (Mead, 1913) although these terms carry subtle but important differences. Wenger (1998: 153) makes the point that we know who we are by what is familiar, understandable, usable and negotiable, while we know who we are *not* by what is foreign, opaque, unwieldy and unproductive; that is by *otherness*. Personal and social identity are thus relational in character, involving simultaneously both a positive and negative positioning. Partly because of this, identity or, better, identities, are not singular and fixed but multiple, dynamic and situationally contingent.
- *Meaning*: as distinguished from information (Baumard, 1999) is the product of learning. Meaning implies the way we understand the world and our place in it. It involves knowing about things, sometimes tacitly: the way they interconnect and the way we relate to them, include connotative codes that they carry. Thus for example higher education regulatory agencies such as the QAA and its procedures carry meaning for higher education professionals over and above the information they have about such agencies. This meaning will vary from location to location to a greater or lesser extent.
- *Discourse*: language too is a form of social practice, one that is both conditioned by and conditions the social structures that give regularity and a certain degree of predictability to behaviour. Examples of such structures include educational ideologies, class structures, and so on. While discursive repertoires are partly exogenous to a community of practice and imported into it, the social construction of reality within a community of practice also involves discursive creation, negotiation and contest as well as simple articulation. While some see *Discourse* as language and practices and *discourse* as language (practices) only, we do not make this distinction: language practices and social practices instantiate each other.
- *Technology*: the role of technology within social practice is not limited to the simple use of tools. The tools and techniques used for achieving ends are themselves bound up in constructivist social processes. The fact that photocopy machines and desktop computers were initially predicted to be irrelevant to office practice (Brown and Duguid, 1991) demonstrates the important interactions between technology and social practice. Within the existing (situated) practices at the time of their invention it was true that they were and would be redundant: it was difficult to envisage any alternative. However the introduction of technologies changes practice and thus the nature of the constructed social world, as brief reflection on the use and effects of email communication in universities will illustrate. At the same time social practice shapes the way technologies are defined and used within the large range of possibilities that they frequently present.

In the next section we elaborate on the aspects of social practice theory that are particularly significant in conceptualizing leadership in university departments.

Social practice, learning and meaning

Perhaps the clearest way to characterize the position adopted by social practice theory with regard to learning and meaning is to delimit what it is *not*. Blackler (1993) contrasts its approach to that of the rational-cognitive model of learning and knowledge. In this model learning is considered to be individual, private, cumulative, permanent, context-independent, acquired by explicit transmission and predominantly rational in nature. Knowledge, in turn, is seen as explicit, codifiable and transmissible. Such foundationalist world views presumably derive from and are reciprocated in the assumptions embedded in the experience of schooling that most of us share.

By contrast, in social practice theory 'knowing' is viewed as inherently connected to the activities engaged in within a context and culture in which the act of knowing occurs rather than having an individual, internal character. Thus knowing is contexted and contingent: what is appropriate and useful knowledge in one context can easily become redundant or wrong in another. As Brown *et al.* put it: 'Activity, concept and culture are interdependent. No one can be totally understood without the other two' (1996: 23). Knowledgeability itself is indexical and metonymic in nature: in the context of social practice it becomes overlain with contextually specific denotative and connotative meaning, and with emotion too (Van Maanen and Kunda, 1989). This is true of knowing about our departmental colleagues, our students, the pedagogical practices we engage in, the way the department is organized and led and in many dimensions of our professional lives.

A corollary of all of this is that, in an important sense, knowing is *distributed* rather than individualized: '"Cognition" observed in everyday practice is distributed – stretched over, not divided among – mind, body, activity, and culturally organized settings (which include other actors)' (Lave, 1988: 1). Knowledgeability and expertise are not simply inside our individual heads but are intimately tied to various aspects of the relationships we have with people, technologies and other dimensions of context. There is a parallel here with our discussion of leading and leadership in Chapter 2. Expertise in, say, lecturing well relies on the lecturer having well-substantiated understandings of his or her students and other aspects of the context, knowing about the pedagogical tools available there, shared meanings about aims and processes and sets of stable personal relationships. It also requires certain sets of compatible attributes in the other participants involved, for example the students. As Hart-Landsberg *et al.* say 'expertise is socially distributed among workers, jointly constructed in close articulation with features of the work activity and environment' (1992: 5). In addition, what actually *counts* as expertise is socially constituted; a point we made earlier in relation to leading.

Experienced academics recruited to new contexts frequently report the experience that the new situation, different technologies, changed students and disrupted sets of meanings leave these once-expert practitioners feeling temporarily disempowered, deskilled and filled with self-doubt. Ontological security becomes disrupted in these circumstances and can require considerable time to recover. The conclusions from the ethnographic study of the English university 'NewU' (Trowler, 1998) indicated that changed circumstances are not, however, disruptive for everyone. Here the study concerned the same context but in changing times. Some academics found themselves 'sinking' in the new situation but others were able to 'swim' quite easily. The difference was a factor of the compatibility between the characteristics of the new situation and the set of relevant structural and agentic conditions within the individual academic's situation. For example some individuals were in a position to profit professionally from the changed situation and found that aspects of it were compatible with their previous experience, view of the world and dominant educational ideology. Thus new or changed situations can be empowering as well as disempowering.

The social practice approach, then, adopts a *constructivist* as opposed to a transmissive perspective on learning, including professional learning. Knowledgeability and expertise are dynamic, not just in the sense that new knowledge is continually being created but also in the sense that once created they change. For this reason Blackler (1995) suggests we use the word 'knowing' rather then knowledge. Apple is right to note that 'Concepts do not remain still for very long. They have wings, so to speak, and can be induced to fly from place to place. It is their context which defines their meaning' (1993: 49). In discussing the implications of this in work contexts Brown and Duguid distinguish between canonical and non-canonical practice. Canonical practice is that which is described in organizational charts, training manuals and formal descriptions of practice. Descriptions of espoused, canonical practice are requested by and presented to quality monitoring organizations such as the QAA. Non-canonical practice refers to the complex and diverse practice on the ground, which is necessarily different from canonical practice because, at one level, canonical knowledge can never capture the complexity of practice on the ground, as we noted in Chapter 1. Also, and more significantly, it is necessarily different because of the dynamic character of knowledge, knowing and expertise discussed above: new ideas, developed understandings, work-arounds, re-interpretations and reconstructions of tasks, projects and roles mean that the relatively static nature of canonical practice can never keep up with non-canonical realities. The insight that policy 'implementation' necessarily involves policy (re-)making is necessarily true for this as well as for other reasons.

All this means that important aspects of learning when joining new communities of practice involve accessing largely tacit, distributed knowledgeability, rules of appropriateness, taken-for-granted understandings and conceptual appreciation that are specific to the workgroup. Learning to become an organizational member is far more a question of socialization than to do with formal learning along transmissive, rational-cognitive lines. Social practice theorists stress the importance of *legitimate peripheral participation* in real contexts for acquiring new knowledgeability and skills: of undergoing a process of socialization in the context of practice so that learning relates not only to the form but to the deep substance: the meanings and subtle aspects of practice (Brown and Duguid, 1991; Lave and Wenger, 1991). The veracity of this was highlighted by our study of the organizational socialization of academics new to university contexts. We found that 'learning how to go on' (Giddens, 1983: 75) in an organization occurs through being involved in the cultural undergrowth of an organization (Trowler and Knight, 2000). In this way new entrants gain understandings of what is considered an appropriate pace of work, what is important and what not, the appropriate (and inappropriate) discursive repertoires, taken-for-granted understandings of phrases such as 'at 2:1 level', 'bare pass' and 'appropriate experience for credit exemption'. Where academics are excluded from deep social engagement in this way, as is the case for deaf academics in HEIs (Trowler *et al.*, 1999), there are important, and quite debilitating consequences: what is taken for granted or invisible to everyone else can be problematic because there is no access to overheard comments, asides and gossip, which are so important in forming judgements (see pages 48–9). In the 'normal' case these clues contribute to:

> the internalization of institutional or institution-based 'sub-worlds' ... the acquisition of role-specific knowledge ... Secondary socialization requires the internalization of ... semantic fields structuring routine interpretations and conduct ... At the same time tacit understandings, evaluations and effective colorations of these semantic fields are also acquired.
>
> (Berger and Luckmann, 1966: 158)

Tacit knowledgeability

Because meaning is at least partly constructed within workgroups engaged in social practice it is situated, distributed and, importantly, largely tacit. Polanyi says, 'we know more than we can tell' (1983: 4). Like the pattern recognition abilities involved in recognizing a human face, much knowledgeability can be learned but not easily explained and, like the interpretation of facial features, knowing carries with it a layer of connotative codes which are also partly developed in situ. Sternberg (1997) has argued, for example, that knowing about the way that things are done and other people in the organization is far more important to success in leadership and other roles than are formal qualifications or intelligence quotient (IQ) scores. Such knowledgeability is acquired through socialization rather than formal instruction:

> Suddenly to find yourself in a system whereby you have to contact some technician if you want the slide projector and another one if you want the television and this is what to do if you want the printing. Again, I

suppose it's people who have been in a place for a while get to understand and know the systems, which admin. person deals with different
parts of the course.

(Respondent 7, new academics study, female, teacher education,
unchartered university, England)

However, tacit knowledgeability has a deeper and more important significance than knowing about organizational responsibilities, processes and
routines. As concepts and ideas are worked and reworked in their application, meanings and discursive practices are developed in a way that is largely
invisible to the individuals and workgroup involved but extremely perplexing to outsiders, who may have come across what appears to be the
'same' idea elsewhere. Tacit knowledgeability based on socially constructed
meaning developed through practice is an intrinsic part of the symbolic
universe of any community of practice and is often surprising to novices and
outsiders:

> I'm new to the country and . . . when I came here there was a Christmas
> party . . . For the first time in my life I was in a room where the sub-
> ject of the Teaching Quality Assessment [(TQA)] [came up] and every-
> body, even people who I thought can't possibly be interested in this,
> were totally focused on [it]. The person who was giving the results was
> . . . like Santa Claus coming with the presents. It was incredible. He had
> a few jokes before he'd actually reveal it. It just reminded me of . . .
> you know when they train managers in those American professional
> videos where they get the team together, they get them excited . . .
> There was absolutely no question that there could be a problem, that
> maybe they shouldn't all be committed to this [exercise], that they
> shouldn't all be thinking it's the end of the world if they [didn't get
> a good score] and there was no criticism at all of the way that points
> were dealt out, it was just 'did you get a high point or did you get a
> low point?'

(Respondent 2, new academics study, female, social science,
chartered university, England)

General understandings of intangible cultural characteristics are usually
tacit too: 'In terms of initiation into the sort of central philosophy or the
culture about approaches to students, well that was by osmosis, we picked
that up through centre discussions really' (Respondent 8, new academics
study, female, teacher education, unchartered university, England). While
many important assumptions remain tacit and intangible the initiate usually
soon knows when they have transgressed them.

Those with leadership responsibilities, of course, acquire tacit knowledgeability too, as discussed in Chapter 2 and developed in Chapter 10.
It allows individuals to 'automatically take appropriate action in a given
situation, without having to make an effort of analysis to decide what approach to apply' (Baumard, 1999: 63). Baumard discusses the Greek notion

of *metis*: a form of intuitive, wily intelligence. Found in the prudence of the politician and the skill of the ship's captain navigating dangerous seas, it is invaluable in transient, unpredictable, ambiguous situations that are not amenable to logical analysis. For local leaders it is a form of tacit knowing that is crucial in 'the shadowy zones of human interaction' (1999: 67). This reminder of the discussion begun in Chapter 1 is some way removed from the explicit, rationalistic approach adopted by much of the leadership theory addressed in Chapter 2.

Professional identity

Situating an understanding of identity in workgroup processes, which are themselves considered in the context of organizational and social structures, leads us to think carefully about the nature of identity. For social practice theorists learning involves not just the cognitive dimension but the whole person, the identity, because learning is an aspect of social practice that is bound up with social groups, situations and activities in which it occurs (Lave and Wenger, 1991: 53). Identity is never static, however, rather it is protean and dynamic in character (Weick, 1995).

Identity at any given time can be seen as a work in progress that weaves together the past, present and future, one's own sense of self and a response to the representations of others (Mead, 1934). Krappmann calls these representations the 'social identity' that the individual must negotiate in interaction and that they must in some way accommodate to achieve a 'balancing identity' between this and their personal identity (Krappmann (1969), quoted in Somekh and Thaler (1997)).

In HEIs the workgroup and the classroom are the sites of much of this identity work for academics. The comments made by Maclean about this based on his study of children are also relevant to university academics. He points out that people:

> are positioned by the actions they undertake as group members, by their relative centrality to the group's activities, by the power they wield and the restrictions placed on them as a result of group membership, and by the boundaries which separate members of a group from members of another . . . Membership of a group helps to constitute identity, but it is an identity which is restated and renegotiated with each action.
>
> (Maclean, 1996: 172)

Important ways in which this identity work is done within a workgroup include: using the discursive resources available to the group to send messages and achieve goals; acting 'politically' to change the character of the group, including one's own role in it; constructing and reconstructing relationships with others, who are sometimes alienated or oppositional; and giving messages about the 'self' through actions. These forms of behaviour operate reciprocally so that identity construction is always a social activity.

Both individual agency and the forces of social structure are important in this process. Professional identities are constructed within parameters conditioned by social structures but they are none the less personal constructions. Moreover, the individual comes to new situations from earlier social contexts, bringing with them personal and professional identities shaped in those contexts, which may or may not be in conflict with potential or emerging identities in the new workgroup. Wenger talks about an identity trajectory:

In summary, the temporal notion of trajectory characterizes identity as:

1. a work in progress
2. shaped by efforts – both individual and collective – to create a coherence through time that threads together successive forms of participation in the definition of a person
3. incorporating the past and the future in the experience of the present
4. negotiated with respect to paradigmatic trajectories
5. invested in histories of practice and in generational politics.

(Wenger, 1998: 158)

The nested character of social practice

The predominant depiction of the cultural character of universities is that all can be characterized in terms of one of four cultural types, although authors disagree about the characters and names of these types (Becher, 1988; Birnbaum, 1988; Cameron and Ettington, 1988; Bergquist, 1993; McNay, 1995). New entrants are perceived as quickly learning the values, ethos and organizational saga (Clark, 1972; Van Maanen and Schein, 1979) and, like older hands, coming to enact pre-existent recurrent practices, which themselves instantiate taken-for-granted values, attitudes and assumptions (Masland, 1985; Smart and Hamm, 1993).

An alternative to this functionalist view of culture as something static, to be learned and conformed to, is, as Grbich notes, to see 'culture as dynamic and unbounded, comprising a diversity of groups each with the capacity to develop unique mini cultures' (1998: 69).

In this alternative model culture is constructed as well as enacted and, rather than being culturally homogeneous, HEIs are characterized by multiple cultural configurations (Alvesson, 1993), which are dynamic in character. Rather than having one culture or an unequal mix of two, there are many cultures operating throughout the institution, as we suggested in Chapter 1. The lived reality in one department or service section is quite different from that in another: in some senses the group members may as well be in different organizations. As McDermott and Varenne put it:

Life in culture is polyphonous and multivocalic; it is made of the voices of many, each one brought to life and made significant by the other, only sometimes by being the same, more often by being different,

more dramatically by being contradictory. Culture is not so much a product of sharing, as a product of people hammering each other into shape with the well-constructed tools already available. We need to think of culture as this process of hammering a world.
(McDermott and Varenne (1995: 326), quoted in Tierney (1997: 6))

The diversity and dynamism of an institution's cultural configuration derives largely from the small workgroups within it. They are the sites of cultural 'hammering', the powerhouses of university life; places where culture is both enacted and constructed and where personal identity coalesces and is shaped and reshaped. It is here that recurrent practices become embedded and developing meanings are shaped as individuals work together on the issues of professional life where ideologies are 'fired' by issues as they arise and battle lines are drawn up.

An HEI, then, may be envisaged as a 'community-of-communities' (Brown and Duguid, 1991: 53); overlapping and nested in character. It is also, though, an open system, with sets of values, assumptions, recurrent practices and attitudes brought into the daily life of workgroups by the individuals who compose them and influencing in important ways the processes of cultural construction and enactment, identity formation, policy interpretation and implementation and the 'reading' of behavioural signs and symbols. A focus on the local level should not blind us to appreciating the systemic character of social life, to 'the ways in which action is structured and order made possible by shared systems of rules that both constrain the inclination and capacity of actors to optimize as well as privilege some groups whose interests are secured by prevailing rewards and sanctions' (DiMaggio and Powell, 1991: 11).

Like the university as a whole, workgroups too are open natural systems rather than closed ones, that is their members and the context they work in are subject to influence from cultural, ideological, technical and other characteristics of environments beyond the group and the organization. Individuals operating within a workgroup bring with them characteristics from their background, sets of values, attitudes, assumptions and recurrent practices that may or may not be similar to or compatible with others flowing into the group through its other members.

One way of conceptualizing this is to use the metaphor of a river. There is flow into it and from it as well as movement within it. Impediments to the flow (rocks in the river, which represent contentious issues within the institution) cause eddies and realign the flow into new configurations. Notice, though, that over time the flow may realign, or even erode the impediments. Cultural flow into and through each institution is dynamic and complex and close attention must be paid to the important streams if the participant hopes to come close to understanding the nature and impact of the configuration in any particular context.

Metz has noted the importance of these sorts of external linkages in relation to other minority groups:

Where workers, or a significant portion of them, participate in a strongly defined common ethnic or community culture, they will inevitably carry its values in to the workplace. Where ethnicity . . . [or other minority status] is clearly visible to others, it will shape workers' actual experiences and so shape the daily round to which the worker subcultures are a response.

(Metz, 1986: 20)

Linkages into the workgroup are not necessarily homogeneous or integrative in nature, as Metz implies, and do not necessarily serve to cement shared values and embed recurrent practices. Rather they are often fractured and in tension: there are road blocks and road rage, to switch the metaphor, as well as considerate driving, although usually the rules of the road are well understood and adhered to. Resulting conflicts and clashes are inevitable and can be a source of dynamism and learning within the system, as Engestrom points out, and so should not be considered aberrant and dysfunctional, as functionalist theory would have it.

Social practice theory: implications for leaders

Social practice, learning and meaning

We saw earlier in this chapter that learning is intimately connected to the development of meaning and, in Chapter 2, that leadership has recently been seen as the 'management of meaning' in much of the literature in this area. The discussion above, however, suggests that this notion needs to be problematized for the following reasons:

- Meaning is dynamic in character and hence interventions aimed at managing meaning must also be continuous and dynamic, making it a far-from-simple or easy task.
- Meaning is created socially and not simply 'received' from others higher in the organization.
- Important 'stages' of meaning construction are largely inaccessible to leaders beyond the local level of the workgroup. While the public face of organizations exists 'front-of-stage', negotiations, deals and compromises are conducted 'back-stage' while gossip is purveyed and stories are exchanged under-the-stage. The last is particularly elusive for formal leaders.
- Meaning is situated: that is it is intimately connected to the interplay between identities, technologies, assumptions and practices of particular workgroups. Meaning-management interventions can have unpredictable consequences in different locations.
- Such interventions will always be interpreted, or 'read', by those on the ground.

It is possible to argue, though, that local level workgroups can be 'captured by the discourse' imposed from above (Bowe *et al.*, 1994), that is the way they think about issues and, importantly, what becomes 'unthinkable' and unsayable, can be structured by the discursive repertoires that seep into local workgroups from senior management and more widely. Thus, for example, in the UK the discourse of subject review and the research assessment exercise, with their grading of departments and disciplines in institutions, may colonize the evaluative criteria and language we use to assess the work of ourselves and others. The quote from respondent 2 in the new academics study (p. 54) indicates that this might have happened in the department referred to there. Displaced and increasingly marginalized would be earlier evaluation methods and criteria, more traditionally located in disciplinary norms, such as the reputation of individuals derived from their work, knowledge about success and failures of particular projects in university departments, and so on.

However a study by one of the authors (Trowler, 1999) cast doubt on the validity of an unreconstructed 'capture' thesis, noting the existence of discursive 'struggle' in universities: discursive displacement, resistance, reconstruction and negotiation as well as acceptance. The sources of this struggle lie in structural locations often outside the university and higher education system, and in the processes occurring within workgroups at the local level. Universities are, as we have already noted, dialogical entities (Eisenberg and Goodall, 1993), that is they are composed of a multiplicity of discourses with plurivocal meanings brought to bear by participants whose utterances are intertextually shaped by prior texts and anticipate subsequent ones (Bakhtin, 1986; Fairclough, 1992).

So leaders do not have an unchallenged privileged position in meaning construction and organizational learning. However *local* leaders have potential advantages over institutional leaders deriving from their intimate connection to ground-level, meaning-creation systems. They can:

- explore the unintended deleterious effects of current practices, values, attitudes and assumptions with those who practise and hold them;
- make interventions that are sensitive to their impact on identities and on pre-existent sets of meanings;
- make the tacit explicit, including exploring cases where there is a threat of discursive capture. They can highlight the power of the taken-for-granted words, phrases and other aspects of discursive repertoires in daily use in workgroups.

'Reading' practice

For local leaders these insights have more than simply theoretical significance. They bring to the foreground the fact that actions, both their own and those of others, occur in a web of localized meaning. Tierney illustrates this in his discussion of the semiotic aspects of leadership (Tierney, 1987, 1989), introduced in Chapter 2. The meaning intended by a person acting or speaking is often not what is received by the person 'reading' its meaning. Tierney gives the example of Sister Vera, the new President of a small, US, Catholic liberal arts college. She saw her mission there as changing the family-like culture and practices of the college to more business-like arrangements in order to get the college on a sound footing for the future. Unfortunately for her almost all of her actions were interpreted in terms of the approach of her predecessor, who had a more relaxed, and familiar management style. Thus Sister Vera's 'open door' – literally and (in her mind) figuratively – became its opposite to the staff of the college: a sign of cynicism and the failure of communication because in the other things she did Sister Vera was perceived as uncaring and uncommunicative, especially when compared to her predecessor:

> that which makes a sign a sign is neither the object nor the intention of the speaker about the object. Rather, it is the context and process of signification itself – the shared interpretive activity based on a common set of codes – that endow signs with interpretive power . . . What may be considered a highly charged sign in one organization . . . may acquire little or no meaning in another organization . . . Further, the capacity of a sign to carry simultaneously a sender's intended meaning and its opposite is much more widespread than we realize.
>
> (Tierney, 1987: 234)

The 'NewU' study (Trowler, 1998) demonstrated the importance of under-the-stage processes in developing and transmitting sets of understandings, which can lead to such 'aberrant' interpretations. Informal conversations over coffee, the transmission of gossip, shared confidences, jokes, nicknames and the opportunity to share grievances have important influences on the way signs are understood.

Tacit knowledgeability

This return to the theme of tacit knowing stresses the importance of an awareness of the tacit repertoires of information circulation that exist in organizations and the interventions that may be necessary in relation to them. Baumard (1999) notes that organizations usually suffer from a flood of information while simultaneously suffering a drought of knowledge. Information circulates formally via email, memos, official documents and the rest while the circulation of knowledgeability is more informal, incremental, disjointed, interpersonal and intimately related to practice. Members of communities of practice 'not only have access to the physical activities going on around them and to the tools of the trade; they participate in information flows and conversations, in a context in which they can make sense of what they observe and hear' (Lave and Wenger, 1991: 102).

Lave and Wenger refer to the 'fields of transparency' that relate to the extent to which the significance of artefacts and their relationship and use in social practice is apparent to those who are not yet members of the community of practice. This transparency is achieved largely through informal social processes and for those in positions analogous to deaf people in a hearing community, the social world and social practice remain muffled: 'this notion of transparency constitutes, as it were, the cultural organization of access. As such, it does not apply to technology only, but to all forms of access to practice' (1991: 102). The attempt to maximize access to practice and the transparency of the form and use of artefacts for all members of a community of practice is a key obligation of leaders at the local level, though we have already suggested in Chapter 1 that there are limits to how far this is possible:

the ability of people to learn *in situ* suggests that as a fundamental principle for supporting learning, attempts to strip away context should be examined with caution. If learners need access to practitioners at work, it is essential to question didactic approaches, with their tendency to separate learners from the target community and the authentic [non-canonical] work practices.

(Brown and Duguid, 1991: 49)

Management gurus such as Tom Peters have picked up the significance of this for making organizations more effective and efficient. In his chapter 'Beyond re-engineering: creating a corporate talk show', Peters approvingly quotes Alan Webber in the *Harvard Business Review*:

Conversations are the way knowledge workers discover what they know, share it with their colleagues and in the process create new knowledge for the organization. The panoply of modern information and communication technology – for example, computers, faxes, e-mail – can help knowledge workers in this process. But all depends on the quality of the conversations that such technologies support.

(Webber (1993: 28) quoted in Peters (1994b: 176))

Gee *et al.* (1996: 65) note that management gurus like Peters have seized on social practice theory as a potential solution to the 'problem' of obtaining commitment from workers in 'fast capitalism', which demands ever more time and effort, increasingly including intellectual effort, from workers. For Peters, 'becoming a member of a community of practice is literally a requirement of modern-day job success' (1994b: 174). According to this view the community of practice becomes just another management tool rather than an inevitable part of social practice. In an earlier article Gee and Lankshear write:

The logic of the new work order is that the roles and responsibilities of the middle will pass to the 'front line workers' themselves (formerly, the bottom line of the hierarchy). Workers will be transformed into

committed 'partners' who will engage in meaningful work, fully understand and control their jobs, supervise themselves, and actively seek to
improve their performance through communicating their knowledge
and their needs clearly. Such 'motivated' workers (partners) can no
longer be 'ordered' around by 'bosses', they can only be 'developed',
'coached' and 'supported'. Hierarchy is gone, egalitarianism is 'in'.

(1995: 7)

This vision of a 'post-Fordist' work environment (Jessop, 1989; Ball, 1990)
is reflected in Brown and Duguid's discussion of communities of practice,
in particular their comment, quoting Orr, that 'Occupational communities
. . . have little hierarchy; the only real status is that of member' (1996a: 70).
This characterization of them is more idealized than realistic.

Professional identity

Given that identity construction is an inseparable aspect of social practice,
that there is a sense in which all work is also identity work, then social
practice involves an identity dimension as a concern with the task or issue at
hand. The implication is that the way university staff interpret and approach a novel issue is conditioned by their contextually related identity
positioning, and engagement with new tasks also involves further identity
work and new positioning *vis-à-vis* others. One of the implications for this is
that practices become non-canonical: that is the gap between espoused
practices and actual ones increases, with inevitable implications for the
implementation gap – the disjunction between policy as articulated ('the
vision') and as practised.

Moreover, because identity formation is also conditioned by influences
outside the workgroup, for example by the forces related to gender socialization discussed above, there will inevitably be clashes and contradictions
related to identity even in long-lived and coherent workgroups where the
social construction of reality, and identity, has been ongoing and collaborative over some time.

Leaders need to negotiate these and be aware of identity issues involved
in all social practice in this regard. One successful Canadian leader illustrated this in her response to our electronic enquiry:

The most important factor that HELPS me to lead is my ability to find
and use the passion within individuals based on their value systems.
And . . . this is different for every individual . . . I have had individuals
come to my team because their current leader no longer wants them
. . . for whatever reason. I have been able to work with the individual
to find what inspires them and to move them to being a valuable,
contributing member of my team.

(Female, new leader, Canada)

Nested practice

The nested character of culture and practice has implications in two main areas: equal opportunities and power. In terms of the former, the socially constituted inequalities between men and women, different ethnic groups, able-bodied and disabled people that exist in the broader society can easily be instantiated in the daily practices, decisions and policies of workgroups. Pervading this are unequal power relations in their various dimensions. Thus, for example, we found in earlier studies that assumptions among male academics and students about gender meant that women often found themselves in a position of having an unequal share of tasks in the area of student support and counselling and in teaching as against research. This has, of course, not gone unnoticed by female academics (e.g. Deem, 1996; Letherby, 1996). Meanwhile unequal power relations mean that it is rather difficult for those who find themselves in this position to challenge and change it, which is a point we deal with in more detail below.

For leaders, then, the issue concerns recognizing and challenging practices and assumptions that may have their roots outside the workgroup but that have important influences on its practices, the effects of which are deleterious to equality of opportunity. Any understanding of live realities in universities needs to be informed by critical theory, i.e. an approach that is sensitive to the ways in which 'injustices and inequalities are produced, reproduced and sustained' (Ozga, 1999: 47). Importantly, such an understanding can act as a guide for practice for leaders, particularly at the departmental level, so that the illumination of inequality and the injustices resulting from power flows can make leaders' decisions more sensitive to these aspects and enable them to work for change.

Criticisms of social practice theory

We do not, however, treat social practice theory unproblematically. There are a number of areas in which its tenets need to be critiqued and revised, at least as far as their application to higher education is concerned. We briefly deal with these criticisms next.

Communities of practice: boundaries and functions

In attempting to apply the notion of the 'community of practice' to university life it quickly becomes apparent that drawing the lines between communities of practice is difficult if not impossible. In one sense everything is a community of practice. Wenger (1998: 6) notes that we all belong to communities of practice: at home, at work, at school and in our hobbies: 'In fact, communities of practice are everywhere'. Wenger rejects the idea of 'encumbering the concept' with a single restrictive definition (1998: 122), yet acknowledges the danger of the concept being stretched so far as to be rendered meaningless. He identifies the indicators of the presence of a community of practice as follows:

1. sustained mutual relationships – harmonious or conflictual
2. shared ways of engaging in doing things together
3. the rapid flow of information and propagation of innovation
4. absence of introductory preambles, as if conversations and interactions were merely the continuation of an ongoing process
5. very quick setup of a problem to be discussed
6. substantial overlap in participants' descriptions of who belongs
7. knowing what others know, what they can do, and how they can contribute to an enterprise
8. mutually defining identities
9. the ability to assess the appropriateness of actions and products
10. specific tools, representations, and other artifacts
11. local lore, shared stories, inside jokes, knowing laughter
12. jargon and shortcuts to communication as well as the ease of producing new ones
13. certain styles recognized as displaying membership
14. a shared discourse reflecting a certain perspective on the world.
                                                                (1998: 125–6)

Reflection on this list soon raises a number of issues. Firstly, within any university department or even faculty there will be layers of 'communities', right down to the level of dyads, for which these characteristics are more or less true. In practice a circle cannot be drawn beyond which one can say 'within this lies the "true" community of practice and beyond it there is no such community'. Secondly, even at the very local level, say a research project team, there may be dissent and individuals to whom some of these characteristics do not apply, although they could not be considered to 'not belong' to the community of practice.

Thirdly, the word 'community' has now accrued multiple meanings and its connotations of warmth and closeness make it simultaneously attractive and unhelpful (Brown and Duguid, 1996a: 53). In discussing communities Wenger (1998), for example, makes frequent reference to terms such as 'mutual engagement', 'joint enterprise' and 'shared repertoire'. Bauman adopts a critical perspective on this:

> We are being told repeatedly by the learned opinion of many social scientists, by the born-again enthusiasts of the 'pre-reflexive togetherness' they once assigned to the pre-modern and pre-civilized past, that 'community' is the most likely candidate to fill the gap . . . The idea of community has been recovered from the cold storage where modernity . . . confined it, and restored to a genuine or imaginary past

glory . . . Community advertises itself as the cosy, burglar-proof home amidst the hostile and dangerous city.

(1995: 275, 277)

By contrast any account of university life needs to be sensitive to the often-conflictual nature of the social dynamics in these organizations and the operation of power; things that the discourse of community tends to occlude. It is necessary to question the tacit functionalism of much of the work in neo-institutionalist and activity theory thinking, articulated in this quote from Wenger:

> [Individuals in] a community of practice . . . make the job possible by inventing and maintaining ways of squaring institutional demands with the shifting realities of actual situations. Their practice:
>
> 1. provides resolutions to institutionally generated conflicts . . .
> 2. supports a communal memory that allows individuals to do their work without needing to know everything
> 3. helps newcomers join the community by participating in practice
> 4. generates specific perspectives and terms to enable accomplishing what needs to be done
> 5. makes the job habitable by creating an atmosphere in which the monotonous and meaningless aspects of the job are woven into the rituals, customs, stories, events, dramas and rhythms of community life.
>
> (1998: 46)

Vaughan's (1996) study of the space shuttle Challenger launch decision shows how the socially constitutive nature of workgroups' operations can operate in ways that can be dysfunctional, in that case fatally so. Rules of appropriateness and recurrent practices, which have the effect of progressively normalizing deviance, can be developed and become taken for granted. Only when the consequences become apparent, as happened dramatically with the explosion of the Challenger space shuttle, are these processes brought to the surface.

The problem of intersubjectivity

Social practice theory has focused on the ways in which mutual knowing and shared sets of meanings, both denotative and connotative, are generated and used in small workgroups. In everyday interaction we are only too ready to make the assumption that intersubjectivity has been achieved (Blum-Kulka, 1997), although this has long been recognized by scholars within linguistics (e.g. Dretske, 1981; Smith, 1982) to be a complex matter.

The conclusion of a study of interpretive processes occurring between deaf and hearing academics (Trowler *et al.*, 1999) led to the conclusion that we need to reconsider the operation of mutual understanding in 'normal' settings, too. Since all workgroups within a university setting are open systems into which alternative cultural currents, sets of assumptions and understanding flow, we need to acknowledge that there will be limits to the homogeneity of participants' mutual knowledgeability. Indeed, it could be argued that in universities in general there are as many sets of understandings of any specific issue as there are participants engaging with it.

Power

A third and important weakness of social practice theory is the largely rhetorical nature of its acknowledgement of the operation of power in social contexts. This applies both to power working on groups and individuals, including leaders, and its use by them. Lukes (1974, 1979) distinguishes three dimensions in the operation of power, each of which is apparent in the dynamics of workgroups. The first, most tangible dimension involves individuals or groups securing outcomes to behaviour or decisions that operate in their interests. This is close to Weber's definition of power, which involves physical or psychical compulsion with the intention of securing behaviour that will lead to desired outcomes or inflicting sanctions for deviance: making the 'other' do what they would not otherwise do (Gerth and Mills, 1970: 180).

Lukes's second dimension involves agenda-setting and, importantly, exclusion from the agenda. Here individuals and groups exercise power through the creation, reinforcement, reproduction, exclusion and undermining of sets of values and the practices that stem from them in order to delimit the parameters of what is conceived of as sensible, normal, possible and desirable. This dimension of power has been elaborated by Bachrach and Baratz (1962).

The third dimension involves the exercise of power through what has more recently been called 'discursive capture' (Bowe *et al.*, 1994). In a much more fundamental and 'invisible' way, the socially constitutive power of discourse is used to shape not only what is, and is not, on the agenda but what can and cannot be thought about (Foucault, 1975). As Ball puts it, 'We read and perhaps respond to policies in discursive circumstances that we cannot, or perhaps do not, think about' (1994: 23).

In this dimension knowledge, knowing, discourse and personal identity become intertwined in the fabric of social life, which is permeated with power relations. There is a 'network' or 'web' of power in operation, which is largely invisible to participants.

The reader will, no doubt, be able to reflect on instances of the operation of each of these three types of power and their consequences in his or her professional experience. Each type of power operates both at the level of interpersonal interaction and at a more macro-level: in the institution and beyond. Much of this is invisible in social practice theory other than at

a rhetorical level. Thinking about social practice, including leadership behaviour, is richer when informed by an appreciation of the operation of
power in its different forms.

These criticisms of social practice theory, conceptual and substantive,
should not be taken to mean that it has no value; only that care needs to be
taken in applying the approach to higher education situations. It is a key
argument of this book that the concepts and approach of social practice
theory are valuable in helping leaders reflect on practice in the ways elaborated earlier in this chapter.

Conclusion

It is clear that leaders cannot hope simply to shape culture in the interests
of organizational efficiency and effectiveness in the rather simple ways advocated by Deal and Kennedy (1982) and others. Neither can organizational policies be simply determined by the 'top team' with the expectation
of unproblematic implementation on the ground. Organizational cultures
are too localized, diverse, dynamic and rooted in extra-organizational structures, such as the disciplinary communities to which academics belong as
well as to their departmental communities, for the levers of organizational
change to be predictably effective. Likewise policies are too subject to interpretation and affective response and too liable to accrete connotative codes
to be unproblematically implemented in the way that top managers intended. Leaders at whatever level (and this discussion implies that local
leaders are considerably more important than is often recognized) would
do well to develop skills that might equip them to interpret and conceptualize the social worlds they operate in and to understand better the likely
consequences of actions, policies, statements and the rippling effects of
environmental change. Wenger puts this rather well: 'The combination of
engagement and imagination results in reflective practice. Such practice
combines the ability both to engage and to distance – to identify with an
enterprise as well as to view it in context, with the eyes of an outsider'
(1998: 217).

To use Hopkins's (1992) metaphor, workgroups and departments in universities are sailed, not driven; steered from the stern. The leader needs to
read the wind, the currents and the trim of the boat, tacking and changing
with that reading. Murphy (1994) uses a different metaphor to make a
similar point, talking about leading from within the web of human relationships rather than from the apex of a pyramid. Good leaders are in the thick
of the action and understand that action well: they have 'thick connec-
tions'. Perkins talks about 'knowing your way around':

> knowing your way around . . . certainly calls for knowing that and know-
> ing how. But it depends on much more as well – having a sense of
> orientation, recognising problems and opportunities, perceiving how

things work together, possessing a feel for the structure and texture of a domain. It encompasses not just explicit but tacit knowledge, not just focal awareness but peripheral awareness, not just a sense of what's there but what's interesting and valuable . . . Better than knowing that, knowing how, or like names for knowledge, knowing your way around resonates with the notion of a learning environment.

(1996: v)

In contrast to most studies of leadership, then, this book attempts to shift the focus off the figure – the individual leader – towards the ground around him or her.

4

Learning from Other Places

Well done is half stolen.

(Davenport and Prusak, 1998: 53)

Preview

The first three chapters have 'stolen' ideas from the worlds of sociology, psychology and organizational and management studies and brought them together in discussions of social practices, change and leadership that have suggested that all three may be more complex than has often been assumed. Even if our position were plausible, a critical response could be that whatever organizational studies, sociology and psychology might suggest to us, this is a vision that is not grounded in studies of *educational* organizations. In this chapter we claim that research into secondary schools confirms that the positions we have developed are applicable to educational settings and that it previews issues that are central to good departmental leadership in higher education.

Secondary schools and HEIs

Secondary schools are different from universities and departments. They have no research missions; in most countries their curricula are prescribed; high stakes assessments of student learning are normally done on a national or state-wide basis; and they are smaller than almost all HEIs. In addition, school architecture, timetabling and routines combine to make for a much more collegial environment than is found in most HEIs, where cell-like separation is more common (Tompkins, 1992) and the involvement of a dozen different teachers in any one child's curriculum requires a more diverse pattern of staff interaction than can be found in most HEIs. Finally, children as learners are different from students as learners. The significance of that depends on whether you emphasize the similarity of formal learning, regardless of the learners' age and the educational setting, or the differences between secondary school children and students. Consider here Knowles's (1990) claim that adult education should be based on its own distinctive principles, which together are described as andragogy. A response is that there is nothing special about the principles and that 'andragogy' is a redundant concept: it could be said that all Knowles has done is described good pedagogy, which is as appropriate to young children and secondary school learners as it is to adults (Davenport, 1993).

Although they are smaller than HEIs, schools are complex organizations and teachers are grouped into subject departments and work in other teams, especially for pastoral care and curriculum development tasks. In similar ways teachers resemble tutors: both have formal academic knowledge attested by at least one degree; both are involved in work that demands non-routine decision making; both have to accept that their teaching work has uncertain outcomes that may not be easy to recognize; and both have multiple roles and priorities that are not always clearly specified or readily reconciled with each other. The intrinsic rewards of the job matter greatly to teachers and tutors, although a price of investing so much of the self in the work is that frustrations can be all the more debilitating. Teaching, in higher education and high schools, is emotional work and when it does not satisfy the emotions there are serious implications for faculty vitality and creativity (Hargreaves, 1998; Knight and Trowler, 2000a). And finally, schools and higher education appear to be in crisis as global economic and socio-political changes threaten funding, intensify professionals' work, raise doubts about the adequacy of present performance and promise that institutions and teachers who do not adapt to lifelong cyberlearning will crumple into obsolescence. Trepidation in the face of such change forces operating on schools and HEIs alike has led to calls for more investment in professional learning and for better, inspirational, efficient and transformational leadership.

There is a century of international research into school-teaching, learning, curriculum and assessment, much of it funded on a scale that is unknown to researchers into higher education practices. HEIs can learn from this research because the specific differences between schools and HEIs are less significant, we think, than their shared purposes and types of work.

School effectiveness

The following 12 characteristics of primary schools (Mortimore *et al.*, 1988) are fairly typical of the products of school effectiveness research (SER) in general. Effective schools are marked by:

- purposeful headteacher leadership;
- involvement of the deputy head;
- involvement of teachers in school policy and planning;
- consistency among teachers;
- structured teaching sessions;
- intellectually challenging teaching;
- a work-centred environment;
- a limited focus within teaching sessions;

- maximum communication between teachers and students;
- record keeping;
- parental involvement; and
- a positive school climate or ethos.

In secondary schools the second point should be extended to include heads of faculties (where they exist) and/or departments.

Although research based lists such as these have set the norms against which school effectiveness is judged, SER is vulnerable to several criticisms. Firstly, effectiveness has usually been based on pupil performance in public examinations or tests. Quite properly the raw scores have been adjusted to control for the well-known influences on achievement that are outside the school's control, such as socioeconomic status (SES) and achievement scores on entry to the school. The residuals are then taken to be 'the school effect', although there is some unease with this assumption (Coe and Fitzgibbon, 1998) and greater unease with the idea that educational effectiveness can be equated with test scores and little more (White, 1997).

Secondly, sceptics also point out that some schools are in circumstances where they have so little room for manoeuvre that a totally different concept of effectiveness ought to be deployed. Gewirtz (1998) shows how a school serving a deprived community might be judged to be effective simply because it keeps going as a place of some safety. Teddie and Reynolds (2000) also report that effective schools serving high and medium SES areas are also led differently from those serving low SES groups. There are problems, then, with a one-size-fits-all notion of school effectiveness, which echoes our earlier emphasis on the significance of contingency in social practices, change and leadership.

Thirdly, once allowances are made for the continued upward creep in public examination scores, it appears that only a minority – perhaps 14 per cent – of high schools are consistently effective, where that is defined as outperforming what might have been expected on the basis of the students' characteristics on entry (Sammons *et al.*, 1997; Gray *et al.*, 1999). And fourthly, recent SER work consistently finds that in high schools there are 'variations in outcomes between departments (and sometimes within departments) in the same school which are almost as great as the difference between schools' (West, 2000: 52). In other words, those wanting to make a difference to educational outcomes might do better to target departments, not schools. It is a point to which we shall shortly return.

Notwithstanding these limitations, SER has been a fertile source of prompts for thinking about good education. However, when it comes to trying to improve schools, other limitations emerge. For example, SER speaks in terms of norms and averages, which may not be helpful in specific cases, and its findings tend to be at a level of generality that requires a great deal of interpretation. It is one thing to have research based lists of the characteristics of effective schools but it is far from obvious how to use those descriptions to create effective schools.

School improvement

School improvement research (SIR) is informed by effectiveness research, but it is primarily about finding feasible ways of improving student learning and sustaining actions that are situationally sensitive and appropriate. It is about praxis, the fusion of practice and theory; the particular and the general; reasoning about aims and reasoning about means.

Time and time again, researchers have concluded that the quality of school leadership makes a disproportionate difference to school effectiveness and is central to school improvement (for a review, see Leithwood *et al.*, 1999). There is a distinct tendency to see effective leaders as those who are person-centred; who facilitate rather than dictate; who encourage collegiality and share responsibility; who emphasize the importance of the emotional quality of work; who encourage innovation and accept that errors come from ambition and good intentions; and who believe that professional learning is at the centre of improvement and that it depends on beliefs that improvement is possible, given effort and good thinking. Despite this general agreement about the characteristics of good leaders, SIR shows that school improvement has many forms. McCulloch *et al.* (2000) observed that English secondary schools, departments and teachers creating their own microrealities by responding in their own ways to structural changes. Schools start from different levels of effectiveness and take different trajectories accordingly; in one school organizational and behavioural issues must predominate while in another the quality of classroom teaching is rightly the focus. With improvement there is not a right starting point or a right route to take, but it is the sustained commitment to thoughtful improvement itself that matters (Fullan, 1999; Gray *et al.*, 1999; Teddie and Reynolds, 2000). Whoever the leader and whatever the starting point and the trajectory, there is a common danger 'that schools . . . seem to have almost unlimited interest in the process of structuring and restructuring . . . in focusing on the management arrangements *per se*, rather than as a means to improving the quality of teaching and learning' (West, 2000: 54). It is exactly this focus, on the quality of classroom teaching and learning, that distinguishes the minority of schools that consistently improve from the majority of inconsistent 'average' performers. Nor can improvement be tightly planned, although leaders should have a good sense of direction. There should be a flexible balance between planning and responsiveness, so that the school can respond to turbulent environments and to teachers' bright ideas and enthusiasms. Leaders need the 'ability to galvanize staff energies behind a small number of agreed priorities while simultaneously retaining the capacity to encourage development on a wide range of fronts' (West, 2000: 49). However, the weight of evidence is that there are attractors, to use the language of chaos and complexity theories, that pull improvement into the form of organizational reforms and away from hard-to-sustain attention to the quality of individual teachers' work to help learners to learn. The key messages of SIR are about good leadership and diversity in the face of powerful attractors that divert attention from the crucial matters of learning and teaching.

This review of SIR has helped to make it clear why we regard educational improvement, wheresoever it be, as praxis: contingent and changing, a matter of reflecting and doing, and of making mistakes and learning. Improvement cannot be captured by a recipe or scientific laws but it does not follow that leaders are stranded in uncertainty. SIR indicates that instead of depending on recipes it is important that leaders get the ingredients of improvement into place. Then 'the hard part is taking the risk to *trust* the process as you embed it in complexity theory' (Fullan, 1999: 24). This ingredients- or process-led approach is based on the belief that human systems are inherently complex and non-linear (Stacey, 1996; Lewin and Regine, 1999), an insight that explains that, 'Successful innovations . . . fail to be replicated because the wrong thing is being replicated – the reform itself, instead of the conditions which spawned its success' (Fullan, 1999: 64).

Important though SER and SIR are, researchers have come to think that educational improvement efforts must give as much attention to the department (or activity system, or community of practice) as to the school itself.

Leading departments

Good departments exist in poor schools and bad ones in good schools. Siskin, studying large US high schools, wrote that, 'One can move a few yards away [from one department], into the territory of another department, to find a starkly contrasting atmosphere' (1994: 110). It is 'the department, rather than the school [that] effectively marks the bounds of "major interactions" for most teachers' (1994: 69). Work collated by Harris *et al.* (1997) and done by Sammons *et al.* (1997) provides British evidence that variations in pupil achievement that are attributable to departments can be greater than those attributable to the school. This is not an attempt to make the school redundant as a unit of analysis. School policies affect departments, students, parents, the community and teachers. But teachers are also intimately affected by the ways in which school-level factors are worked out in their communities of practice. Accounts of secondary school change should include the school, the teachers and the departments, just as we have suggested that leadership and change in HEIs need to be explored at macro-, meso- and micro-levels.

There is agreement that 'if . . . the "goofy logic" of focusing change at the school level is resisted and, instead, the department is regarded as the unit of change, then the role of head of department is of major importance' (Busher and Harris, 1999: 315). Rather predictably it is harder to say exactly what makes for a good head of department, since we would expect it to be somewhat contingent, situated and shifting because schools are at different levels of effectiveness, have different improvement trajectories, different priorities and are led in different ways. Research confirms the

Table 4.1 Main factors contributing to success identified by maths and English heads of departments (after Sammons *et al.*, 1998)

Maths departments	English departments
1. The department works as a team (high commitment and high community)	1. The department works as a team (high commitment and high community)
2=. Appropriate curriculum (Given the constraints of a National Curriculum)	2=. High quality teaching in most lessons
2=. Good classroom management	2=. High expectations of student achievement
4. Teacher commitment and effort	4=. Quality of teachers
5. High expectations of student achievement	4=. Good classroom management

Table 4.2 Main barriers identified by maths and English heads of departments (after Sammons *et al.*, 1998)

Maths departments	English departments
1. Large classes	1. Administrative loads and paperwork
2. Administrative loads and paperwork	2. Large classes
3. Inadequate resources	3. Inadequate resources
4. Teacher expectations of pupil achievements are too low	4. Little parent and community support

expectation that leading a school department appears to vary according to a school's particular circumstances and improvement trajectory (e.g. Busher and Harris, 1999). Nevertheless, Sammons *et al.* (1998) found that 47 heads of maths departments and 39 heads of English were substantially in agreement about the factors helping and hindering their work. They reported a correlation coefficient between the English and maths leaders of +0.70 for success factors and +0.83 for barriers. Tables 4.1 and 4.2 summarize the most frequently mentioned factors.

Similarly, Turner and Bolam (1998), while warning of the danger of relying on general lists of the skills and competencies of good leaders without appreciating the contingencies that affect what they do, suggest that all heads of department need:

- knowledge of people;
- situational knowledge;
- knowledge of educational practices;
- conceptual knowledge in the form of sets of ideas and theories that are used to understand and analyse situations and possibilities;

- process knowledge or 'know how' to do with team-building, monitoring, evaluating, scheduling, etc.;
- control knowledge, in the sense of self-knowledge, metacognition and skill at reflecting.

If the enormous potential that exists for improving schooling by helping heads of departments to lead better is to be exploited then eight problematic areas need attention. They echo themes raised in earlier chapters and anticipate issues to be considered when dealing with higher education in later chapters.

- Neglect. Concern with school effectiveness and improvement have meant that the business of leading departments has been neglected by researchers and policy makers. Published advice on being a head of department is necessarily decontexted and tends to have a strong management emphasis (Gold, 1998).
- 'Effective preparation for [the head of department role] . . . appeared to be fortuitous and most off-the-job training that was available was invariably offered after the job was taken up' (Earley and Fletcher-Campbell, 1989: 227). Adey and Jones (1998) confirm that there is a lack of training for heads of departments and add that they tend to be appointed on the basis of proven teaching skills, which need not be good predictors of skilled leadership. In Britain the government has sponsored a definition of national standards for subject leadership. However, any implication that learning to lead can be adequately done as a formal and decontexted activity ignores the substantial evidence that teachers (McCulloch *et al.*, 2000), like others (Becher, 1996; Eraut, 1997), mainly learn informally and on the job. 'The most powerful forms of teacher development are fostered most directly and powerfully by conditions unlikely to be found outside the school' (Leithwood *et al.*, 1999: 150). How is on-the-job leadership learning to be provided for prospective departmental leaders?
- Heads of department lack time (e.g. Brown and Rutherford, 1998) and often have to resort to corner-cutting coping strategies (Gray *et al.*, 1999).
- They face role ambiguities. Headteachers hope for a commitment to whole-school policies and practices (Sammons *et al.*, 1997) but many heads of department did 'not consider that their role extended beyond that of advocacy for their subject' (Glover and Miller, 1999: 336). Another conflict is between managing and leading with Glover and Miller reporting that, 'Subject leaders were less aware of the transformational as opposed to the transactional approaches to leadership' (1999: 333). Thirdly, they frequently resist close examination of teachers' work and are uneasy about classroom observation, even though a departmental approach to improving learning and teaching implies greater openness among colleagues.
- Educational improvement means continually asking more of teachers but getting anything more than surface compliance from them means appealing to their intrinsic motivation. However, the psychic rewards that a teacher values can be compromised by paper-pushing and prescriptive

leaders who set goals, regardless of the teacher's preferences and beliefs and then expect too many outcomes too quickly (Hargreaves, 1998). Successes are more likely where the departmental culture centres on helping children to learn well and supports teacher initiatives in pursuit of it. Equally, where teachers believe they have the capacity to succeed – where they have the 'learned optimism' (Seligman, 1998) that they can make a difference in most situations and that their fate is not to be perpetual victims of structural factors – then improvement initiatives have better chances of working. Positive beliefs can be strengthened by the good interpersonal relationships that are associated with true collaborative cultures and good, person-centred leadership. They can also be sapped by toxic departmental cultures and by poor leadership. There are three main problems here for leaders. This emphasis on beliefs, emotions and intrinsic motivation runs counter to the command-and-control thinking found in many educational hierarchies; there are no quick-fix recipes for changing beliefs and building trust, nor are there guarantees that even patient and empathic leaders can vitalize all teaching; small, manageable projects are more likely to bring success than are root-and-branch reforms (Leithwood *et al.*, 1999), which implies that change and improvement come slowly as teachers tinker to improve their practices (Huberman, 1993).

- Some research evidence (Harris *et al.*, 1997) suggests that while some effective departments do have the sorts of beliefs and cultures identified in the last bullet point, other effective departments rely on everyone working to the same structures and routines. This leaders' dilemma – whether to rely on fostering collaborative success cultures or to use positional authority to secure compliance with sound operating procedures – is a reminder of the point that school improvement in general is the art of practical reasoning, or praxis.

- Good departments should be learning organizations in the two limited senses of: having a departmental view of teachers' learning priorities; and sharing learning, not treating it as personal property to be amassed in a miser-like fashion. However, opportunities for off-site learning are restricted in quantity and quality and further compressed by inexorable intensification. Furthermore, we said earlier that learning organizations need people to make their tacit knowing explicit and share it (Nonaka and Takeuchi, 1995). This is not simple and it certainly doesn't just happen: skilled leading is called for.

- Headteachers and senior management teams are not always united, which makes it difficult for departmental leaders to have a sense of direction (Sammons *et al.*, 1997; Brown and Rutherford, 1998). Even when senior managers agree on improvement strategies, it is rare to find that a plan to vitalize all departments is among them. Strategies for improving the school by improving departments might include: identifying lead departments that had volunteered to be watched piloting an innovation; leader shadowing, where one leader spends a week observing or sharing another's leadership activities; and benchmarking, where heads of departments identify knowledge and practices in other departments from which they could learn. The other side of the coin is that headteachers can be obstructed by recalcitrant or inert heads of department. In some cases school improvement depends on waiting for some heads of department to leave (Gray *et al.*, 1999).

Conclusion

It would be as unwise to criticize assumptions that the institution is the most important unit of analysis in improvement thinking and then proceed as if it were good enough to substitute 'department' wherever 'school' or 'university' would previously have been used. Departmental effectiveness is related to the school's effectiveness and individual teacher effectiveness is also important. Indeed, research into schooling tends to swing between a concern with teacher effectiveness and a fascination with school effectiveness. The department lies between the teacher and the institution. Research into improving secondary schooling is increasingly concerned with how departments make a difference to students, teachers and schools. We take that to support the case we began to develop in Chapters 1–3 that better higher education means taking academic departments far more seriously. In the following chapters we work out some implications of seeing quality improvement in higher education in terms of the quality of departmental leadership.

Part 2

Issues

In Part 2 we shift our attention to the ways in which leaders in higher education can operate successfully in its current turbulent environment, focusing in turn on the key areas in which they are likely to be involved. We begin with the assessment of students' work and the issues for leaders in addressing it.

5

Leading and Assessment

Even the most sophisticated and expensive assessment technique – the assessment center – accounts for only 10 per cent to 20 per cent of the variance in management promotion rates.

(Hunt, 1991: 255)

Put your faith in the process – not in your estimate of the final outcome.

(James Gleick, quoted in Lewin and Regine (1999: 17))

Preview

Even when trustworthy assessments can be made, as at assessment centres, they are not as useful as might have been expected. Might it be, then, that the quest for highly trustworthy or reliable judgements of achievement is out of proportion to their usefulness? If so, there are interesting possibilities for leaders who have an interest in improving the quality of student learning. The first section of this chapter sets out the way in which we shall talk about assessment and the second is a compact review of the nature and purposes of assessment. To get an idea of how compressed that review is, you might scan the shelves in your library for books on research methods in social sciences. You should find hundreds of them. The assessment of human learning and performance is no less complex and raises virtually the same issues. The third section lays out some characteristics of department- and programme-level assessment systems and the fourth considers what a team leader or head of department might do to improve the way student learning is assessed. A recurrent theme is, 'Get that [low stakes] assessment right and good learning does follow' (Knight, 1999: 104).

Terminology

'Assessment' does not have exactly the same meaning in all English-speaking countries. We use the word to describe the collection of evidence for making judgements about achievement. Notice the implication that assessment is not an objective activity. It is about judgement. Loose and informal judgements are fit for some assessment purposes, but when it comes to high-stakes purposes assessment should be similar to judgements in legal processes: it should be impartial, informed and fair.

'Testing' is one way of collecting evidence. Examinations are one type of test. Tests are usually used to make a summary of achievement after learners have completed an assignment, course or programme. They usually have time limits, which are frequently tight enough to favour those who work fast. They are overwhelmingly used to identify individual, unaided achievement. In this explanation of 'testing' we break with a US usage (Knight *et al.*, 2000) and treat tests as special types of assessment situations in which a variety of assessment methods might be used. The same general methods might also be used to promote conversations about the improvement of learning.

In the USA there is a tradition of testing that has tended to restrict the assessment of learning to short-answer, multiple choice or other fixed response tests of the more reliably measured aspects of achievement; subject matter knowledge, for example. This approach has its place but it also has considerable limitations (Sternberg, 1997). It has a high opportunity cost because it displaces assessment for other purposes – such as learning improvement – and it occludes complex or fuzzy forms of learning – such as critical thinking – that cannot be properly captured by general, content-free, highly reliable instruments. It also depends on views of humankind, cognition, affect and reality that are increasingly challenged. There has been a reaction to the narrowness of testing in the form of a growth of interest in 'performance' or 'authentic' assessment. One view of performance assessment is that it 'includes any technique that requires students to generate their own responses rather than to select among responses that have been provided for them' (Palomba and Banta, 1999: 116). Both authentic and performance assessment approaches tend to draw on a wider range of methods than testing and to present 'real-life' assessment situations that allow judgements to be made about learners' achievements in terms of the wide range of learning goals that is valued by state, provincial and national governments. Cuming and Maxwell (1999) have observed that some supposedly authentic assessments are pretty contrived and sterile and argued that it is important to remember that the original concept referred to the assessment of authentic (or realistic) achievement. Authentic assessment is increasingly valued in the assessment of complex achievements in realistic conditions. Walvoord and Anderson (1998) provide an excellent account of ways for departments to get a better match between assessment methods and their undergraduate course goals, which echoes Erwin's position that 'deciding what to teach and assess is one decision, not two' (1995: 51). Outside the USA performance and authentic assessment are well established, although a false consciousness that assessment is necessarily about producing reliable judgements for high-stakes purposes has been a constraining force. In the next section we develop the position that although testing is sometimes appropriate, and although there are many occasions when reliable, high-stakes performance assessment is in order (whether it is assessment of laboratory skills, faculty teaching accomplishments or departmental research standing), assessment is important as a part of learning conversations. Grading, by which we mean the award of marks, may contribute to learning conversations but it is not necessary for them and it may even scupper them.

The complexities of assessment

When assessment procedures are touched the whole educational enterprise feels it. Things that can be creatively left in tacit form in the curriculum have to be acknowledged when it comes to thinking about assessment. Both dilemmas and differences that can be hidden in the fuzzy Discourses of teaching and learning have to be clarified if assessment is to take place. To the requirement that teams and departments come clean about what they value is added the necessity of finding assessments to match.

This is a chapter about the assessment of student learning and more besides. The principles developed here apply equally to the judgement of teaching accomplishments, academic achievements, departmental effectiveness and student satisfaction. Questions of purpose – of why we are assessing – take similar forms, whether the topic is the assessment of student learning, the development of employability performance indicators for British universities or the appraisal of academic staff performance. Assessment methods get used for many different purposes and similar questions about their fitness for purpose arise in contexts as diverse as social science research, staff appraisal, departmental review and accreditation, teaching evaluations, academic grading and psychometric measurement: Brown and Knight (1994) give details of common assessment methods, Walvoord and Anderson (1998) list 63 but do not describe them and *The ASSHE Inventory* gives a page to each of 137 assessment initiatives in Scotland (Hounsell *et al.*, 1996).

Assessment as conversation

Where assessment is a part of conversation about ways of improving future understandings and performances, it is more likely to be an informal, low-threat (or low-stakes) exchange between people who may be equals. The conversation may be face-to-face or it may be asynchronous and based on paper or electronic media. It does not matter much whether these learning-centred conversations are about how a university's research profile might be strengthened, or about writing better history papers, or about increasing part-time MBA students' satisfaction with their academic programme. Each would be based on some assessment of present performance that is then shared in order to make a difference. These conversations are examples of formative assessment in which giving and receiving feedback are the central processes. Chapter 6 elaborates the idea that the quality of feedback in these conversations is crucial to the quality and amount of learning that is (or is not) inspired.

An important implication of this view of assessment is that '[I]t is hard to see how any innovation in formative assessment can be treated as a marginal change in classroom work' (Black and Wiliam, 1998: 16). That is all the more true given their review of 681 research publications on formative assessment in school settings that showed 'conclusively that formative assessment does improve learning' and argued that if best practices were achieved in mathematics on a nationwide scale that would raise 'average' countries such as England and the USA into the top five (1998: 61): the possible effect size of 0.7 is 'amongst the largest ever recorded for educational interventions' (1998: 61). Naturally, this promise is not to be attained without meeting a number of conditions. For example, Black (1998) has concluded that formative assessment was best when it related to clear criteria and where the comments were not accompanied by marks or grades, and Brown and Knight (1994) identified more than a dozen beliefs and practices that were needed if formative assessment were to work in higher education. It is because formative assessment is not a cost-free practice that it may promise rather more than it delivers. There tends to be a rather naïve assumption that something like Habermas's ideal speech situation will operate, so that prejudices and power relations are set aside as well-informed and committed people engage in a collective search for better learning. Certainly these ideals are not realized in the early years of schooling, when teachers' formative intentions founder because young learners defer to authority and overlook feedback for improvement in their concern to get praise for achievements (Torrance and Pryor, 1998). The same might be said of college students too. It might be thought that replacing the teacher as the source of feedback by a fellow student would stop students focusing on the authoritative grade and make them hear the learning message. In the sense that work with children indicates that the quality of learning conversations between peers tends to be better than those between teachers and children, this is likely. Yet power is present in all relationships and substituting peers for teachers alters, but does not obliterate, power relations. Less valued groups and lower status individuals may tend not to be heard in peer conversations and peer suggestions can be regarded as poor and cheapskate substitutes for the teacher's expert authority. The hopes for assessment as conversation may be inflated, although they faithfully reproduce the ideal of the learning community that a university is supposed to be. Notwithstanding practical shortcomings, Black and Wiliam's summary of the potential of assessment as conversation is a compelling one.

It is especially attractive because conversational or formative assessment is low-stakes assessment. If no one is going to get fired, promoted, or awarded a degree as a direct result, then the assessments need not be overwhelmed by the 'objective' measurement procedures that are necessary for reliable, high-stakes assessments. That is very useful because if it is true that 'most of the problems of modern society are *affective* and *emotional* [and] . . . it is time to begin shifting our educational interest and energy in the direction of the affective side' (Astin, 1999: 174, original emphasis), then there is a major assessment problem: these qualities and achievements along with 'transferable skills' that governments would like higher education to promote, are not susceptible to reliable, high-stakes assessment – or are, but only at a prohibitive price. Yet to be taken seriously they need to be assessed. What high-stakes assessment cannot do, formative, low-stakes, conversational assessment can. And should.

Assessment as accountability

Where assessment is a way of holding others to account for their achievements, whether that is in order to celebrate achievement through the award of a degree, to identify and damn poor teaching, or to find the university adding most to the employability of its undergraduates, then everything changes, except the assessment methods, although the same methods will feel very different when used for these two different purposes (learning and accountability). When assessment is high stakes, then it ought to be objective and scientific with authoritative assessors to pass down final judgements of attainment. Feedback may or may not follow, but if it does it is usually at a time (at the end of the semester or term) or in a form (a grade) that makes it virtually useless for improvement purposes.

Accountability judgements that lead to an award, such as a degree, diploma or certificate, are seldom made with an eye to directly informing further learning. In some systems they take the form of a pass/fail statement, or of a degree grade and nothing else. Where they are accompanied by transcripts and grade point averages (GPAs), there is little to be inferred about what needs improving, let alone how to do it. One reason is because US transcripts seldom do more than list the courses that students have taken and that is not necessarily particularly illuminating (Adelman, 1990) and, 'grade-point averages – despite the patina of objectivity that quantification lends them – too often represent a meaningless averaging of unclear assumptions and unstated standards' (Walvoord and Anderson, 1998: xi). Nor do degree classes or GPAs say what the learner did well or what was not mastered, let alone suggest ways of improving future performances. The scope to contribute to new learning is further limited by the fact that summative judgements frequently come at the end of the learning line. Even in school systems where curricula are carefully designed so that this year's work builds on last year's, insufficient use is made of summative judgements from one year to the next in the learning plans drawn up by the next teacher down the line, so high-stakes assessment often has little more than a symbolic effect on school practices (Airaison, 1988). In loosercoupled higher education systems progression is more likely to be based on the assumption that learners will develop by exposure to a succession of cafeteria-style courses than upon purposeful responses to summative assessments from earlier modules.

Yet accountability driven assessment is intended to bring about improvements in learning. The mechanism is indirect. It is based on the idea that management and measurement go together; that you can't manage what you can't measure. Measurement allows underperformance to be identified. When underperformance is defined as doing less well than average, there is a continued press for improvement, since the mean, mode and median are all defined so that average and above average achievements are balanced by below average achievements: there are always losers to identify and cajole into improvement. In this norm-referenced system, improvement and accountability bring about improvement by naming the above average and shaming the below average.

An alternative to the in-built failures of norm-referencing is criteria-referenced accountability: thresholds or benchmarks are set and performances are judged against them. This approach has no problem with the idea of a 100 per cent success rate. In fact, high success rates are causes for celebration, not for mutterings about 'decline of standards'. Achievements are usually defined at different levels of achievement, which means that students can see exactly what they need to do in order to sustain a level or to improve on it. Setting out learning goals and levels in this way can help students to see what they have to do to achieve a level, help them to identify what they need to learn to do better and make it possible to teach learners how to become skilled at self-assessment. The clarity and step-wise nature of the criteria are widely reckoned to be motivating (James and Gipps, 1998).

Criteria-referenced assessments can be highly reliable, and this approach is at the heart of the British system of National Vocational Qualifications (NVQs) and General National Vocational Qualifications (GNVQs). However, as the development of these awards has shown, that which should be assessed in terms of validity remains hard to do reliably. For sure, the reliability of assessments of authentic, workplace or simulated performances can be raised to very high levels by the use of multiple assessors making multiple assessments of any one element of achievement. In practice, the costs work against high reliability. The National Curriculum in English schools was intended to produce reliable and valid criteria-referenced assessments of achievement to sustain children's learning. In practice, tests of low-level skills and facts in maths, science and English have been privileged (James and Gipps, 1998). The costs of reducing the threats to reliability even in something as familiar as essay marking are considerable (Breland, 1999; Fleming, 1999). That and the absence of common curricula, shared notions of graduate standards (Elton, 1998), shared understandings of the contribution of higher education to human development (Chickering, 1999), and of shared meanings within subjects and disciplines (Wolf *et al.*, 1997), lead us to say that whether the approach is norm- or criteria-referenced, the high levels of reliability needed for accountability purposes are only affordably attainable as far as subject matter knowledge and low-level skills are concerned.

Table 5.1 summarizes differences between the accountability and the conversational approach.

Table 5.1 Dimensions of difference between conversational and accountability approaches to assessment

Aspect	Conversational ◄――――――► Accountability	
Basic ontology	Has roots in constructivism and poststructuralism	Tends towards realism and positivism
View of measurement	Some reject the term 'measurement'. Others use the language of informed estimates, provisional judgements and plausible accounts	'Scientific', highly reliable and objective measurement is the Grail
Standards of measurement	Estimates, judgements, accounts or measures must be as fair as they can be and as they need to be for the purpose at hand	'Scientific', highly reliable and objective measurement is the Grail
Assumptions about achievement and ability	Patterns of achievement cannot be predicted: everyone may learn well, work hard and meet the criteria for success (and if there is a 'normal' distribution, it is not shaped like the classic bell curve)	Achievements and ability are normally distributed in the shape of the bell curve: grades should tend to fit that distribution
What is assessed?	Anything can be assessed in the sense that information can be collected to inform assessment conversations about any learning goals	Things can be assessed scientifically (reliably). So a lot that we claim to value is not assessed and as a result is not taken seriously
Who assesses?	Conversational partners: sometimes this is the teacher, sometimes other students and sometimes you assess yourself	Experts, which is to say teaching staff
Language of assessment	Reactions, responses and suggestions: provisional	'Final' language (Boud, 1995) – firm, authoritative verdicts
Feedback	Ideally fast, personal, engaging and intended to help the learner see ways of doing better on a different task next time	Often very specific and not very transferable to future work. May come when the course is done and there's no chance or incentive to use feedback for improvement. Feedout to others, rather than feedback?
Assessor–assessed relationship	Rooted in collegiality	Appropriate to patriarchy
Purposes	Motivating (extrinsic and intrinsic), helping, affirming, supporting	Labelling, celebrating shaming, sorting, motivating (extrinsic)
Forum	May be one-to-one and more or less private	Frequently public – for example, in England, naming and shaming schools.

Combining conversational and accountability approaches

Few people think that the same piece of work can be judged for account-ability and improvement purposes. It is a commonplace in psychology that we learn from making mistakes. It follows that situations that discourage us from taking the risk of making mistakes or that encourage us to hide defi-ciencies, inadequacies and errors by 'faking good' are not ideal for learn-ing. So if we are to collect evidence for improvement, it is important that the people who are being assessed feel that it is safe to disclose material that shows them falling short of their aspirations. By and large, then, it should be clear and public, in advance, whether assessment procedures will be for accountability or conversational, summative or formative purposes. People being assessed need to be confident that anything they disclose for con-versational assessment purposes will not resurface later and be used for accountability purposes. One of the costs of the apparent spread of low-trust work environments (Sennett, 1999) is that learning is a casualty of the image-management campaigns that can dominate working lives. This anticipates a theme of Chapter 9, which is about continuing professional development.

We identify three ways in which conversational and accountability pur-poses can be combined. A common but limited approach is to assess for accountability and then find ways of getting improvement feedback from it into the system. The limitations of this approach are that accountability assessments often do not provide data that help improvement, nor are they always timed to feed into the next learning cycle. If these limitations are overcome, accountability data can be useful for improvement purposes, always remembering that the need to have reliable measurements has meant that there are important things about which these data are silent (because they could not be assessed with sufficient reliability). A second is have formative assessments leading to summative reassessments. The third, which is our preferred option, is to keep the two apart, to assess some achieve-ments summatively, so as to satisfy the needs for certification, licensing and bean counting, and to assess others formatively.

Departmental assessment systems

A major problem is that most academic staff do not understand that al-though assessments can provide good data for some inferences about under-standing, skills and dispositions they more commonly provide limited and even misleading data. Even where the difference is understood, we believe that there is a strong tendency to exaggerate the security of assessment data. Consider, for example, attempts to produce statements of intended learn-ing outcomes that are to be arranged in hierarchies to describe different levels of performance. Such taxonomies proliferate, although they are far less precise than they might appear and attempts to use them for high-stakes assessment are compromised by the differences in meanings that communities of practice attribute to these statements of achievement criteria. Of course, the limitations of the criteria vanish if they are predominantly used for low-stakes assessment and recognized as fuzzy indicators that help to give learning a broad direction and that become a heuristics for assessment conversations. If the attempt is made to try and develop fuzzy indicators into reliable measures of the sort associated with Newtonian science, problems proliferate. Some fundamentally problematic points include the following:

- It can be assumed that a common language can be found with which to describe outcomes, when often there is a proliferation of languages, leading to a babble, as has been found in attempts to identify the character of 'graduateness' (HEQC, 1997).
- There is a tendency for outcomes to multiply through fission, with goals being divided and sub-divided until hundreds or thousands of outcomes have been written (Stenhouse, 1975).
- Not only are there objections to the idea that invariant taxonomies can be constructed, so that remembering is always below analysing, but it is also challenging to write statements of levels of achievement for the same outcome and arguably impossible to do so unambiguously (Greatorex, 1999; Price and Rust, 1999).
- Even if good achievement criteria can be produced for different aspects of complex activities, such as counselling, writing a paper or designing a house, skilled performance involves some kind of 'meta-skill' of appropriately coordinating those constituent skills. How might that be assessed?
- Since all performances are strongly contexted, how is a performance to be assessed such that judgements about the skill are separated from the particular context? Many of the disputes about the pace of child development can be traced to the problem with distinguishing an ability from the context in which it is, or is not, manifested.
- Subjectivity plays a pervasive role in judgement. How can assessments be reliable when outcome statements, no matter how carefully they may be written, need to be interpreted to help assessors to decide whether an ability is present in a given, contexted performance (Wolf *et al.*, 1997; Price and Rust, 1999)? The common response is to write more and longer criteria, which makes them less usable and provides more degrees of freedom for disputes about grading.
- Unlike can be aggregated with unlike. How can contexted assessment judgements be combined so as to allow reliable summaries of achievement to be constructed (Mitchell, 1997; Dalziel, 1998)?

Yet departments and institutions have to produce some robust judgements of student learning and these are better based on criteria-referencing than on the pernicious bell curve of norm-referencing. A working solution involves reducing the unreliability of criteria-related assessment to acceptable but affordable levels. Strategies include:

- concentrating on subject matter that is sufficiently regular that the scope for argument about better-and-worse and right-and-wrong is lessened;
- assessing things that are well embedded in the Discourses of a community of practice;
- making standards, criteria and methods of judgement as explicit and public as possible;
- conspicuously inducting students into programme assessment practices and expectations;
- ensuring that procedures look fair by means of the even-handed application of assessment rules and by having more than one grader making judgements in circumstances that appear to be free of bias for or against any learner or group of learners;
- establishing a rule-based system that leads to final judgements that are derived from repeated assessments of the designated understanding, skill or whatever.

To all intents and purposes these established procedures are sufficient to produce grades in which we could have a high, but not complete, confidence. But not only are the procedures more expensive as attention moves from the assessment of information recognition, through to the assessment of understanding and on to the assessment of fuzzy skills and qualities, but they do not really work when it comes to trying to assess polymorphous things such as reflection, professionalism, interpersonal skills and self-motivation.

The simple answer is not to try and assess reliably that which cannot be reliably assessed at an acceptable cost. The following principles give an indication of the nature of an assessment system that is responsive to the extended goals that higher education needs to espouse and that is intended to support learning rather than to measure it.

Ten assessment principles

1. Higher education institutions and departments make claims to be developing an extensive set of understandings, qualities and skills (e.g. Stephenson, 1998), so assessment methods should be equally extensive: students should get information about their achievements in terms of all programme and institution goals.
2. Point 1 calls for a multiple-strategy approach to assessment, using a range of methods to profile a range of achievement.
3. That which can be assessed reliably and at reasonable cost should be assessed reliably so that it is possible to communicate something of students' achievements to employers and other stakeholders in a secure way.

4. That which needs to be assessed but which cannot be judged with certainty should be the subject of assessment conversations with peers, tutors, and – inevitably – with oneself.
5. Assessment conversations do not have to be accompanied by the panoply of reliability that attaches to high-stakes assessments. There is the potential to use the academic time and resources they save to improve the overall quality of assessment, learning and teaching. Principle 10 identifies one area where saved resources could be reinvested.
6. Students should be shown how to make claims to achievements that draw on assessment conversations. These claims will often take the form of portfolios (Tait and Godfrey, 1999; Wright and Knight, 1999).
7. Those responsible for programmes, whether they are departments or teams, should have assessment plans that identify repeated opportunities across the whole three- or four-year programme for assessing achievement against programme goals. This is a necessary addition to and prerequisite for course-level assessment planning (cf. Toohey, 1999).
8. Programme assessment plans should attend to progression in student learning in at least two ways: by providing fuzzy achievement criteria that indicate features of more advanced, less advanced and highly valued achievements; and by reducing the social, conceptual and organizational scaffolding that are available to students as they move through the programme.
9. As at Alverno College, Milwaukee (Mentowski *et al.*, 1991), students should be inducted into these assessment principles, which will pervade their programme of working, reflecting and learning.
10. Principles 6–9 imply that regular academic counselling should be designed into programmes. The time for this comes from time saved by reducing the clutter of inappropriately adopted reliable assessment techniques.

Leading to better assessment practices

It is a cliché of curriculum studies that although it may be true that any subject can be taught in some intellectually worthwhile form to any child, it is not true that any teacher can do it. Likewise, it is one thing to propose ten assessment principles and another to know how best to respond to them. In some departments and teams it would be wise not to act, on the grounds that all available energies must be devoted to maintenance, repair or building defences against another threat, or because interpersonal relationships are too fragile. However, those who say things like this may be talking up their own powerlessness in order to protect themselves from having to do things that they fear. One reason for the increase in ways of calling institutions, teams and departments to account is the suspicion that an 'excuse culture' has been used to avoid actions that external stakeholders want and that are unpalatable to some insiders.

Nevertheless, there is a range of actions that can be taken to begin assessment reform, running from tinkerings to transformation. Organizational analysts, such as Weick and Westley (1996) frequently recommend that leaders look for 'small wins' and take an incremental approach, and research on reforms in schooling also indicates that it is both sensible and potentially effective for leaders to encourage small-scale changes. We noted in previous chapters that the educational changes that really happen and last (in contrast to ones that are planned and pass) often come from teachers routinely tinkering with their practices, much like a mechanic who continually improves an engine by forever adding new parts, replacing old ones, and tuning the lot (Huberman, 1993). It is all the better if assessment reform is associated with the development of an improvement culture in which people talk about how they might deal with problems and do things better. Here the leader facilitates and energizes these problem-working activities and is as much a coach and motivator as monitor or manager (Rosenholtz, 1989; Nias *et al.*, 1992). As Chapter 4 suggested, there is no one right way to get started in the business of improvement so a leader might start assessment reform with any of the suggestions that follow. Possibilities, which are listed in order of complexity and ambitiousness, include:

1. *An assessment audit.* When students follow a programme that only gives them a restricted choice of modules or courses, it is easy to do audits in order to get a better sense of their cumulative experiences of assessment and learning. Nowadays, there is so much choice that these are the minority of students, which makes audits much harder. They are not, though, impossible because some patterns of choice are much more popular than others. Perhaps half a dozen combinations will account for 80 per cent of the students for whom a departmental chair or team leader is responsible. Audits can be based on these courses and action can be based on what audits show about students' de facto curricula. This is an approximation but an approximate idea of what the whole assessment and learning experience looks like is better than none.

   Audits might focus on any or all of the following:
   * *Assessment methods or techniques.* It takes a good range of methods to assess a good range of learning goals. An audit will show if some methods are being over-used (essays, lab reports and solving well-structured problems like those done in the lecture are the mainstays of many assessment regimes).
   * *Assessment scaffolding.* Is there progression in assessment so that structure and scaffolding are reduced? When that happens students are led to be more independent, to identify and define problems and issues for themselves, and to apply, spontaneously, understanding skills and qualities from one area to another.
   * *Assessment balance.* What is the weighting between summative assessment (high-stakes and graded, possibly based on tests), conversational or formative assessment where the teacher gives ungraded improvement

feedback and conversational assessment where other students are the source of learning feedback?

2. *Establishing achievement criteria at course level.* We are sceptical about the idea that criteria can be so precise that graders need make no inferences, although this becomes more likely the closer assessment moves towards being an 'objective' test of factual knowledge. Yet that does not mean that criteria are useless, only that they need to be regarded as fuzzy statements (Kosko, 1994) that deal in probabilities and approximations. When accounts of what better work looks like can be shared and used in the form of fuzzy criteria, they help to focus attention on learning, to indicate what should be given priority in teaching and learning, and offer a language to draw upon in assessment conversations.

As Walvoord and Anderson (1998) illustrate well and in detail, it is no great slight on academic freedom to ask colleagues to make explicit what they are hoping to do in their course and to say how they recognize different levels of success in terms of those course goals. While it is a good discipline to try and express these criteria precisely and unambiguously, we have already made the point that many learning goals have to stay in fuzzy language, which is the starting point for discussion, not its endpoint. That implies that it is not enough to publish criteria. Students need to talk about them and practise using them. This course-level work on criteria is not nearly as powerful as aligning course criteria with a single programme framework (see point 7, below).

3. *Sponsor a series of electronic or paper 'practice notes' that summarize good practice in assessment.* Walvoord and Anderson (1998: 114) give an example of a briefing sheet for students engaged in peer assessment. This could be extended to other aspects of assessment practice (and to learning and teaching practices as well). Notes should be short, direct in style and realistic in expectations.

4. *Investigate the feedback that students get on their achievements and that they are aware of getting.* This could be the first stage in an action research project, where the intention is to use an inquiry to bring about improvements. Three things that might be aimed for are: disseminating the idea that feedback for improvement should be endemic; working towards a situation where teachers' feedback meets the standards in Box 5.1; and looking for ways of helping students to see the importance of giving and receiving peer feedback.

5. *Improve student evaluations.* Although student course evaluations are mandatory in most institutions they are usually summative assessments that can contribute little to improvement conversations. Perry and Smart (1997) provide substantial summaries of the limitations of many evaluation procedures and of the frequent misuses of evaluation scores, and we shall return to this theme in Chapter 6. One way of improving assessment is to collect more and better information from students about how they see the assessment system. Sambell and McDowell (1998) have used student focus groups to get a better understanding of ways in which assessment

---

Box 5.1   Aspects of good feedback in assessment conversations

- Achievement is not predetermined by a fixed level of ability. Achievement is related to effort, to our strategies and to the social and other resources on which we draw (Dweck, 1999). In other words, feedback is based on the presumption that improvements are possible.
- Good feedback identifies things that, if they were changed, could make a difference to performance on a different topic. It is not cluttered with lots of detail about specifics: it consists of headlines, not footnotes (Walvoord and Anderson, 1998).
- Good feedback does not use 'final vocabulary' by trading in firm, authoritative terms that limit thinking (because final language leaves no room for manoeuvre) and that may label learners in ways that make them 'learn helplessness' (Boud, 1995; Seligman, 1998).
- Judgements and improvement advice that are related to known and understood criteria have more weight and meaning than those that appear to be arbitrary. Criteria can be especially useful for explaining ways in which future work could be improved (Sadler, 1989).
- Good feedback is fast feedback – on the spot by preference, otherwise within days.

---

processes could be brought more into line with students' various learning and emotional needs. More radically, base student evaluations on the principles of assessment conversations and reduce the importance given to apparently reliable and actually misleading questionnaire-based course evaluations.

6. *Organize professional development sessions on assessment matters.* Three possible interventions are:
   - Faculty learn about assessment methods that will often be new to them and have opportunities to study examples, talk about them with colleagues, take part in simulations, watch videos showing the methods in action, or hear students or staff talk about their experiences with these methods.
   - Instructional development professionals explore beliefs about learning, teaching, assessment, and achievement with faculty. Colleagues who believe that assessment is about reliable grading of achievement will see little value in assessment conversations that do not produce a set of accurate marks. Again, if you (wrongly) believe that human achievement is 'normally' distributed in a bell curve and that ability is a fixed attribute, then you will be uneasy with criteria-referencing and the possibility that everyone might succeed.
   - Consultants work with faculty on pressing assessment problems, such as identifying course goals and then describing what would count as evidence of achievement in terms of those (fuzzy) goals.

7. *If course learning goals and the language used to describe them can be related to a programme-wide set of learning criteria it becomes possible to capitalize on the resultant curriculum coherence, continuity and progression.* It is not necessary for programme-level criteria to include all course goals because some will necessarily be specific to particular courses. Nor would each course have to address all of the programme goals. Benefits of programme-level assessment could be:

- Students can be inducted into a common set of assessment criteria that become a well-understood point of reference in most assessment conversations and judgements.
- It is possible to get better assessments of how well students can transfer their achievements from one context to another by setting tasks that required achievements from one course to be the basis of performance – perhaps to a higher level – in another.
- A common set of fuzzy criteria makes it easier for faculty to communicate with each other, to plan for progression in learning and to think in terms of programme-wide improvement.
- There should be greater consistency in high-stakes assessments.

In the UK there have been a number of attempts to produce regional or institutional statements of key learning goals and accompanying descriptors of levels of achievement commensurate with different awards (master's degree, bachelor's degree, diploma, certificate). Ellington (1999) describes how such criteria have been customized by departments in his university, which have been expected to relate their programme goals and standards to a common institutional framework. A similar deductive exercise is needed when programme goals have to be nested within criteria, standards or descriptors produced by outside professional bodies or accrediting agencies.

An alternative to deducing programme achievement criteria from institutional descriptors is to induce them from current practice. Walvoord and Anderson (1998) give pages of examples of ways in which teams have gathered information about existing course assessment processes and criteria (or 'primary traits', as they call them) and then negotiated descriptions of common ground, from which have grown programme-level assessment criteria. Although doing it this way round is still difficult, it has two advantages over the deductive approach. One is that the criteria are based on what faculty already do and the second is that teams and departments can more easily feel ownership of the goals that emerge. Apart from the time it takes and teachers' common feeling that they lack the expertise to do this, the major limitation is conservatism. A synthesis of existing goals and standards may not produce programme criteria that have the breadth that is now expected of undergraduate provision. So, leaders who want to locate course-level assessment within a programme-wide set of criteria will need to complement the inductive approach with a request that the team also looks for ways of describing, assessing and teaching things of importance (for example, independence, information and communications technology (ICT) literacy, incremental self-theories, team working) that might not be represented in present practice.

8. *Benchmarking and networking.* Benchmarking involves identifying better or best practice and aiming to match or beat it. That can be done by an academic version of industrial espionage but networking makes for better learning. There are two sets of communities in which most teams and departments can learn. One is the institutional community, which implies the identification of superior assessment practice in another so that others could learn from the leaders or, better still, learn with them by joint development, problem-working and sense-making activities. The other community is the national and international subject community, comprising historians, midwives, architects, equestrians, and so on. The principles are the same as for the institutional community, although cost considerations mean that networks will tend to be virtual rather than physical.

Benchmarking can be simple and unthreatening. If it is treated as sharing information about practices and problems (Woolf and Cooper, 1999), benchmarking is a good way to improve assessment, learning and teaching practices, with the only difficulties being working out how to make something that worked *there* work *here.* Adopting better practices means faculty changing their assumptions about what is right and proper, which can threaten individuals and cause conflict in the department. Best practice will often be based on assumptions about teaching and teachers, learners and learning, assessment and knowing, that are quite different from those in currency in the department. So it is evident that using benchmarking to try and change tectonic beliefs about assessing, learning, and so on, will be harder and less liable to succeed than using it as a source of hints for better practice. There is much to recommend benchmarking as a contribution to tinkering but, as we suggested earlier, there are also times when more fundamental changes are mandated.

There is clearly a great deal that can be done to improve good assessment practices while retaining established frameworks. For example, if there is only a limited range of achievements that HEIs can assess reliably enough to certify, then there are swathes of student achievements that are important and valued but that are not described by existing high-stakes assessment methods. We have suggested that these achievements should be formatively assessed, either by peers or by faculty, which leaves a problem with documenting them for employers and graduate schools. These are achievements of value but because they cannot be reliably assessed they ought not to be endorsed by universities and colleges. One way of dealing with this problem would be if transcripts, letters of recommendation and other references referred to the range and depth of learning entitlements in a programme and identified the accomplishments that those entitlements would normally stimulate. This would help stakeholders to appreciate the sorts of achievement claims that might be made and to know that they had a grounding in planned curriculum experiences. Of itself, though, this information would not be sufficient, since learning entitlements may hold the promise of some learning achievements but not the certainty. This might be tackled by expecting that learners would learn to: make claims to having certain accomplishments at certain levels (learners would refer to programme criteria and use them to formulate their own claims to achievement); make other claims that would be based on out-of-class learning that went beyond programme assessment criteria; and provide evidence to substantiate those claims.

It would only work if students were inducted into this model of learning and claim-making from the beginning of their programmes; if programme assessment criteria were available to help guide their claim-making; if all teachers on the programme made students aware of the relationship between any one module and the overall programme assessment/learning criteria; if opportunities for reflecting on learning achievements, learning claims and learning needs were built into the programme; and if there was systematic teaching about portfolio-making, accompanied by individual academic and careers guidance. Dalhousie University in Nova Scotia, Canada has introduced a first year option in which students take a credit-bearing module on making a skills-related 'Career Portfolio'. In this module they learn about the skills that the university and prospective employers value, about the sorts of evidence they might collect about their achievements, about reflecting on their learning and on their needs, and about making portfolios to substantiate their claims to achievement. Dalhousie recognizes that out-of-class learning also contributes to skills development and students are encouraged to consider how their work experiences can be used to substantiate claims to achievement. The first year students in this module are guided by fourth year students, who take credit-bearing modules that have two primary aims. One is to help them to finalize their own portfolios and the other is to equip them with the group leadership and communication techniques, skills and strategies needed to mentor the first years. Ideally, these two 'bookend' modules would be linked by scheduled review and planning sessions throughout the sophomore and junior years. Some of this review and planning work ought to be done in small groups, action learning sets or on a 'buddy' system, but there also needs to be one-to-one work with an academic adviser.

Such assessment reform can be a substantial and disruptive undertaking. Where Knight (1995) offered advice on creating learning portfolios, Trowler and Hinett (1994) argued that disproportionate efforts were needed for success. On the other hand, it may be that departments that are responsive to government calls for highly skilled, flexible and self-directing graduates will *have* to move in these directions, accepting costs now in anticipation of benefits – such as survival – in the future.

Conclusion

This chapter has made the claim that leading assessment is necessary to sustain student learning that engages with the broad range of goals associated with modern higher education. Many piecemeal improvements can be made without great expense or trouble but because assessment does so much to determine what students regard as the 'real' curriculum, major reforms may be needed if ambitious learning goals are to be taken seriously. At the same time, systemic assessment reform demands, and should evoke, change in the curriculum, learning and pedagogies, which is the subject of Chapter 6.

6

Leading Learning and Teaching

There is a general increase in awareness about the importance of teaching, so fewer faculty can ignore this aspect of their performance. The need to report annually and present a portfolio on each course, including student evaluation of the conduct of the course means that faculty give this matter some priority. [Sources of difficulty include] Workload. The amount and standard of productive scholarship required to attain tenure &/or promotion is greater than ever, causing some faculty to minimize their attention to pedagogical questions. Perception, certainly in some faculty, that they are good teachers and it is the students who criticize them who are wrong. My own scepticism of the value of many of the devices used to solicit student evaluation of a course . . .

(Male, web survey, experienced leader, Canada)

Preview

Many points about the improvement of learning have been made in Chapter 5, since where assessment procedures are in the service of good learning goals, good learning tends to follow. It was also suggested that a department's goals will mainly be a selection from subject and disciplinary expectations, official mandates and injunctions, and a more general concern to promote human development (Chickering, 1999). There is no further discussion of goals. Attention is concentrated on the ways in which goal-directed learning happens. The following section is essentially a digest of various literature on the characteristics of good learning in the pursuit of these complex, demanding and extensive goals. A convenient, alternative ten-point account is published by the Joint Task Force on Student Learning (1998).

The subsequent section contains suggestions for ways of making team or department plans for good student learning. Because good learning needs time and involves practice it is advisable to plan for the whole student learning experience, or to have an overview of that part of the experience organized by the team or department. This is not, then, a chapter about individual modules, units or courses but one about academic programmes in which learning synergies can be achieved because there is curriculum consistency, coherence and a progression in learning expectations. The final section considers some implications for leaders. The following 12 propositions about good learning permeate Chapter 10 and influence the analysis of leaders' own development in Chapter 11.

Twelve propositions about good learning

1. Under the influence of human capital theories that say that better educated nations are more competitive and prosperous nations, governments have taken the view that schools and higher education should do more than teach for subject matter understanding (SCANS, 1991). Learning should now be extensive and support the development of highly skilled, flexible graduates with a bent for achievement and a commitment to lifelong learning (NCIHE, 1997). Modern higher education curricula should, according to this view of official knowledge, be concerned with the development of a wide range of understandings, skills, efficacy beliefs and self-theories, and strategies.

2. Following the constructivist accounts of learning developed by Piaget and Vygotsky, we see learning as acts of sensemaking (Weick, 1995) within communities of discourse. This implies that learning is much more than the energetic collection of information, although there are students and teachers who think and act as if that were the name of the game (Entwistle and Ramsden, 1983; Prosser and Trigwell, 1999). Good learning – and good teaching – depend on those learners discarding the alternative conceptual frameworks that privilege the collection of information over the construction of understanding.

   Not all of the understandings that learners construct have equal practical usefulness. In some disciplines it is possible to operate on a realist agenda and say that some understandings are right and that others are wrong. In other subjects there are competing accounts, and while it may not be possible to say that one is right and another is wrong, that is not the same as taking up the position of pure relativism and saying that 'anything goes'. Different understandings can be appraised in terms of their adequacy within the community of discourse, of their coherence, power and reach (Sayer, 1992). Hecht *et al.*, writing of US higher education, argue that, 'If your department supports an "open" [extended choice] curriculum, it is even more important to develop a consensus on the mega-meanings of the discipline' (1999: 139). Good learning in education settings involves an awareness of what learning is and of what sorts of learnings are preferable.

   This provides another reason for having some forms of fuzzy criteria of the types described in Chapter 5; namely that they help students to recognize constructions that are valued. They also contribute to learning because learning is understood as a goal-oriented activity and so it helps to be explicit about the selection of goals that academic staff are concerned to promote.

3. Learning takes place within communities of practice and activity systems that have their own sub-cultures and discursive repertoires. Clearly, the lecture theatre, website and library are all sites of learning that may provide fresh information and perspectives and it would be idle to ignore their historic and continuing significance. However, what counts as knowledge is affected by the rules of the community, so that questions about the use of natural science knowledge have often been rejected as scientific questions, as in the case of bioengineering and atomic science. It is also affected by the local group, so that ideas that do not fit with embedded thinking and practice are discounted, as is the case where a university department that prizes poststructural literary criticism is indifferent to Leavisite analyses, or where a department committed to SER discounts evidence that the key to educational improvement may lie in support services for young, at-risk families.

4. Learning, like thinking and feeling, is always situated and often does not transfer smoothly from one context to another. The person who learns to be a good head of department in one context is not invariably a good head in a different context, as our respondent quoted on page 41 noted. So, too, the Brazilian child street trader who can swiftly calculate the price of coconuts fails on formal tests of multiplication (Nunes and Bryant, 1996). The situation in which learning takes place provides a structure, often comes with social support to help us and usually provides plenty of practice, which allows the emergent learning to be consolidated. This has often led to claims that children would learn more and better if only their work was more securely located in concrete, real-life and familiar situations (see, for example, Edwards and Knight, 1995).

Although there is much sense in that position, it is limited because we think that education is about the abstraction of learning from specific contexts, the manipulation of generalizations (whether they be in the form of skills, procedures, concepts or laws), and the application of knowing to new circumstances. If versatility and flexibility are the business of education then new ideas, laws, procedures and skills should be encountered, practised and secured in any convenient and educationally compelling contexts. However, the test of learning within this view of education is in the transfer, in the ease with which situated cognition is retrieved from memory and deployed to new communities of practice, novel problems or fresh tasks. In Laurillard's words, 'situated cognition is not enough' (1993: 19). Programmes must be designed to help learners develop heuristics, routines and dispositions that help them to identify the possibilities of transfer and means of doing so (De Corte, 1996; Ohlsson, 1996). Work in schools has shown that programmes that teach for transfer by developing students' heuristics, routines and dispositions *and that help learners to know that they are developing them* make a powerful contribution to all aspects of learning (Scardamalia, 2000).

5. Learning needs mental activity and engagement. Astin (1997) concluded that one thing characterizes effective teaching and learning in higher education, namely that learners engage with their work. Implicit in this is the idea that once a new concept, skill or understanding has been constructed there is a need for massive practice, tuning and automation so that performance becomes expertly smooth, fast and accurate. For example, one model identifies seven epistemic tasks involved in higher-order talking and writing: describing, explaining, predicting, arguing, critiquing, explicating and defining (Ohlsson, 1996). It would be reasonable to expect a programme to provide systematic opportunities to learn ways of doing these tasks, to practise them repeatedly, especially by deploying those processes on novel problems. Time is needed for practice, just as it is for reflection.

6. Learning involves challenge and scaffolding. The idea that learning involves a challenge is such a consistent finding in research into learning in higher education (Terenzini, 1998) that it is worth marking it as a separate proposition.

   Challenging learning may exasperate the learner but it is not intended to do so. Our thinking is influenced by Vygotsky's concept of the zone of proximal development. This imaginary region is composed of tasks that the learner can only do if they are structured for her or him, or if they are done in collaboration with others. Some learning takes the form of becoming able to do those tasks with less scaffolding and then with none, with others and then alone. As Guile and Young (1998) observe, this zone has both a social and a cognitive dimension, and so learning challenges can come from fresh intellectual demands (as with the need to apply concepts that have previously only been understood in other contexts), or from fresh social demands (doing a task alone and in a restricted time), or from both (working alone and without the aid of the intellectual scaffolding that breaks the task into bite-size pieces).

   Challenging programmes will have fuzzy criteria that try to identify the ways in which more difficult concepts and material are introduced while there is progressively less support from faculty, who expect that learners will bring more material into play as their answers become more securely based. And, to develop an earlier remark, they will also be programmes where students do not complain of an excessive workload because tutors know that when learners are faced with more than they can process well, they use satisficing or coping strategies (Chambers, 1992): they stop trying to understand and concentrate on coping.

7. Learning criteria will embody a notion of progression in learning. Perry (1970) saw development as a transition, which not all students complete, from dualistic 'either-or' thinking to complex coordinations of multiple perspectives. Prosser and Trigwell (1999) add to this that students' concepts of what counts as learning tends to change from a 'collecting information' view to a quest for personal understanding of

public matters. These two accounts of changes in the nature of thinking that are often associated with undergraduate education are not the only ones, nor do they completely describe what is involved in progression. As Case (1985) showed in his neo-Piagetian work on school-children, within-stage development takes place and is important. A student might remain a dualist, information collector but become much better at working independently, quickly and accurately. From some points of view that is a greater achievement than developing more relativist thinking while remaining dependent, dilatory and disorganized.

As it is understood here, progression means designing courses within programmes so that students encounter more demanding learning experiences as they move through their undergraduate years. The related concept of match (see Bennett *et al.* (1984) for discussion) is used to refer to the tasks that learners are set and to the (fuzzy) criteria applied in their assessment. A set of good assessment criteria for a course gives an indication of the ways in which different performances will be judged. An overall set of programme criteria gives a general indication of the core achievements that will identify the successful graduate, although the criteria are likely to describe the minimal requirements for the award of a degree. So, although one form of planning for progression does involve identifying any distinctive criteria that should mainly be addressed by final year courses, another approach relies on planning programmes so that a progression of learning experiences is built in. Later in this chapter we shall argue that planning in terms of learning experiences, as opposed to learning outcomes, has distinct advantages.

8. Learning involves conversations (Laurillard, 1993; Barnett, 1994), whether they be face-to-face, electronic, dialogues between the learner and print or interior dialogues that involve reflecting, analysing, criticizing, synthesizing and evaluating. It is about interactions and as such it is an inescapably social process (De Corte, 1996). In that vein, Laurillard argues that:

> [a] 'conversational framework' for describing the learning process is intended to be applicable to any academic learning situation: to the full range of subject areas and types of topic. It is not normally applicable to learning through [direct] experience, nor to 'everyday' learning, nor to those training programmes that focus on skills alone, all of which tend to occur at the [direct] experiential interactive level only.
>
> (1993: 102)

Literal and metaphorical conversations can give learners new ideas or information that can either enrich existing ideas and structures by being assimilated to them or by challenging them so that the existing ideas and structures get accommodated to the new material. Feedback from others is especially important in learning conversations, whether it takes the form of fresh material, questions, suggestions or challenges.

Skilled learners supply their own feedback as they reflect on their knowings, think metacognitively about their learning and strategically plan what to do next but reflecting with others has considerable learning advantages (Cowan, 1998). ICT developments are transforming the possibilities for learning conversations. In 1997 Chickering and Ehrmann showed how the seven principles of good practice in undergraduate education (which are deeply supportive of learning conversations) could be enriched by ICT, and by 2000 Scardamalia was describing sophisticated ways of engaging young children, older children, teachers, experts and student teachers in complex, knowledge-working processes that sustained high-level thinking on a topic that is notorious for encouraging a surface, trivial, 'hunter-gatherer' approach to learning: dinosaurs. Programmes that plan ICT into learning can make for superior learning conversations.

9. Reflecting, which we take as a special case of learning conversations, is important to learning, whether it takes the form of a private dialogue or of a public conversation. The literature on reflection, which is well summarized by Eraut (1995b) and Cowan (1998), has been shot through with discussions of the relationship between reflection *on* practice, *in* practice and *for* practice; with the relationship between thinking and practice; and with stages and cycles of reflection. Some people are probably edified by these issues. Less frequently considered is the quality of reflection. Reflecting does not invariably lead to good quality conclusions. The same can be said of the awareness of our own thinking and learning strategies, which we call metacognition (Flavell *et al.*, 1993). Metacognition is generally esteemed but it does not invariably lead to learning. Scrutinizing our thought processes and learning strategies may simply confirm a position and encourage the conclusion that there is nothing that needs to be done or little that can be done to bring about any further gains. Learning is helped by helping people to keep upgrading their metacognitive awarenesses and to reflect more rigorously.

Figure 6.1 suggests that reflecting well involves questioning assumptions about causes and considering different ways of seeing things. It draws on attributional theory to say that when reflecting people may construct explanations in terms of causes that are outside themselves and essentially beyond their control or attribute achievement to internal causes, to things that are to do with themselves rather than to external forces (Pintrich and Schunk, 1996; Dweck, 1999). Internal attributions can, in turn, be to things within their control, such as effort, or to those that are thought to be beyond it, such as ability. The assumption is that metacognition and reflecting involve an interplay between thinking about self and settings, agency and structure, internal and external attributions. It also makes a distinction between single-loop learning and double- and triple-loop learning (Argyris and Schön, 1974; Snell and Chak, 1998). Single-loop learning is about learning

Figure 6.1 Six areas for mindful reflecting. The darker shading denotes areas that are less readily accessible to reflection.

Stable or changeable factors at work?	External attributions to unchangeable factors ←————→	Internal attributions to changeable factors
If changeable, are they under one's control?	Beyond one's control ←————→	Can be affected by thinking better, more effort, etc.
Single-loop learning (learning within the discourse)		
Double- and triple-loop learning (opening the discourse to scrutiny)		

within established discourses or parameters and involves 'becoming more skilful; registering that one's actions are not achieving their goal, adjusting one's actions to increase the possibility of achieving the goal' (Snell and Chak, 1998: 340). Although double- and triple-loop learning are separated in the literature, they are joined in Figure 6.1 because they both involve going beyond the givens and asking questions about the terms of engagement themselves. Double-loop learning is about 'choosing to learn different types of skill . . . Reframing problems from a position of deeper insight' (1998: 340) and learning from self-evaluations of past performance. Triple-loop learning entails 'becoming aware of the limitations of *all* grand frameworks' (1998: 340, original emphasis) and creating new ways of thinking about particular problems. For much of the time, single-loop learning is usually going to be appropriate, but metacognition and reflecting should also be open to the double- and triple-loop perspectives that fundamental assumptions may be in need of change.

The darker shading indicates areas of thinking that can be more penetrating and more empowering, although there may be a tendency for people to think in terms of the more lightly shaded areas. An implication is that one goal for learning, in the sense of developing the quality of metacognitive thinking and reflection, would be to habituate learners to using a model such as this as scaffolding to help them become more sophisticated in their learning and assessment conversations.

10. Good learning comes from good working, not from good genes. It is extraordinarily damaging to believe that: human ability is biologically determined; high scores on a psychometric indicator of ability, such as an IQ test, show whether someone is generally destined to succeed or fail; and smartness is fixed, so that you can't get what you don't have. The damage takes several forms. The main harm lies in the way that this entity view of ability leads those who do not come out in the top 5, 10 or 15 per cent to think that there is little point in trying to succeed.

So people who get labelled 'dumb' and who come to believe it, quite literally go on to learn helplessness (Peterson *et al.*, 1993). Persistent failure is corrosive, but that is especially so when failure is attributed to a lack of ability. As Dweck (1999) has shown, those who believe that ability is not fixed by the genes but is a combination of some threshold level of intelligence with mindful work strategies (which we might call metacognition or reflective practice) and persistent effort are people who cope best with difficulties. She describes this 'threshold ability + effort + strategy' view as an incremental self-theory and points out how much more empowering it is than the entity view in which most people are predestined to mediocrity or worse. (Incidentally, that predestined successlessness is exactly the message of norm-referenced tests in which scores are standardized to fit the bell curve.) This fits with Resnick's (1999) concept of 'practical intelligence' and with Sternberg's (1997) critique of the multiple failings of IQ tests and his alternative concept of 'successful intelligence'. The list could be continued by referring to those who have drawn attention to the highly significant part that our learned and improvable interpersonal and social repertoires play in life and work success (for example, Goleman, 1996, 1998).

This is not a claim that anyone can learn anything, let alone that learning can invariably be quick and enjoyable. It is a claim that those people who believe that mindful efforts can make a marked difference to their learning, and who have abandoned the view that they are pinned down by the malign effects of a bad mixing of their parents' genes are more persistent in the face of learning difficulties than those who are under the influence of entity theories of ability and success. One thing that their undergraduate programme ought to be doing, then, is helping students to realize that, intellectually, they are likely to have what it takes to succeed and that to capitalize upon it is a matter of thinking strategically and being persistently effortful.

11. Design motivation into the curriculum. The metaphor of the football coach motivating his team is a vivid and misleading one, even though student course evaluations frequently identify interest and enthusiasm as two of the three key features of good teaching (Perry and Smart, 1997). Of course, it is good that students can be enthused by individual teachers, but it is desirable that they regularly experience uncharismatic motivational support by, for example, being encouraged towards incremental theories of ability, through improvement-centred feedback and through the social support of learning and assessment conversations. These forms of support are consistent with goal-setting theory (Latham *et al.*, 1997). That theory says that people are more motivated by goals that they value (which are often goals that they have had a chance to choose or shape); work towards goals that are challenging but achievable (within their zone of proximal development); and are more likely to persist with goals when they get useful feedback on performance and valued appreciation of achievement. There are also parallels here with

the conditions in which motivation is more likely to be intrinsic – fuelled by the rewards of the work itself – than it is to be extrinsic, which is where the work is done either to avoid punishment or to get rewards such as higher wages or better marks. Intrinsic motivation is associated with believing that the work itself is personally valuable, meaningful and important, with time to do the work properly, and with sufficient skill to be able to perform well, and even to experience 'flow' (Csikszentmihalyi, 1990).

These are views of motivation that direct our attention away from questions about how every teacher can be turned into a virtuoso performer and charismatic figure towards the ways in which the processes of learning, assessment and teaching treat learning as important and possible, and support and reward it. Teacher performances may motivate but so too should programmes, albeit in rather less obvious ways.

12. Teaching contributes to learning. The relationship between teaching and learning is much less clear than might have been assumed. Research in school settings has established that direct teaching, which includes face-to-face work and tightly structured mastery learning sequences, is effective with subject matter that can be broken down and encapsulated in drill-and-skill form (Peterson, 1979). Factual and rule based material and skills coaching can be well served by direct teaching. However, when evidence has to be appraised, where judgements are to be made, and where there are uncertainties, complexity and ambiguities, then the emphasis shifts from the teacher as didact to the teacher as skilled organizer of appropriate learning activities. Where the subject matter and learning goals are not well suited to direct instruction, it is important to think of teaching as an act of planning and facilitating appropriate learning experiences, of which classroom teaching is one, but only one. Moreover, classroom teaching then comes to mean instructing and coaching, motivating, giving feedback, suggesting and asking.

Programmes of teaching improvement that concentrate on classroom performance miss the point as far as higher education is concerned, since the goal should not, in the main, be for students to master material whose cognitive demands are low enough for direct instruction to be an appropriate method of supporting learning. Good teaching is about more than good performance and attempts to improve learning through the improvement of teaching quality need, therefore, to look at the provision of good learning experiences and learning environments (Knight *et al.*, 2000).

Implications for leaders

Table 6.1 summarizes some implications of these 12 propositions for the design of programmes as sets of learning experiences.

Table 6.1 Twelve propositions about learning and some implications for heads of departments (mainly about auditing and then developing progrommes)

Proposition about learning	Implications for leaders
1. Learning should be extensive and include subject understandings, skills, efficacy beliefs and strategic thinking	Working to get broad programme learning goals accepted. Establishing how these goals are *really* supported and developed across the suite of courses that students typically take.
2. Learning involves constructing understandings that are acceptable within communities of practice	Courses and programmes that mainly deliver information are suspect because learners need to process it – to work on it, apply it, analyse, criticize and appraise it – if they are to be best placed to construct meanings. Check learning activities against this criterion. Fuzzy learning criteria are one way of signifying what is valued within a community of practice. Check that courses have criteria that are compatible with and that contribute to programme criteria.
3. Learning is a natural outcome of the normal workings of communities of practice or activity systems	This has substantial implications for faculty development; see Chapter 9. Try to find whether there are messages in the way that the department normally works that contradict the programme's formal learning messages. Are there things in the ways faculty talk to students, in faculty availability and office hours, in the use of teaching assistants, and so on?
4. Learning is situated and hard to transfer	Faculty should be encouraged to make the quality of students' reflection and metacognition a priority by: • being aware of the programme goals that can best be developed in their courses • providing learning activities which call for the use of skills, concepts, etc. that have been developed elsewhere • talking routinely with students about how learning gets to be transferred • ensuring that students have to reflect on their own learning, preferably with reference to fuzzy learning criteria.
5. Engagement and practice make for good learning	Key learning goals should be regularly revisited across the programme, which can be seen as a spiral curriculum. Check that there is a spiral of practice, so that things encountered in a simple form in Year 1 are re-encountered in a more challenging form in the final year.

Table 6.1 (*cont'd*)

Proposition about learning	Implications for leaders
	Engagement involves processing information but it also suggests that there is a commitment that is greater than just complying with assessment requirements. Investigate the motivational characteristics of the programme (see point 10, below)
6. Learning involves challenge and scaffolding	Work with students and then with faculty to try and identify: • what is frustratingly difficult about the programme and courses (this is about identifying places where scaffolding is defective or absent) • whether a story can be told that explains how final year work is more challenging than first year work and whether it is a story that does not rely on there simply being more to do • whether any courses are not challenging; 'bird' courses
7. Progression	Work with students and then with faculty to try and identify whether a story can be told that explains how final year work is more challenging than first year work and whether it is a story that does not rely on there simply being more to do. Programmes need to be planned to provide progressively more challenging learning experiences. Learning criteria should encourage students to move from knowledge acquisition to developing understandings, and from dualism to complexity.
8. Learning is conversational and interactive	Check whether there is plentiful, timely and helpful feedback to students and recurrent opportunities to think with others, face-to-face, in writing and electronically.
9. Learning involves reflecting well	Learning diaries, journals, portfolios, reviews and the like are all important and they have more power where they are understood, fuzzy criteria that can be used as starting points and where staff and students share a map of areas for reflection, such as the one in Figure 6.1.
10. Learning is not limited by fixed abilities	Try to get colleagues to convey incremental views of ability to students and to encourage the attributions of learned optimism. This should extend to advising students and working with them on portfolio-making.

Table 6.1   (cont'd)

Proposition about learning	Implications for leaders
	Work for assessments that allow achievement and that have the possibility of a 100 per cent success rate. Ask that as far as possible feedback avoids final language.
11. Motivation is something designed into curriculum, rather than something added by charismatic teaching	With students, and perhaps with recent graduates as well, identify ways in which the programme could more consistently encourage enthusiasm and persistence in the face of difficulties and discouraging features could be removed.
12. Teaching contributes to learning	Recognize that improving classroom performance is one part of improving teaching (and the observation of classroom performance usually does not provide very reliable information) Appraise, at course and programme levels, the quality of thinking and planning for student learning Try to find out more by the contributions to learning (and the impediments to it) from things outside your team or department

Non-implications

These principles can be unscrupulously used to give dodgy practice a respray that gives it a meretricious sparkle. 'New learning environments' promise student empowerment through resource based learning and ICT technology, emphasize collaborative and cooperative learning, praise reflection and the associated peer- and self-assessment, and celebrate the flexibility that comes from extensive choice from many modular learning packages. But it is a learning discourse that may be an attractive way of legitimizing the business of cutting teaching costs, with the result that quality is compromised. In fact resources saved by emphasizing empowerment and learning over teaching and following ought to be redeployed to help students become more autonomous as learners. These principles can cost more than traditional methods. A department may need fewer faculty to manage a course based on them but it is likely to find that start-up costs are greater, that resource costs increase, that more support staff are needed and that there are greater demands on central learning support provision. Increased costs often fall on students as well: where once they would have been given offprints to read they now get a uniform resource locator (URL) and, because most people are not used to reading complex papers on screen, they print papers out at their own cost.

Planning for learning: outcomes and entitlements

This section explains that the conventional approach to planning for better learning is based on the identification and measurement of learning outcomes. It argues that this approach has its uses, has definite limitations and that it should be complemented by another.

Understanding curriculum

Once 'curriculum' was an up-market synonym for 'syllabus', which was a list of content to be covered, perhaps with a schedule and advance notice of examinations attached. In the USA a syllabus might contain details of the instructor (*sic*), course purpose, objectives (*sic*), resources and readings, evaluation and grading, learning tools and 'how to study for this course' (Grunert, 1997: 81). Elsewhere this might be called a curriculum, which we take to be an account of the content to be studied, its organization, the learning and teaching methods and the arrangements for evaluating student learning. Where Grunert's concern is the course, ours is the programme as well.

Skilled curriculum makers are alert to the distinction between the planned curriculum, the created or 'delivered' curriculum and the understood or 'received' curriculum. The three are not the same. Curriculum intentions become changed as they are created in teaching and learning situations and assessment regularly shows that what learners understand is different from what was planned and created, in ways that social practice theory explains well (see Chapter 3). Following Fullan (1991), we hold that the 'slippages' between the three are not eradicable: curriculum must always be somewhat loosely coupled. Despite the lessons of the great school curriculum projects of the 1930s (Stenhouse, 1975), it often seems as if managers and planners think that the gaps can be entirely eliminated.

In the next section we recall that higher education is expected to foster a range of fuzzy learning outcomes, such as independence, creativity, flexibility and critical thinking, and that these are difficult, expensive and sometimes impossible to assess reliably for high stakes and summative purposes. Our position is that curriculum planning in higher education cannot be based on a learning outcomes approach, although that approach has its place. That is followed by the suggestion that the best way to plan for good learning is to base curriculum on the concept of student entitlement to learning experiences that are embedded in their programmes of study.

The limits of learning outcomes in curriculum planning

The problems with curriculum planning in terms of learning outcomes have largely been described in Chapter 5, where problems in using them for assessment purposes were discussed. In sum, the argument is that employability, an increasingly important goal of higher education, is a more extensive concept than is often allowed and that many aspects of employability are hard to capture in the language of learning outcomes. In particular, the notion of key or transferable skills is more problematic than is usually recognized and it is hard to describe complex and contexted achievements in neat ways, let alone to assess them cleanly.

The argument that follows is that a new approach is needed to curriculum planning. There is an alternative to the vexed business of trying to define graduateness or employability in terms of the products of education, statements of skills and other outcomes. There are two parts to the argument. The first is to accept that some educational products, especially subject understanding, *can* be fairly pre-specified and assessed in terms of outcomes statements. Skills, beliefs and reflective thinking cannot. The second part is to trust the process where it is not wise to talk in terms of unambiguous and reliably measurable products. In the remainder of this chapter we concentrate on constructing a curriculum in terms of processes that make for employability and to which all students should be entitled.

In this account, graduateness has two principal components:

- Subject-specific understanding and skill in the use of appropriate techniques and procedures. In many cases the language of outcomes can be used to describe this curriculum component and established assessment practices can provide sufficiently reliable and valid high-stakes judgements.
- Key skills, efficacy beliefs and strategic thinking. Given the problems with trying to describe achievement in the language of outcomes and the attendant concerns about getting affordable, reliable and valid judgements, this part of the curriculum should not be constructed around outcomes statements. Consequently, there should be no high-stakes assessments of learning outcomes.

A process view of curriculum

Professor Lawrence Stenhouse was a pioneer in curriculum research and development in the UK. With considerable simplification his thinking can be reduced to the advice to choose worthwhile content with which to engage children in worthwhile ways. Outcomes would largely look after themselves if the processes of worthwhile engagements were sound. In the USA, Professor Eliot Eisner also rejected the language of performance objectives, outcomes, false certainties, reductionism, atomization and bogus precision in measurement and assessment. He too wanted to consider the sorts of things that children would be doing, which he described as 'process objectives'. Although their positions have not been influential in state-mandated school curricula in western nations, they have been mentioned to make the point that there is a scholarship that provides an alternative to the outcomes model of curriculum planning.

This does not mean that there is no place for targets, benchmarks, indicators or criteria. Learners gain by knowing what they might construct from the considerable, organized variety of teaching, learning and assessment processes with which they are expected to engage. That does not compromise the process view of the curriculum. The status of these indicators is different from that of outcomes descriptors. Where outcomes descriptors are intended to provide comprehensive and accurate definitions of valued learning and will be central to the process of reliable high stakes assessments, indicators in a process model are as different as a sense of place is from a global positioning system display. Indicators in a process model are simply that – indicators. If a defining image for the outcomes approaches to curriculum and assessment is a technical manual prescribing systems operation in loving detail, then indicators are texts to be appreciated and interpreted.

Teaching entitlement

It is convenient to start with teaching entitlement on the basis that if teaching processes are consistent with the broad goals to which HEIs subscribe, then the learning will tend to follow. The five recommendations that follow, and that constitute a view of the teaching to which students should be entitled, are essentially a digest of international mainstream research on the characteristics of effective teaching. Two good summaries are by Chickering and Gamson (1991) and Svinicki *et al.* (1996). Knight *et al.* (2000) draw on the same sources as they make detailed suggestions for ways of working these ideas out in practice.

- Teaching should use different media because continued learning in professional life happens through a variety of media. For example, students could be entitled to experience teaching in face-to-face mode, through audio-visual media, in the form of online conferencing and by means of asynchronous ICT. This greater teaching bandwith also goes well with research showing that different people have different preferences in terms of the learning media that they use by default.
- Students should be entitled to varied teaching methods, both in the interests of good learning that is faithful to broad curriculum aims, and because they embed working practices that are hallmarks of flexible, learning and skilful graduates. Lectures are a very important teaching method, as long as they are used to teach things that are best taught by lectures. The same goes for the extensive array of computer-assisted learning techniques.

And for seminars. These three methods are powerful in proportion to their being fit for a learning purpose.

One-to-one or paired tutorials are an important entitlement for two reasons. They may not be necessary to help students reach a better command of the subject matter but they are important in the same way that mentoring in the workplace is important: to promote reflection; to guide reflection away from the easy paths of ritual analysis; and to identify fruitful activities, possible priorities and provisional goals. On the basis that 'to teach is to learn twice', teaching methods should include more experienced students teaching less experienced ones, as at Dalhousie University, where senior year students help freshmen to begin the metacognitive process of making skills portfolios.

Work experience should be there, especially for students taking non-vocational subjects, but it should be there under two conditions. One is that planned work experience should be understood as an addition to all the other work experiences that students have and the second is that there should be no planned work experience unless it is grounded in good practice. Our research identifies features of good placements and also indicates that it is vital that students are mindful about what they might learn from a placement before starting and that the quality of post-practice reflection is an important complement to mindful preparation.

- In some countries teaching is often called 'instruction', but students should be entitled to teachers who do more than instruct. They should also be entitled to facilitating, caring, problem-posing, enthusing, conversing and clarifying.
- Good teaching is scaffolding for learning. As learners pass from being novices to being experts they can work with less teacher-provided scaffolding and learn how to erect their own. This autonomy is something that employers repeatedly say they want in new hires, as well as being a valued attribute in academic life. Consequently, students should be entitled to be taught about the scaffolding that they begin by using and then they should be learning how to work with less and then how to make their own scaffolding to help them work on new structures. That means becoming better at strategic thinking, goal-setting, taking responsibility, self-evaluation and self-knowing.
- Research into the characteristics of good teaching performances produces few generalizations but they are persistent: good teaching is interesting, clear and enthusiastic (ICE). Leaders cannot guarantee that all teaching performances will be ICE but students should be entitled to teachers who look at what they intend to do and reflect on ways to get ICE in it.

Learning entitlement

In many ways the learning entitlement is the flip side of teaching entitlement. The important distinction is that learning space is far greater than teaching space. Institutions that plan programmes in terms of student learning hours (SLHs) often allow seven or eight learning hours for one teaching hour. The SLH:teaching ratio is not sensitive to the informal learning that takes place outside formal study time. That is especially important where HEIs have broad learning goals and where a lot that is valued (beliefs, reflecting and some skills development) cannot be tied to an SLH formula, let alone to a teaching hours one. The design of environments that encourage it must be systemic and, as US research reviews have shown, take account of the psychosocial qualities of the whole learning environment, including students' living and recreational patterns. This section identifies some of the other features of good student learning environments in HEIs with broad learning goals.

- The prime learning entitlement is to teaching that carries with it the full complement of teaching entitlements.
- Learning must be designed to be extensive in the sense of attending to understanding (not just to knowledge); to skills (both subject-specific and general); to the development of self-beliefs (about capacity and contexts); and to a reflective cast of mind (the development of metacognitive awareness, strategically deployed). It is an entitlement to breadth of intentional learning.
- The value of learning is limited in all sorts of ways where it is about writing down teachers' understandings and rehearsing them in expected forms at predictable times for conventional purposes. It is well appreciated in some subjects that what matters is being able to draw on learning that comes from disparate sources at different times so as to get a purchase on identifying, shaping and working on a problem. This is evocative of the workplace, where neatly formed problems do not present themselves, let alone come attached with memos that identify a standard solution (for there are no solutions but only approximations) in the notes made in one lecture course. Consequently, students should be entitled to learning that makes a call on application, fuzzy thinking, problem-working (not problem-solving), synthesis and understanding-in-action.

  That – and much else in this section – has considerable implications for the assessment entitlement. The day of 'tell me what I told you' and 'tell me what the books [which I too have read] say' assessments should be over, save only where these are used as checks that students have a sufficient toolkit to tackle some worthwhile and authentic matters that sprawl across course boundaries.

- Learning happens outside class and outside campus hours, just as most workplace learning is not through formal means but by engaging in communities of practice. That might be of slight interest were high quality graduates those who understood their subject and no more. Once they are identified in terms of an extensive model, student learning environments need to be planned differently in two ways. Firstly, attention has to be paid to making the most of the whole institution as an environment for employability and life learning. This implies that student services are understood as part of the mainstream institutional mission. Secondly, there needs to be learning time (and appropriate teaching time) given over to collating experiences and identifying the learning that can be constructed from them and around them. Reflection, for example, becomes a reflection on living and learning, not just on course learning.

* Implicit in this is the imperative for there to be a student entitlement to supported personal review and planning. This resonates with best practice in professional learning and development. Portfolio-making is recommended as a good focus for this metacognitive, reflecting learning. The institution is responsible for providing these entitlement opportunities throughout academic programmes but not in the same way as it is responsible for student development of subject matter understanding. Firstly, person-centred counsellors are needed to support this approach to reflecting. Secondly, these metacognitive products, especially the portfolios, are not to be graded and may not even be seen by academic staff. The process has to be trusted, and not validated by assessing any written products. Thirdly, there are two reasons why there should be opportunities to reflect with peers: dialogue with peers is more authentic than dialogue with those who have positional authority; and the more we have to try and tell others about a topic, the more that things which we felt tacitly can be brought to the surface, become 'known', communicable and understandable. There may also be ethical and moral reasons why review and reflecting should involve peers. Fourthly, given the importance of self-evaluation in the workplace and in career management, for that reason, if for no other, institutions should be helping students to become skilled at self-review and reflecting, which should complement social processes of review and reflecting, and not displace them.

Leading for better learning and teaching

The leader who has initiated changes in assessment has already initiated changes in learning and teaching. This chapter has offered a view of what good learning involves and claimed that some pedagogical practices are more desirable than others. It also described an approach to planning that is less cumbersome than the learning outcomes model.

A fair objection to that entitlement approach is that many governments and HEIs expect to see courses planned in terms of levels of achievement with respect to key learning goals. The fact that those with power command it does not mean that the approach can be made to work, but it would be prudent to humour them by taking a more-or-less acceptable taxonomy off the shelf and spending a strictly limited amount of time laying it over the programme. Two things need to be understood. Firstly, even if a lot of money is spent, reliable assessment of many of these outcomes is simply not possible, and in most cases time and money will not be available. So taking up a taxonomy from elsewhere should be done in the realization that the model's inherent limitations, discussed in this chapter and in Chapter 5, will have to be lived with. Secondly, curriculum planning for effective learning will still be easiest if it is done in terms of student entitlements to learning, teaching and assessment experiences. When that is done, the new curriculum can be appraised against the off-the-shelf taxonomy in order to see how the programme promotes achievement of those outcomes. By and large, entitlements of the sorts described in these two chapters will allow teams to say that their programmes energetically advance the outcomes described in most statements of graduate attributes and achievements. Planning the curriculum in this way is easier and avoids a lot of the wrangling that usually goes with attempts to work in terms of outcomes and criteria-identifying levels of learning achievement.

As with assessment, there are many starting points, including: audits; supporting small-scale changes where small wins are likely; giving programmes an ICT makeover; responding to student evaluations; and so on. Although much can be achieved by little more than making learning, assessment, teaching and the curriculum subjects to talk about, care about and tinker with, most teams and departments really need to reconstruct their programmes. However, leaders who responded to our electronic enquiries often said how much institutions do to thwart departmental action. The quotation that heads this chapter alluded to high workloads and faulty ways of appraising faculty work (see also Chapter 9). Another leader said, 'Incidentally, support from my own institution was very mixed' (male, new leader, USA), and an experienced, male leader in the UK told of an 'unforgiving/unsupportive external regulatory/accountability environment – lack of resources – inappropriate structures – element of lack of support from (due in part to constraints on them) from other managers/leaders'. Another had problems with the 'Lack of monetary teaching awards to serve as motivation & lack of "development" time for creative uses of technology in courses' (female, experienced leader, USA). This makes it all the more important that those wishing to improve learning and teaching try to respond to the dozen propositions about good learning in subtle ways that do not overwhelm faculty.

Nevertheless, leaders can demand more when they can say that the team or department *has* to respond to pressure from central management or state bodies. The experience of an experienced female leader in the UK was that she was helped by:

> strong internal quality assurance guidelines; own interest (as HoD [head of department]) in developing a quality culture within the department; the 'big stick' of potential QAA assessments; Subject Quality Groups within the department in which staff see the student feedback, external assessors comments and assessment results of everyone else (in the Group's) modules, and can offer suggestions on improvement of learning, teaching and assessment.
>
> (Female, experienced leader, UK)

Structures can inhibit as well as help:

In order to be transparent about the quality of programmes my institution has set in place a number of systems such as course scrutiny panels that sometimes make it very difficult to be innovative if the courses one's staff are proposing does [*sic*] not obviously fit the 'standard' model. Of course it is important to ensure proper safeguards for the students. This should not be at the expense of innovation or diversity.

(new leader, male, Scotland)

Other factors that have helped leaders to have some success in improving learning and teaching were:

dedication/loyalty of faculty members to dept, goals and to me, personally; stated mission of the university includes excellence in teaching; written student complaint policy that notifies instructors who are not performing well in the classroom

(Female, experienced leader, USA)

having a 'clear sense of strategic tasks and responsibilities – membership of/participation in external support/professional networks – reasonable grasp of issues around quality enhancement'

(Male, experienced leader, England)

The ability to see long-term. I was also able to develop relationships with key government officials who also understood the key issues confronting higher education. I was then able to follow this vision (need to respond to accountability issues in higher education) by hiring good people.

(Male, new leader, USA)

These quotations could be read to say that quite a lot of luck has been involved in improving learning and teaching by means of curriculum reform. Agreed, they also point to the importance of vision, but when it comes to trying to build on that vision there are resource and logistical difficulties. It is no less a matter of concern that few leaders are skilled in the art of curriculum development and those who are confident as course developers are likely to be less so as programme developers. There is a remarkable shortage of published advice on curriculum development in higher education, although the account of Boyatzis *et al.* (1995) of the making of the MBA programme at Case Western Reserve University is recommended. This, then, is a point at which to get help from colleagues in central units whose brief is to secure assessment, learning and instructional development in the institution. For the new head of department wanting to make an impact it might be easier to start with improving the research effort, which is the subject of Chapter 8. But give faculty development colleagues notice that in 18 months time curriculum will come to the fore and their expertise will be needed.

7

Leading Research and Scholarship

The priorities of American higher education have been significantly realigned since World War II. The emphasis on graduate education and research has cast a long shadow over undergraduate education at many large universities. The prime focus of these institutions moved from student to professor, from general to specialized, and from loyalty to campus to fealty to profession. Colleges and universities followed . . . a 'snake-like procession' as one institution after another . . . pursued the same path.

(Glassick *et al.*, 1997: 8)

[Building a successful research culture means] thinking together, sharing clarity about goals, developing vibrant investigative relationships. Getting balance right in developing individual and developing the group, looking ahead to anticipate challenges.

(Female, new leader, England)

Preview

The pressure to publish or perish is endemic so leaders need to work with colleagues to construct and sustain networks that make for a commitment to scholarship. To do this it is necessary to develop ways of talking about research, sharing ideas and expertise, and working together on proposals, projects and publishing: to nourish a knowledge-building system with research its prime concern. Ramsden's (1998b) analysis of the correlates of research productivity identifies factors that are similar to those associated with teaching and learning quality. However, with research it is also important in many teams and departments to break with assumptions that research is large-scale, funded, positivist inquiry. It may be, particularly in natural science disciplines, but 'research' has also become popularized and can take a variety of forms. Departments and teams can therefore raise their research profile by encouraging faculty members to understand better the opportunities for research and to appreciate ways in which research can be integrated with their other concerns. This can be reflected in formal staff evaluation procedures and should also inform low-stakes formative research appraisals. There may be some scope to support research activity by making the team's operations more efficient, but not if it is at the expense of network-building and conversing.

Research as a parasitic activity?

Blackburn and Lawrence (1995) have shown that publication and research have become priorities for baccalaureate or liberal arts colleges. In most HEIs faculty now have to show that they are active as published researchers and, as Blackburn and Lawrence found, they want to spend a greater proportion of their working week on this work.

Although there is a view that research contributes to teaching, many are sceptical: research and teaching compete. Huber (1992) said that it is as believable as claiming that being a good theologian correlates with excellence as a preacher. Ramsden and Moses' (1992) study of Australian academics questioned the idea that research and teaching achievements were associated with each other, although they, like all researchers in this area, had problems in finding acceptable measures of teaching and research. Smith and Webster (1997) were similarly unconvinced that research achievements signalled teaching skill and Bailey (1999) found that in a sample of 107 academic staff in an Australian post-1987 university there was a modest association between motivation for teaching and motivation for research (+0.486) and a weak association between self-efficacy in the two areas (+0.142).

Tensions between research and teaching have been widely reported (e.g. Boyer, 1990; Rice, 1996; Knight and Trowler, 2000b). Kennedy, former President of Stanford, said (1997) that the public expected students to be the priority, whereas faculty expected research to be. Blackburn and Lawrence (1995) found that the greater the research orientation, the smaller was a department's or institution's perceived commitment to teaching. Huber argued that because university teachers are judged by their research achievements, then this 'is the only profession in which you can become a success without satisfying the client [the student]' (1992: 11). He added that '[P]rofessors are hired as teachers but evaluated as scholars' (1992: 147). In American research universities the picture could be more worrying.

New members of the academic professions are acutely aware of the ways in which research and teaching vie for their attention (Boice, 1992; Menges *et al.*, 1999). Sykes (1988) blamed the research culture, academic freedom and tenure for 'profscam', a system of higher education that favours tenured, productive researchers, who have little teaching, great freedom and good rewards, at the expense of the students (who are taught by teaching assistants in a system that does not rate teaching highly) and of part-time staff (Leslie, 1999). Obviously, there will be differences between the disciplines, since research and teaching come more comfortably together in some than in others, and there will also be variations between different colleges, departments and individuals because their situations, capabilities and perceptions will also combine in more or less harmonious ways. Yet, it still looks as if research activity can be at the expense of pedagogical activity.

> the research universities have too often failed, and continue to fail, their undergraduate populations ... Recruitment materials display proudly the world-famous professors, the splendid facilities and the ground-breaking research that goes on within them, but thousands of students graduate without ever seeing the world-famous professors or tasting genuine research. Some of their instructors are likely to be badly trained or even untrained teaching assistants who are groping their way toward a teaching technique; some others may be tenured drones who deliver set lectures from yellowed notes, making no effort to engage the bored minds of the students in front of them.
>
> (Kenny, 1998: n.p.)

This burgeoning research culture can threaten faculty who were appointed primarily to teach and who may be clustered in newer universities. Ramsden's Australian evidence is that many academic staff publish little, which suggests low levels of research activity: in the early 1990s, '[T]hree quarters of respondents in the older universities published no books, 60% no book chapters, and 20% no articles' (1998b: 357). The Higher Education Research Institute (HERI) Faculty Survey said that in 1998–99 25.3 per cent of faculty in the USA reported 'spending 0 hours doing research and/or scholarly writing per week', compared to a figure of 20 per cent in 1989–90 (*The Department Chair*, 2000: 17). Less active researchers may see demands to do research as a threat to teaching excellence and as an assault on their identities (Lucas, 1994; Bailey, 1999) although Halsey (1992) is not the only one to report that most faculty want to combine teaching and research, even if they usually wish to teach less (Blackburn and Lawrence, 1995). So many leaders will be intent on increasing the proportion of staff who do research and most will want to help their colleagues to create departmental ways of sustaining commitment to teaching and research. At the same time legislatures everywhere are demanding more attention to teaching and related matters and there are continued pressures on student fees and funding.

A reconciliation of research and teaching?

Boyer's *Scholarship Reconsidered* was an attempt to find ways of resolving a 'conflict of academic functions [that] demoralizes the professoriate, erodes the vitality of the institution, and cannot but have a negative effect on students' (1990: 2). He argued that academic work was a blend of four forms of scholarship, each of which should be addressed when evaluating faculty performance. The four are the scholarship of discovery, integration, application and teaching. 'Discovery' approximates to what is often called 'research' and 'teaching' speaks for itself. 'Integration' is to do with interpreting, drawing together and bringing out new insights. Boyer saw it as an interdisciplinary activity, although many disciplines need an integration of the knowledge constructed by sub-disciplinary communities. Application involves problem-working and engagements with the worlds of practice. These four forms overlap. So knowledge creation is primarily about the scholarship of discovery but new knowledge can also be created through teaching, application and integration. Application and integration are very much about using knowledge, although teaching can be seen as a special case of this. Integration is plainly about synthesizing knowledge, as is teaching. Application frequently demands integration too. According to this view scholarship involves discovering, synthesizing and using. Boyer's attempt 'to give scholarship a broader, more efficacious meaning' (Glassick *et al.*, 1997: ix) implies that faculty should take all four roles seriously and that institutions' appointment, evaluation and reward systems should do likewise. (In passing we suggest that there may be other scholarships to add to Boyer's four – a scholarship of leadership, for example. If so, it too should be encouraged, evaluated and rewarded, although there is little evidence that HEIs do take it that seriously.)

It will probably prove impossible to get Boyer's four forms held in equal esteem, and it may be risky for a faculty member to declare that for five years the scholarship of integration is to have priority over the other three forms. An alternative is to consider how the four forms can coexist in a 'synergistic system' (Kenny, 1998: n.p.). One distinguished scholar argued that his research benefited from his teaching:

> My books would have been quite different – and to me less valuable if I had produced them in solitude or after talking only with professional colleagues. It was not just that thinking about how to teach students to read responsibly led me to ideas that I would otherwise have overlooked. Responding to students' rival readings actually changed my opinions about how to appreciate a given novel or work of criticism. For this and other reasons, teaching and publishing have always felt absolutely inseparable.
>
> (Kenny, 1998: n.p.)

This sort of realization underpinned the Boyer Commission's recommendation that American research universities should plan, 'to make research-based undergraduate learning the standard' (Kenny, 1998: n.p.). A problem with this, though, is that it implies that undergraduate courses should reflect the research activities of faculty rather than be maps of the disciplinary territory. In some large departments interests and territory may coincide but elsewhere the search for synergy would imply a skewed curriculum. In one sense that need not be a matter for concern, since it can be argued that teaching about the discipline's structure and methods does not depend on any particular content and, in addition, that skills, beliefs and metacognition can also be fostered through many topics. A second recommendation by the Boyer Commission is to involve undergraduates in the research process, principally by providing more opportunity for enquiry and less occasion for instruction. This is consistent with the position we took in Chapters 5 and 6.

Attempts like these to rectify the balance between research and other scholarly activities certainly made a much-needed case for taking other forms of scholarship seriously but the problem of how to do it received less attention. Boyer suggested that individuals might spend some years when one area of scholarship was foremost in their work and then move to another in later years (Boyer, 1990; Rice, 1996). That helps to resolve the problem of role conflict for the individual but there are at least two substantial difficulties. One is that it relies on appointment, tenure and rewards committees changing their behaviours to reflect these more subtle models of academic careers. Rice (1996), Director of the American Association for Higher Education's Forum on Faculty Roles and Rewards, identified groups of universities that have begun to address this substantial task. Until this subtle career model is widely accepted, ambitious scholars will play to the belief that the research portfolio is the passport to a rich career, even if the employing institution apparently endorses a four-fold valuation of scholarship. In practice 'it is in research grants, books, articles, papers and citations that every university defines its true worth' (Kenny, 1998: n.p.).

A second difficulty with Boyer's suggestion is that it gives little guidance about what departmental leaders might do. How might they help teams and departments to be effective in all four forms of scholarship without exacerbating stress in the workplace? We have given something of an answer in earlier chapters, where we set out the general claim that collaborative cultures are valuable in academic life. We amplified that claim in Chapters 5 and 6, where we argued that collaboration is central to the enhancement of learning and teaching quality. It is a good, basic principle for leading a team's research effort, a point that is developed later in this chapter.

Plainly, there is more to be said than that, but the few handbooks on leading academic teams are not very helpful. They tend to be written in cookbook fashion and to combine lofty advice – '*Aim for co-operation*' (Tucker, 1993: 274, original emphasis) – with common-sense observations, such as, '[A]pplied research is also likely to bring the department into contact with outside agencies' (Hecht *et al.*, 1999: 246). In fact they don't have much to say about research: there is one index reference to it in *The Department Chair as Academic Leader* (Hecht *et al.*, 1999), plus a scattering of other unindexed allusions. There is a greater shortage of enquiries into leading departments' and teams' research efforts. Our treatment of this topic has been helped by our informants' comments and is largely derived from the ideas developed in earlier chapters.

The popularization of the scholarship of discovery

The past 30 years have seen an expansion of what can be regarded as legitimate academic research, much as in the UK the range of legitimate cuisine has been transformed by the popular acceptance of Indian, Thai, Chinese, French and Italian dishes. And just as chicken was a post-war delicacy but is now the staple of poor carnivores' diets, so research opportunities are plentiful because, for example, it is now recognized that expensive, large-scale social surveys are no longer the only ways of doing social research. In some quarters they are shunned, as vegetarians despise chicken, and cheaper and accessible forms of social enquiry such as case studies, action research and ethnography have become accepted as powerful forms of research. The anthropologist need not go to the South Pacific but can study street-corner society in Darlington instead. The collapse, in many subject areas, of the certainties of the positivist project has produced views of knowledge and knowing that take the local, specific, shifting and partly glimpsed as worthy matters of enquiry, and that take seriously the interplays of espoused logic and logic-in-use (e.g. Schön, 1987). And the availability of high-technology, low-cost machinery brings data capture and data analysis within reach of all faculty, with voice recognition software, telephone interviews, email surveys, Optical Mark Reader (OMR) technology, remote sensing systems and web searches cutting the cost of data collection and processing. Changing epistemologies and associated changes in research methods have popularized the scholarship of discovery in many, but not all, fields of study.

Ramsden (1998b) suggests that research, in the sense of discovery, should be feasible or affordable, make a worthwhile contribution to significant questions, and be interesting, especially to the researcher. What he does not say is that it has to be large-scale work in distant places using positivist paradigms. Leading a research culture frequently involves colleagues becoming more skilled at scanning the commonplace environment for opportunities to test or refine theories, to propose conceptual distinctions or developments or to explore the impacts of policies or practices. Important work can be done with one subject, despite a quaint belief that it depends on large samples (Dukes, 1970; Chi and Koeske, 1983). It is important that departments and teams appreciate this.

Although this popularization means that most faculty can be active researchers, activity is not evidence of quality and getting a good research profile involves a lot more than doing copious amounts of fieldwork. Consider our experiences as tutors on Lancaster University's Doctoral Programme in Higher Education and as journal referees. We see lots of reports of small-scale research. They are usually accounts of thorough work, based on sensibly designed inquiries and careful analytical procedures. The biggest problem is that as they are presented these reports often have no obvious appeal except to the writer and close colleagues. Ask the question 'who cares?' or 'so what?' and the parochialism of the work can be seen in stark relief. The ground is there but the theory isn't. In most cases, though, it is possible to see that the particular could be connected to the general and that the case study, action research project, ethnography or evaluation could be represented as a test of, extension to, modification of or contribution to theory or established practices. One of us argues that it is best to begin small-scale work by thinking about the general claims that might be made about the sorts of findings that can fairly be anticipated (Knight, 2001). If that is so, then there is a stronger case for saying that leaders could regularly remind colleagues of the potential pay-offs in thinking early about the presentation of small-scale research findings to national and international audiences. Here, one characteristic of a research culture is that all enquiries begin with the assumption that they should lead to publication in high- or mid-level outlets.

For example, a team or unit may regularly secure funds to investigate the workings of policy developments in say, the care of the elderly in a city or region. After six years there is a substantial set of reports to funders and a far bigger archive of interview, questionnaire and statistical data. Although ten papers have been accepted by practitioner journals, the unit has not really capitalized on the work it has done. The data could be reviewed to give purchase on substantial policy and conceptual debates to do with welfare provision in an ageing society at a time of global change. The team could increase the exchange and use value of their work if their specific enquiries were systematically presented in terms of more general and more appealing theories, issues and concepts. Doing that would not be cost-free but it quickly emerges that the pay-off from raising the research profile would cover the cost of a more ambitious publication strategy and enhance the unit's standing for future bids for funding.

When a 'democratic' view of the scholarship of discovery is allied to an understanding of the ways in which the local and particular can be presented as contributions to thinking, policy and practice at large, then teams and departments are well placed to see themselves as serious operators in the scholarship of discovery. Leading the research effort involves helping colleagues to construct concepts of research that they can see as having a meaning for them and their professional work. Another side of the leader's work is fostering the knowledge-building networks that can productively draw together elements of professional life that are often disconnected.

Integrating the team: research as shared learning

One of our informants explained how his team's research profile was improving as he emphasized the importance of research, set an example and provided help:

> Since I took over as HoD 20 months ago, I have made academic research and, more importantly, publication a major priority in the department. I have done this by 'walking the talk', i.e. doing it myself, despite my heavy workload. This has set the tone for the rest of the staff and although not all are yet research active (and some may never

be), we are probably approaching 50% of departmental staff who could now be described in that way – and this percentage will increase. We had no-one entered in the [national research assessment exercise] last time, and should have 6 (out of 16) in next time round. This has been facilitated by my appointing someone, as a Professor, who is much more experienced than I am in research, is an excellent communicator and is able to help both myself and colleagues with their work. We make a very good team. Like everyone else, I wish I had more time.

(Male, new leader, Scotland)

The pressure on time can have more serious effects, which is why we will finish this chapter with some suggestions for modest time savings. A Canadian man who has recently taken on a department said:

I have functioned more as an editor of research proposals than a leader of research initiative . . . I carry the same academic load that I did prior to my 'promotion'. I have virtually stopped any direct involvement in research. This provides some time, but does not deliver a great deal of satisfaction.

(Male, new leader, Canada)

Again:

The major stumbling block to research is the workload that we are experiencing. We just barely keep our heads above water with what we HAVE to do to serve our clients [so] research is a 'Boy it would be nice to have time to . . .' kind of activity . . . I have pursued my own research and scholarly activity but efforts to stimulate such activity elsewhere have been thwarted to some extent due to lack of resources or . . . other priorities.

(Female, new leader, Canada)

But where heads of department said that they were making progress with their departmental research programme, they often said that a team or collaborative approach was important for research growth, as the second quotation at the head of this chapter indicated. Another head of department was excited by a growing understanding in the department, 'that team research pays big dividends: projects move faster, ideas are generated. Team spirit' (male, experienced leader, Canada). It seems to be increasingly common for teams and departments to approach research collectively and aim to draw everyone into it by holding seminars or brown bag lunches when people report on their projects and findings. Obviously that signals that research is valued. It can help researchers to get some helpful feedback on their work and it can provide some intellectual exercise for people who learn about work that would otherwise have passed them by. Research students can also benefit from involvement with these seminars, and everyone may gain where local practitioners participate. Yet a departmental seminar programme of this sort does not do as much for a research culture as it could. The principal drawbacks are:

- The specifics of other people's research projects can be deeply uninteresting.
- The topics can be specialized enough to deter colleagues who are not specialists in the area or polymaths.
- Reporting project findings closes down more thinking than they normally stimulate.
- Reports of interim findings have the same limits as reports of final findings but without the authority.
- They have restricted power as learning experiences.
- Some researchers have the view 'that they are in post to fulfill their own objectives only . . . [without] understanding other people's point of view' (female, new leader, England).

Although such seminars obviously recognize that knowledge is dispersed and that one way of learning is to share the knowledge and knowing, their power is limited. Too often knowledge is understood as specialized conclusions and sharing takes the form of a 'show and tell' exercise. We recommend a shift from presenting the outcomes of enquiries to sharing concepts, procedures, ideas and problems. Instead of retailing knowledge, seminars would be ways of creating it. This alternative model is based on the idea that seminar programmes should be designed to stimulate the maximum amount of thinking that could be useful to the widest possible audience. They would be open to all: technicians, administrative and secretarial colleagues, research students and other members of the community. They would use various learning techniques to stimulate research thinking and help colleagues construct proposals or work on draft reports, papers or presentations. Programme activities could include the following:

- *Perspective sharing.* People present summaries of ideas and concepts that they are currently excited by in their own thinking and enquiry. On the basis that there is nothing as practical as a good theory, this conceptual enrichment has the potential to inspire new ways of approaching familiar research settings and new possibilities for locating research data in the wider world of academic discourse. Whereas traditional seminars retail finished products, this puts powerful research tools into people's hands.
- *Reading group activities.* This is a development of the first idea. Instead of summarizing concepts, faculty could draw colleagues' attention to fresh and powerful books or papers that have the potential to stimulate research in a number of areas. For example, many social science projects could be more interesting if their authors were aware of Dweck's work on self-theories (1999), Wenger's book on communities of practice (1998) or Hargreaves's paper on the emotions and professional work – teaching in this case (1998). The aim would be to review a key reading in order to see how a team's research and teaching activities could borrow and learn from it.

- *Project-making.* This is an exercise in group problem-working. Individuals or teams come to the seminar with a possible research topic and some thoughts about conceptual perspectives that could permeate it. A skilled facilitator helps to release collective creativity and understandings to identify feasible and promising ways of turning the topic into action. Ideally, a self-selected group will then contribute to bringing the concept through 'to market' and act as an advisory or steering group thereafter. This displaces workshops on 'grantmanship' (Lucas, 1994: 165).
- *Constructing better working habits.* Many of us have learned some deeply unhelpful ways of working. For example, it is usual for writers to wait until they have a substantial and large block of time in which to write; to try and read everything before writing; to hover endlessly over the exact wording of a paragraph; to plan, plan and plan rather than to write; to fail to see that half of writing is done through conversations with others as a part of normal daily intercourse; and to try and do things alone, so that no one gets to see plans, fragments or drafts. For most people, these are the practices of the damned. There are better alternatives. Departmental research learning programmes can be public sites in which these practices can be tackled or, more sensitively, they can be places where people are encouraged to look for sympathetic colleagues who will privately read drafts, talk about ideas and advise on different ways of writing. It can be helpful to everyone if those colleagues are not expert in the research topic, since both people then learn: one from asking and the other from having to put specialized ideas into a form accessible to a less expert audience. There is more on these lines in a later section on 'buddy systems' (p. 131).
- *Themed seminars.* Teams and departments that are skilled at medium term planning may be able to schedule a series of formal seminars on a topic that is designated as a research priority two or three years down the line. The question, 'How could this contribute to our research proposal?' is asked of every seminar in the series.
- *Mid-point tuning.* This differs from presentations of interim findings in terms of the intention behind it, which is to seek advice and guidance. Presenters talk about where a project has reached and, rather than inviting comment on the findings to date (which can be done by email) look for help in seeing how to bring it to completion: perspectives, analytical tools, possible outputs and extension work.

This model of a research knowledge-building network can be a relatively unthreatening way of insinuating into the practices of discovery older faculty who were appointed to teach, not to be active in this form of research. It also provides a way in which people can contribute in distinctive ways to the scholarship of discovery. There can be a tendency to assume that the 'researcher' is the person who has an idea, develops it, gets the grant, manages the enquiry and analysis, writes it up and gets the kudos. Many people, though, are better at some parts of this research process than others.

Some, like those older faculty who may not see themselves as proper researchers, read widely (perhaps to keep their teaching fresh) and can contribute powerfully to the conceptualization, analysis and writing stages. Others, who were often appointed more for their professional qualities than for their academic distinction, may like being out in the world of practice and can collect data far better than their less office-wise colleagues. These 'brown bags' and seminars expand the space in which all can contribute to research learning through their own expertise. As such they embody our earlier ideas about distributed leadership and collegiality in communities of practice.

Faculty who work in the natural sciences might consider that they already work in teams, that their research processes are naturally, normally and frequently collaborative, and that brainstorming is a common way of learning. Where teams such as these are parts of larger departments there may be value in considering whether all parts of the department could benefit from sharing in this research learning process. And because teams often work on highly specialized topics, the greatest value would come not so much from a pooling of research results as from a sharing of concepts and procedures that have the generative power of inspiring research in other areas of the department.

There are limits to what a knowledge-building network approach can achieve. For one thing, face-to-face networking is important, which assumes that there is a convenient slot in the timetable when everyone can meet in congenial setting. In many cases individualism, factions and contingencies inhibit collegiality. And although team research efforts are normal in many natural science areas the learning potential can be lost when the authority structure operates so that people may learn from the research team leader but they rarely learn as a team. Lastly, there is a danger that these research learning programmes will unthinkingly but systematically exclude the female and younger members of the team or department who are most likely to be on part-time contracts and paid by the hour. The prudent chair will be in a position to recognize that these colleagues are very good value compared to the cost of employing full-time, tenured staff, and explore ways offering some compensation to those part-timers who choose to collaborate in this research learning work.

Conversations about research

Academic staff are usually formally assessed from time to time and, following the ideas developed in Chapter 6 about assessment, leaders might want to consider the potential of learning conversations about research activity – of adding formative assessments to the existing summative ones. Few would disagree with the proposition that the way faculty are evaluated has a powerful normalizing influence, defining what is valued and what is not. There is little point in appraisals that enjoin the individual to be active as a creator, synthesizer and user of knowledge when working practices embedded in departmental life value some forms of scholarship and marginalize others. Research should infuse social practices in the department or team.

High-stakes performance appraisals often seem to be founded on a belief that it is important to deter, detect and discipline the derelict, even though they are a very small minority; even a British government that routinely excoriated school-teachers estimated the proportion of incompetents as no greater than 4 per cent. Since the great majority of academic, technical and support staff already work well, they do not need – and may resent – the disciplinary resonances that these procedures can create. Furthermore, these formal systems are usually over-dependent on one sort of formal reward, which is higher pay. It is questionable whether the main motivator in higher education is pay. Of course, people will always welcome more pay and some have urgent needs for it, but the driving motivation for most faculty is fulfilment or self-actualization in work. So, it is a pity if systems that depend on surveillance and extrinsic rewards are used to 'motivate' people whose work depends on creativity, conscientiousness and the self-drive that comes particularly from intrinsic sources. Recognition, encouragement, appreciation, good interpersonal relationships, a positive emotional climate and the chance to have the 'flow' experience in the workplace are the things that are conducive to professionalism, flexibility and creativity. Good appraisal systems, whether for research or any other activity, recognize that.

Informal appraisals can be valuable, especially where it is understood that the appraiser can be anyone chosen by the appraisee and that the only thing that gets written down is the appraiser's confirmation that appraisal discussions have taken place. These appraisals are professional conversations about making the most of the next six months, year or two years. They are concerned with maximizing opportunities for fulfilment and self-actualization in ways that are consistent with the team or department's research profile. Obviously, they would involve looking backwards as well as forwards, but this would not be in the spirit of checking for compliance with a set of targets contracted at the last appraisal. Where appraisals are about identifying what could be done, it is inevitable that many of the ideas will not work out. Some will, and they should be celebrated as successes and used to generate ideas about subsequent projects. Others will not have worked out. On review it will appear that some of those not-successes are worth staying with, while others flickered and died. Even the not-successes may be useful as stimuli to reflecting and learning.

These appraisals might explore the appraisee's contribution to the department's research activities and recognize that people who may not land the research grants may nevertheless contribute significantly to the collective research enterprise. They might be skilled as a mentor in buddy systems (see below); a good facilitator of research students' learning; a powerful contributor of ideas to the departmental research learning programme; or good at bringing the world of the university and the worlds of practice into an interplay that nourishes research and vivifies teaching. Good appraisals are more sensitive to complexity than are evaluations based on seductive performance indicators such as grants, conference papers, publications and citations.

Formal mentoring needs to be provided for new members of staff, although it is not invariably good mentoring and improvements can be made (Knight and Trowler, 1999; Trowler and Knight, 2000). Here we suggest that something akin to mentoring should involve everyone in the community of practice, although we will develop the point with respect to research alone. A buddy system is an agreement to meet periodically with a chosen colleague to reflect on research activity and plans: it takes the idea of the reflective practitioner, applies it to the scholarship of discovery and capitalizes on the power of reflecting with the help of at least one other person. That person need not be an expert in the specialist research topic. The benefits come from four sources. One is from the formal prompt to take the work of reflecting seriously and to do it mindfully. The second is from having to give an account of research work in a way that makes sense to another person who is representative of the discipline and institutional communities; the principle is that to teach is to learn twice. The third is through responding to questions, and the fourth benefit is the joint creation of ideas, possibilities and priorities.

In conventional mentoring arrangements the mentor is usually a person in authority operating within a relatively high-stakes environment. Not only may the power relationship constrain disclosure but the mentee is prevented from choosing the mentor who seems most likely to be able to stimulate the reflecting that drives learning. In buddy systems positional authority is replaced by skill as a facilitator, with one person helping the other to make some implicit knowing explicit, to create and test ideas. Formal research mentoring can also be seen as a threat to academic freedom in general and to collective agreements, where they exist. In those cases the power of a good idea gets lost by resistance to the surveillance and control that can be associated with imposed mentoring systems. Buddy systems can tap that power without raising the fears. However, although one of our informants said that her department's research profile was improving because 'Two very strong committed faculty members serve as mentors to new faculty' (female, new leader, USA), another view was that, 'Attempts in the department to pair active and non researchers have only had limited success. Some active researchers have been successful at developing links and publishing with new researchers in other departments' (male, new leader, Scotland).

Helping research by cutting waste

In the past 20 years politicians have made much of the idea that public services are saturated with inefficiencies that are so great that their elimination would provide high-quality provision without any tax hikes. Managerialim has been used as the means to achieve efficiency. There are three problems with this. Firstly, as the great re-engineering experiments of the early 1990s showed, things that seem to be a waste of resources, such as middle management layers, often exist because they do have important but unappreciated roles. The parallel is with ecosystems, where it is regularly found that eliminating a 'wasteful' feature, such as hedgerows in England, proves to be a mistake. When hedgerows are grubbed up it is often necessary to use more pesticides because they were home to birds and animals that fed off insects and pests in the fields. Secondly, it is not clear that managerialism is the way to bring about efficiency. It depends on a rather rationalist, reductionist and mechanistic view of how organizations operate, use resources and create value. There are good reasons for believing that even if it is a sustainable view of systems designed to do simple tasks, it is quite inappropriate to complex systems with multiple means for pursuing fuzzy goals. Thirdly, efficient systems lack the adaptive capability: they are evolutionary dead ends. Systems that can adapt and learn, that support creativity and innovation and that are flexible are systems that contain spaces and redundancies (Nonaka and Takeuchi, 1995; Morgan, 1997). In terms of a team or department's research effort there are compelling reasons based on systems thinking and organizational studies for recognizing that there needs to be thinking time, space for people to meet accidentally and occasions for serendipities to happen. A coffee machine in a corridor may be an apparently efficient response to the cost of providing a coffee lounge. It is also a good way of reducing a team's creativity quotient, taking with it a good part of its sociability rating. We noted in Chapter 3 the importance of knowledge acquired in piecemeal and serendipitous ways: a phenomenon highlighted by the study of deaf academics who are largely excluded from these sources of information (Trowler *et al.*, 1999).

The implication is that some claims about how research efficiency can be raised should be sceptically addressed. Many departments have delegated more routine and less demanding work to pieceworkers, such as teaching assistants. In the UK there are departments that, in order to earn the best returns in the 2001 research assessment exercise, have put staff with modest or no publication record on teaching-only contracts: others have recruited 'research-only' professors. The promised efficiency gains may be illusory. These manoeuvres can create a caste system, which is a deviation from the ideal of a community of scholars. They can isolate teachers from research even though it is generally expected that higher education teachers should be at the leading edges of knowledge, although they may not need to be discoverers of knowledge. They are consumers, appliers and integrators of fresh thinking and as such they have much to contribute to teams' and departments' research. Conversely, the discoverers can contribute to the business of reflecting about teaching. So, even if it is easy to mark someone out as a teacher or as a researcher, it is arguable that it is not helpful to interfere with an interplay between research and teaching. The choice of words is a careful one. Good research does not cause good teaching but teaching and research can be in a relationship that benefits both. Blackburn and Lawrence (1995) were not alone in finding that most faculty want to do research and to teach and the psychic rewards of working with students are a source of satisfaction in the same way, albeit to a lesser extent, as they are for high school teachers. These efficiency manoeuvres may also reduce flexibility and adaptiveness (Morgan, 1997) and leave a shrunken group of full-time staff to take on all the administrative, service and committee work that part-time faculty and teaching assistants cannot do. The proportion of time that they can spend on teaching and research is thereby reduced.

In sum, Fordist approaches to departmental efficiency can have their costs and they may be highest in terms of the research efforts that they were intended to protect. More promising areas for efficiency gains are:

- *Writing practices.* Many academic staff could benefit from Boice's (1992) finding that the new entrants to the academic profession who were successful were the ones who wrote regularly. Presumably, they routinely thought about what they might say when they next switched the computer on, which meant that relatively small amounts of time could then be used productively. These are also likely to have been people who saw writing as a way of thinking and who were therefore prepared to write in the knowledge that the text would be revised or even discarded later. Becker (1986) and Knight (2001) make other practical suggestions about how to be more efficient as a writer.
- *Administrative practices.* Time can also be freed up by getting an outsider's appraisal of one's established work habits (Covey *et al.* (1994) provide a good account of time management). For example, many people handle a piece of paper or email several times before they finish with it, yet most material is best treated to the 'one-touch' approach and dealt with there and then, often by being routed to someone else. The 'one-touch' system saves time and also means that colleagues are far more likely to get the fast replies they deserve rather than the hopelessly late replies to which they are accustomed. With that goes the idea that material is treated in proportion to its importance. So, decide that a certain administrative job must fit into a half a day a fortnight, or that minutes of departmental meetings can be dumped unread, or that filing is a waste of time because support staff routinely archive important information (and who else in their right mind saves unimportant information?).
- *Review support systems.* It goes without saying that investment in support staff can free up faculty time, although it is not always clear that the work they do is the most useful work that could be done – obsolete patterns can linger – and that they meet together often enough to share best practices, identify improvements and voice needs. Heads of department can help all aspects of a team or department's work by encouraging support staff to develop their own learning culture for their areas of work. Recognizing that support staff can learn from each other does not imply that they should be segregated from the other learning activities in

the community. Efficiency gains in this area may not save money but they can certainly help academic staff to engage with their four forms of scholarship without having to fret away on backstage activities.

Support systems can sustain research activity when there is a budget for conference attendance and travel, with clear, fair criteria for the award of grants; when calls for papers and conference announcements are placed on a prominent well-kept noticeboard; when research intelligence is routinely circulated to all teams members; and when administrative staff do the proper research costings, get them signed off by the finance officer and manage the monies once the project is under way.

- *Formal meetings.* Meetings eat time, especially in environments where it feels right to have plenty of meetings because of a commitment to collegiality. The advice that leaders should be trained to chair effective meetings is likely to be wasted, because it might be easier to admit to being a poor lover than to being a poor chair of meetings. But they should be trained. There is no shortage of hints on running meetings and a web search will produce a plethora of tips for chairs. In high-trust systems, especially where electronic communication is habitual, fewer meetings are possible, even to the point where they are needs-responsive, and not calendar-driven.

These points notwithstanding, there is seldom a lot of scope for efficiency savings that will make more time for research or teaching. More worryingly, apparent opportunities for savings have a chance of cutting out something that has a great but subtle importance. As a rule of thumb, if an efficiency saving can be made it probably already has been.

8

Administration and Positioning

It can also be observed that with two circumspect men, one will achieve his end,
the other not; and likewise two men succeed equally well with different methods,
one being circumspect and the other impetuous.

(Machiavelli, [1514] 1961: 131)

Preview

In her discussion of work in Australian universities, Currie suggests that
'[T]he hours in themselves do not seem to be the main problem that
concerns academics. It is rather the new administrative tasks and the associated fragmentation of work time' (1996: 107). In that respect these faculty
members resemble school-teachers, who tend to resent the 'back-room'
work that does not have a clear 'front-stage' pay-off. Where others may try
to avoid administration, taking charge of the day-to-day routines, the team
or department leader cannot, and its intrusions on teaching and research
may be particularly resented. Faculty frequently wonder whether administration and its associated paperwork, requirements, deadlines, accountability and meetings are really necessary. In addition, they can easily come to
wonder whether their former colleague has lost sight of their interests and
sold out to an uncaring or hostile system.

  This management work often corrodes leaders' control of their time.
Tasks come continuously from outside the department or team and crowd
one upon another, so that in educational management, as in management
in general, problems seldom get sustained attention (Hales, 1993). Coping
strategies and on-the-fly actions replace the deliberate attention that many
management books depict as the normal and rational ways of doing things,
which can itself be a source of feelings of guilt and inadequacy for leaders
who see themselves falling short of those ideals. As the section on efficiency
in Chapter 7 suggested, there are ways of administering that generally make
life easier. This chapter considers some of them.

Knowledge about administration and positioning

Even the longest book on departmental management (Tucker, 1993) cannot successfully resolve three problems. The first is to do with the nature of general advice. Machiavelli got to the heart of the problem. 'Everyone', he observed, 'imagines he is competent' ([1514] 1961: 136), so general advice to praise, listen or be open is likely to be wasted because most people believe that they already have those qualities. The second is that institutions have their own administrative systems, their own quirks and their own power flows that have to be learned. Institution-specific advice is needed. Thirdly, as we have already argued, a great deal of the knowledge that leaders use is tacit. Besides, as we indicated in the opening chapters, we are sceptical about the claim that good management is the successful deployment of rational, strategic planning. For example, actions may precede, not follow, planning, and anticipate strategy rather than be its outcome. In the same vein, Weick (1995) has suggested that policy comes from action so that we 'walk the talk' before we know what the talk is going to turn out to be, and James Moore, working in the science of complexity, claims that 'We know from studying complex systems that prediction in any conventional sense is not possible' (quoted in Lewin and Regine, 1999: 65). Five other reasons for saying that even the administration of established departments and teams is the uncertain exercise of imperfect power are:

- High-trust systems are preferable to low-trust ones because they are cheaper (reduced surveillance costs) and they support the flexibility from which innovation comes. High-trust systems rely on intrinsic motivation and people's quest for self-actualization through their work, both of which are regularly associated with more and better work. As we suggested in Chapter 2, close supervision is incompatible with these approaches and that, along with the consequent emphasis on self-regulation, leads to diversity of expectations and practices. Consequently, leaders cannot monitor compliance in the ways that Fordist management texts recommend: indeed, the concept of compliance itself becomes problematic.
- Even low-trust teams and departments are relatively loosely coupled systems, partly because of the fuzzy nature of the work of teaching and research and partly because of endemic uncertainties about priorities between poorly defined goals. Not only does it become hard to ensure fidelity of implementation, but it can often be difficult to see exactly where power really is located: there is a 'receding locus of control' in which everyone believes that someone else holds the keys to getting things done.
- Academics may espouse collegiality and democratic ways but, desirable though those are, the dark side of academic freedom and participative decision making is a more-or-less explicit veto culture. Management and administrative practices that depend on full and timely cooperation are always potential victims of this academic selfishness.

- In the opening chapters we emphasized the power that situated, contingent and micropolitical factors have over what leaders do. One experienced informant, asked what made good leadership possible listed, among other things, 'Nice people – humorous, brilliant, open and outspoken, kindly and charitable, sociable and reliable. No assholes. No sneaks. No perverts. No introverts. No plotters. No self-interested prima donnas' (male, experienced leader, Canada).
- Not all problems can be solved, which is why we prefer to think of problemworking rather than problem-solving.

In repeating themes addressed in Chapters 2 and 3 we are not saying that being a good administrator is about eclectic practical reasoning and sensemaking that can only be learned on the job, although there is some truth in that position (Chapter 10). The following section outlines some characteristics of effective administering.

Administering

The constant press of administrative work is one of the major causes of stress among chairs and team leaders and '[B]alancing the administrative and scholarship roles . . . accounted for significant stress among departmental chairs in the US as well as in Australia' (Sarros *et al.*, 1997: 284). Leaders who reflect on the ways that they administer and who construct positive self-theories are better placed to reduce that stress. In their study of 827 Australian heads of department, Sarros *et al.* found that levels of stress were associated with the attitude that the head of department had to the job. Those who were doing it willingly tended to be less stressed, and senior staff, who might be more self-confident, were less perturbed by the work than were the associate professors acting as heads of department. In other words, the job is indeed a demanding one but the way people approach it – their beliefs, explanations, attributions and ways of seeing – make it feel more or less demanding. As one informant said, 'I have not found administration to be unduly burdensome . . . I was determined I was not going to let admin spoil the enjoyment I get from teaching and research' (male, new leader, Scotland). In Chapter 6 we mentioned the significance of attributions and self-theories for good learning and indicated that those people who had 'learned optimism' and who appreciated the importance of good thinking and effort were better than others as learners, especially in the face of adversity. Much the same can be said here. One way of understanding the pressures of the job of leading a team or department is to appraise one's own tendencies to learned optimism or learned helplessness (Seligman, 1998; S. Knight, 1999).

More prosaically, the advice on personal well-being that fills self-help books is worth taking seriously. For instance, trying to cope with administration *and* scholarship calls for: more exercise, not less; better time-management; prioritization; delegation; proper meal breaks; decent office furniture, including two good armchairs and alternatives to fluorescent lighting; good

time management; end-of-week reviews and reflection; and friends to remind you that working harder may not be working smarter. Covey *et al.*
(1994) provide a thorough treatment of most of these themes. An experienced woman head of center in the USA listed five habits that help her to
be effective:

1. Perspective: I try to maintain my perspective. I believe that one's
   sense of humor is an indicator of how successfully one is maintaining perspective. Humor requires having the big picture. If it goes,
   that's a warning sign and a time to back off and get away until it
   returns. I frequently refresh myself in terms of what is important
   and what isn't and try to devote my energy to what is important.
   (Easy to say, hard to do.)
2. Working increasingly on-line has actually helped (after an initial
   info overload.) It forced me to realize that one can't do it all or be it
   all – that life is really much bigger than any of us. So it doesn't bother
   me so much to say, 'No, I can't do that worthwhile thing'. It has
   taught me to set boundaries at the start of a project instead of waiting
   for boundaries to be imposed by another. It is really critical to end
   things and plan for ending things, even good things. Circle of life
   and all that. Knowing how much action is worth how much effort.
3. Priorities – that is part of #2 but deserves its own line separate from
   setting boundaries. Every act is a statement about priorities – what is
   most important long term . . . short term . . . evaluating this constantly.
   Understanding that one does some things for oneself, some to stay
   ahead of others and some because of an external demand (and I
   don't mean 'the President says so' but I mean because economic
   trends are such that if you don't, you cease to exist).
4. Understanding people – I read somewhere that the 3 generations
   currently in the work force each need a different kind of leadership
   (olders want to be told, youngest want to figure it out for themselves). That it is impossible to please even a portion, particularly of
   faculty – so please yourself and your reading of the future. To not
   take dissent personally. To understand that all the people with whom
   you work are 'in process'. That's the perspective thing again.
5. To always have a plan so you feel you can walk away from it all. An
   escape route can give you the courage to do what is right.

The work of support staff

Once support staff comprised secretaries and, in some subjects, technicians.
Technicians remain, ICT experts are now common in larger departments
and secretaries have almost everywhere become administrative personnel
rather than typists, although it is questionable whether their pay has reflected the increased complexity and demands of their work. As this quotation says, they can be extremely valuable:

We have recently hired an incredible office support person and she is taking over a huge amount of the daily administration duties. The downside of this is that salaries to find such a person are relatively high . . . the upside is that I feel it saves a huge amount in the salaries of the people who use her services!

(Female, new leader, Canada)

There is no reason why the principles that apply to relationships with academic staff should not apply to support staff, with two major modifications. One is that support staff will almost always need to work at the office every day and between them they should provide full cover of the phones and enquiries made in person or electronically. Secondly, institutional conditions of service for support staff tend to be more prescriptive than they are for academic staff. Even so, it is good leadership practice to respect people's expertise, to ask for their advice, to involve them in decisions, to encourage them to manage the ways in which they get the work done, and to be considerate. This implies: flexibility in office hours; inviting them to attend departmental meetings, seminars and other events; and asking their advice about how things could be done better and their work made easier.

Support staff reviews, appraisals and promotions can be done in the same way as for academic staff, with the emphasis being on development, learning and nourishing intrinsic motivation. However, because support staff's work is far less under their control than is the case with faculty work, it is easier for them to become swamped by the competing requirements of people in the academic team and to feel a lack of control over their work. Academic thoughtlessness and peremptory treatment of support staff are causes of inefficiency in general and can make support staff feel that they are second-class citizens if faculty are insensitive to their feelings and job needs. It can also amount to institutional sexism because support staff tend to be women and full-time faculty tend to be men.

Just as it makes sense to get academic staff used to meeting to talk together about research, support staff can benefit, as a group, from a forum in which they can share problems and look for ways of handling them, and create and share expertise. For example, extended sick leave means that a job has to be covered, sometimes with temporary help, sometimes without. Managers would be wise to ask their office colleagues to think through with them the best ways of covering the work without unfairness. Equally, problems like providing all-day phone coverage can only be addressed collectively. And just as academic staff benefit from sharing ideas about useful techniques, concepts and developments, so support staff can learn from each other and should have the time provided for them to meet and do it. From the leader's point of view this collective slant on the support staff's work can be something of a safeguard when one of them falls sick or leaves. Job shadowing is another way in which support staff can extend their expertise and periodic job rotation is another, although it is unpopular if it is seen as change for the sake of change.

Forum discussions may help administrators to check that working practices are as efficient as they might be. Work habits that make great sense at one time outlive their usefulness and become a source of inefficiency, and secretarial practices that fitted days when keyboard skills were a craft skill and email a fantasy make little sense today. More sensitively, support staff, like academics, vary in their busyness:work-done ratio and some would benefit from adopting new work practices such as 'one-touch' paper handling, out-of-contact mornings, enthusiastic use of the litter bin as a filing system and revised photocopying arrangements. Someone who does not work in these ways, who never closes the office door, enjoys every conversation as a social event and makes a 'bad day' pile of paperwork that will be dealt with as a matter of last resort will be threatened by these suggestions for change. Group discussions of working practices can make it legitimate to raise awareness of best practice and send relatively unthreatening messages about the unacceptability of self-defeating ones. Reflecting as a group can spur individual thought and inquiry; for example, a study of how the week really is used. In terms of making a difference, it is best if a colleague can be involved as a sounding board, mentor and coach. Staff appraisals can provide an opportunity to celebrate efficiencies that have been achieved and to talk through areas that remain problematic.

Departmental and team procedures

Support staff are most likely to be effective when the procedures that they are expected to operate are well conceived. In many organizations some procedures are cumbersome and others should not exist. That was the great insight of the organizational re-engineering movement of the early and mid-1990s, namely that much that was done need not be, and much of the rest could be done more simply. Leading a team or a department well involves checking that procedural nonsenses are eliminated: that virtually the same data are not requested three times; that inquiries are dealt with on a next day basis (at least); that course evaluations are useful; and that meetings are both many (involving small, working groups) and few (tying up everyone).

A frustrated Canadian informant, experienced as a departmental chair, was not the only one to feel that those above him (unwittingly?) sabotage his attempts to be efficient:

> I have found that those to whom I report consider me (and my support staff) as readily available information sources. We are repeatedly asked for the same data in different formats. Tasks are downloaded with no transfer of resources. I have not developed effective means of dealing with this load. The days just get longer and the quality of what I do simply decreases.
>
> (Male, experienced leader, Canada)

We have appointed more non-teaching staff as 'directors' of this, that and the other, within our Faculty and at the level of the Senior Executive. With nothing else to do but think up how 'we' can improve on everything we do, Heads are inundated with consultation papers, spend huge portions of their working week at meetings, and drown in paperwork. I don't know how we get out of this spiral.

(Female, experienced leader, Scotland)

Dean is run ragged so he has pushed many tasks down to departments which were formerly done by the Dean's office.

(Male, experienced leader, Canada)

Disruptive internal forces combine, especially in Britain, with outside expectations, as a Welsh experienced male leader observed:

A lot of pressure from external (and internal) accountability – admin burden is made more unbearable for a central department given the plethora of external QAA, HEFC [Higher Education Funding Council], and government-related initiatives e.g. e-university; community university; UfI [University for Industry] etc. etc. – current structures and allocations of responsibilities don't always help – but this is not something that is given sufficient formal airing or discussion; it's just assumed.

(Male, experienced leader, Wales)

Another experienced leader in Scotland made a list of things he needed in order to work properly that many of our informants would endorse: '1. More time to develop management skills . . . 2. Better support facilities within the university. 3. Understanding of the academic process by senior university management. 4. Governments realistic/sufficient support of the sector (male, experienced leader, Scotland). The suggestions that follow by no means solve these problems but they do identify approaches that can alleviate some of them. Tucker (1993), Lucas (1994) and Hecht *et al.* (1999) provide more detailed advice.

One way of getting an idea of how well administrative routines are working is to run some audit trails. For example, follow through a student's application for undergraduate or postgraduate study, taking the perspective of the applicant and beginning with the department's website (and look at the department's speed of response to enquiries from the website). This is important for recruitment, since it is cheaper to retain people who have been attracted to make enquiries than it is to advertise to get more people interested enough to enquire. So this audit trail should be concerned with improving efficiency to reduce wastage. Other possibilities for audit trails are: new course approvals (which need to be rigorous and fast enough to meet changing needs); new staff appointments (dealing efficiently with too many applications); research grant bidding teaching (why do we teach like this; Would other approaches be cheaper and better?); and the front of house (signposting, decor, reception, image). In all cases the basic assumptions are those of continuous quality improvement (CQI), namely that it is important to keep looking for ways of doing things better, which includes asking whether everything that is done needs to be done.

Increasingly, departments and large teams are administered by a management group. This reduces the load on the chair or team leader and makes it less likely that there will be bottlenecks caused by work backing up around one person who is the channel through which all business flows. Management teams can be more efficient and they can also be a means by which policy can be explored and provisionally decided. In Chapter 10 we shall also argue that they are training grounds for leaders-to-be. A drawback, though, is when they become perceived as 'senior management teams' whose purpose is to stitch up everyone else so that the interests of one clique prevail. There is no way to prevent that perception developing among the disgruntled, but it can be reduced where the team, including support staff, has some say in who is in the management group, and where the period of service is limited to three or four years. Nevertheless, it is sobering to hear that 'Large numbers of faculty in many countries feel they are not influential in shaping academic policies at their institutions, are dissatisfied with the relationship between faculty and administration, and seem to distrust campus leadership' (Boyer *et al.*, 1994: 22).

Often 'administration' means the people who run the department. The costs of that perception in terms of loss of creativity and energy are considerable. That is one reason why the leader's work should be subject to 360° appraisal and not judged through the more common process of top-down accountability. Whatever conventional performance indicators say about a leader's activity our position, with its emphasis on collegiality, implies that the leader's manner ought not to be ignored when evaluating achievements. So, qualitative data from department and team members – especially from support staff – should be reviewed alongside more conventional performance indicators when it comes to reviewing the leader's work in order to understand better the lines that CQI might be taking in the next year or so.

Positioning the department or team in the institution

If Machiavelli's ([1514] 1961) advice to Renaissance Italian principalities was applied to departmental leadership, leaders would concentrate on manoeuvring for position in the vipers' nest of institutional politics and pay less attention to the intrinsic merits of their actions than to how they would be perceived by their (rival) colleagues. Our informants, though, emphasized substance over image:

> The prime factor is knowing that the persons in the department will provide back-up when something has to be delivered. This gives the department credibility in the eyes of those who make the 'big' decisions.
>
> (Male, new leader, Canada)

I have been heavily involved in a number of university-level committees for many years (and chair one) and my personal style is not to speak unless I have something worth saying. But usually when I do speak, it is to make a point which turns the discussion around, or re-focuses us on the main issue, so that agreement can be reached. I can't bear time-wasting debates. Because of this, I think my views are well respected. I am helped by the fact that my department is one of the most successful in the university in recruiting students, finding them relevant, well-paid jobs, and attracting extra income. So, by inference, people assume I must be a good HoD and this does carry some weight.

(Female, experienced leader, Scotland)

Other leaders agreed that personal style is an important complement to departmental achievements:

I am good at speaking, often with wit and economy and I make some good points which seem to benefit us downstream. Behind the scenes lobbying is also very important here so personal charm is important, and being able to listen to the interminable causes of other departments and disciplines without yawning.

(Male, experienced leader, Canada)

This is consistent with the position of Hecht *et al.* (1999) that the departmental chair needs to be seen as a person with integrity so that good politicking is a way of representing real departmental achievements to best effect. That said, substance and personal style are enhanced by political skill, as the next quotation suggests, and, as the two that follow it show, can be frustrated by deans and other senior colleagues.

Before becoming chair, I served in leadership positions in the faculty senate. I was viewed as a voice of reason in many situations and as someone who was not afraid to take an unpopular position on an issue, in other words, couldn't be bullied into submission. This has given me substantial credibility with the upper level administration. I also developed very strategic alliances with the business community. They are big supporters of me and the upper level administrators are reluctant to cross me. When they have, the business community has rallied to my position. These trump cards are used VERY sparingly, though. In fact, it was only needed once in the last four years. Skills that help: good reputation in previous on campus leadership spots . . . ability to set up key alliances with influential contributors . . . sense of humor that can be used to diffuse difficult situations.

(Female, experienced leader, USA)

Poor leadership at the very top – continuous organizational turbulence and unevenness – often not quite sure when/if a decision has been made . . . or if it will remain a decision! – continuous pressure in relation to resource-related matters.

(Male, experienced leader, England)

In the past, when the Dean has not been supportive those organizational and structural problems have been insurmountable. I think organizational structure is an important factor, but that individuals occupying key positions can exacerbate or eliminate [it]!

(Female, new leader, Canada)

Wryly, an experienced woman leader working in the USA asked, 'What is the difference between a terrorist and a tenured faculty member?' and replied, 'You can negotiate with a terrorist'. Despite these warnings that colleagues, deans and others can undermine attempts to represent departments' interests within the institution, there is a more optimistic tone to the following four pieces of advice.

- *Network.* This is not just in the sense of attending the formal meetings and speaking at them in ways that suggest that the team is sensitive to institution-wide considerations, as well as to its own preferences. As we suggested in Chapters 2 and 3, important though that is, it is also helpful to meet informally with colleagues, one-to-one or severally, and explore ideas for making the best of constraints, pressures and possibilities. In this sense, good positioning is about good thinking with people who will also benefit from good thinking.
- *Good thinking calls for good action.* Politically, it is useful to be seen as a leader who can follow up ideas with the promised paper, proposal, reform or contribution, and on time. Leaders who are full of ideas about embedding the development of significant working practices (or key skills, if you prefer) in the undergraduate curriculum are less plausible if no progress is made to represent those ideas in their departments' curriculum plans and practices.
- *Assume responsibility for good 'upward' communications.* In particular, as Bolton (2000) makes clear, deans need to be informed and do not appreciate stumbling across problems that had been concealed from them or being unaware of what departments are doing well and really plan to do better. Deans, it should be remembered, are often in more difficult, demanding and exposed positions than team and departmental leaders (Sarros *et al.*, 1998) and may be expected to be unhappy with those who make their lives harder. Leaders who are attentive about 'upward' communication are positioning the department well in two ways. Firstly, it bonds the team with a larger grouping, such as a faculty or school, which provides a security that can be denied to lone ranger operations and outliers. Secondly, it reduces the department's exposure on problematic matters. For example, where a leader is timely in discussing an emerging problem with research funding with the dean, it allows the dean to consider ways of offering support and makes it possible for the team or department leader to incorporate the dean, with the attendant authority, expertise and resources, into a strategy to cope with the matter. In contrast, poor communication leads to full grown problems coming to the dean's angry attention.

- *Be cautious about being a 'first adapter'.* It is a temptation to subscribe to an institutional initiative or outside blandishment when there is no pressing need to. Doing so may raise the team's profile in the institution but there is often a much higher cost in being at the front of developments than there is in being in the second wave. Schools in England have seen a decade of government mandates. Those that have quickly embraced each directive have not only had much more learning to do but have sometimes suffered when policy has changed soon afterwards. Schools led by 'early adapters' may have good reputations with officials but they are also ones with stressed and worn staff. And in terms of children's learning they are not necessarily the most effective schools. That said, being in the forefront of change can be smart; but not always, and better quality developments can come from following in the second wave.

Conclusion

We have read plenty of descriptions of the ways in which leaders have tried to cope with administrative pressures and political shenanigans and we have summarized recurrent themes in this chapter. What is missing is a vivid sense of what these suggestions really look and feel like in practice. The complexity and nuances of social practices and complex, contested and dynamic situations are stripped out of the general ideas we have covered here. That does not, we suggest, make them useless but it does mean that leaders have to make them real by trying them out and reflecting on them, preferably with the help of mentors or critical friends. This develops a point made in Chapter 1 about the ways in which implicit knowing is partly formed in daily action by the social practices that pervade departments and teams. Chapter 9 develops this idea about learning in a review of ways of leading colleagues' professional development. Chapter 10 builds on that review with a set of suggestions about how leaders can learn to lead.

9

Continuing Professional Development

Teachers' aversion to inservice education activities . . . is legendary.

(Lieberman and McLaughlin, 1996: 63)

Some of the faculty associates don't realize how little they know about teaching and learning – thus they figure it is for everyone else. That has caused particular stress.

(Female, experienced leader, USA)

Preview

Writers on continued professional learning in academic life often imply that faculty members are insufficiently committed to it, which is far from the case. Academic life is about learning, academic staff tend to be voracious lifelong learners and HEIs invest heavily in knowledge acquisition, development and renewal. In Chapter 7 we made a series of suggestions for sustaining research vitality, which are tantamount to suggestions for supporting academic staff's continuous professional development (CPD) *as subject specialists*. Admittedly, there may be some teams and departments that specialize in teaching and in which faculty members live off academic capital that has lost most of its exchange and use value, but this self-chosen isolation seems to be quite rare. Either as teachers, or as people engaged in the scholarship of integration, application or discovery, most faculty members are continuously engaged in learning more about the subjects they profess.

Lifelong learning has other forms as well. Although there is a common belief that ageing leads to a loss of commitment, there is also evidence that it can lead to new frameworks, insights and values and be a force for new learning in the workplace (Walker and Quinn, 1996; Karpiak, 2000). Career development also prompts new learning, teaching can stimulate continuous tinkering and piecemeal refinements of practice (Huberman, 1993), and a host of changes in the work environment mean that, like rust, learning never sleeps.

So why do so many writers on staff, instructional and professional development take a deficit view of faculty learning in higher education? The most obvious reason is that they are uninterested in advances in the disciplines because they are in the cross-curricular business of advancing pedagogy and of stimulating faculty learning about better student learning. Their complaint is simply that teachers are not sufficiently occupied in the forms of professional development that are *their* business. But it is not quite true to say that academic staff are aloof since most teams and departments do routinely review their teaching, courses and programmes and make adjustments in the light of developments in the discipline, teaching evaluations and institutional quality assurance procedures. From the point of view of the developers the problem is that these occasions for change are often assimilated into existing pedagogies, whereas the developers' diagnosis is that there is a need for nineteenth-century pedagogies to accommodate themselves to the new mandates that are being laid on higher education and to the new teaching and learning methods they need. This chapter takes up these concerns and explores what team and departmental leaders can do to help staff to help students to construct good understandings of the subject/area and develop valued skills, versatile self-theories and regularly used metacognitive awareness. Faculty's professional development as exponents of their disciplines is of no further concern in this chapter.

Teams and departments as sites of educational development

It is not by accident that the team or departmental leader is at the centre of our account of professional learning. As we have implied in earlier chapters, learning and knowing are situated and contexted, which means that they are located in the daily operations of activity systems or communities of practice. However, the dominant provider model of educational development has tended to rely on central teaching development programmes, although 'on the whole, campus programmes designed to assist faculty are almost always too narrowly conceived and even more narrowly implemented'(Schuster, 1990: 6). Webb refers to a preoccupation with activities and techniques, describing developers' conferences as 'lively and boisterous bazaars' (1996: 7) and Edmunstone's study of the British health service found that 'the self-perception of trainers limited their role to direct training or instructing through the medium of "courses", rather than a problem-centred organizational or a strategic and anticipative approach' (1990: 273). Summarizing research into CPD for school-teachers, Bradley *et al.* said that, 'over the past twenty years there have been more negative research conclusions than positive' (1994: 233–4) about the relationship between CPD and educational change. McCulloch *et al.* (2000) found that in-service courses were rated as one of the least important influences on teachers' professional development and Becher (1996) identified seven modes of learning used by people in six professions: learning by teaching; learning by doing; personal research; consulting experts; networking; professional interactions; courses and conferences. He went on to take a sceptical line about proposals that professional standards should be enhanced by the provision of more, formal CPD opportunities. There is little good evidence about the impact of CPD on higher education (Weimer and Lenze, 1991), although our informants regularly said that they used central providers of professional development opportunities, when they could afford it. For example, a Canadian man, new to departmental leadership, said:

> We are fortunate to have an excellent University Teaching Service that provides workshops and other assistance respecting the task of teaching (developing learning environments). Many academic staff used their PD [Professional Development] funds to pay the 'tuition' for this type of class. As far as the support staff are concerned, there are no longer any funds available to provide them with development opportunities.
>
> (Male, new leader, Canada)

> We place a great deal of emphasis on teaching; hence, we are very open to staff going to pedagogical conferences aimed at the tertiary level instructor. Also, we have always funded academic conferences reasonably well, though there is work to be done in this area.
>
> (Female, new leader, Canada)

> Main problem is time. However, all staff are encouraged to undertake as much staff development as possible. This includes formal courses (MAs, MPhils, PhDs), training courses and attendance at conferences (and indeed presentations at them). This approach – especially the conferences – has been successful in raising the self-confidence, knowledge and profile of researchers.
>
> (Male, experienced leader, England)

Nevertheless, there are reasons to be sceptical about the efficacy of courses and workshops, a position that Goleman (1998) has developed with regard to professional learning in general. It is not that courses and workshops are useless but rather that, depending on exactly how they are designed and worked out, they are more or less effective contributors to different professional learning purposes. We see courses and workshops as occasional contributors to professional learning and, like distinguished speakers in an undergraduate programme, they may be stimulating and powerful contributors. There are, as Table 9.1 shows, other sites for professional learning. This extends the stance taken in Chapter 7 on the development of a research culture, where attention was very much centred on ways of encouraging the team or department to behave like a learning community. This is a stance in which the departmental chair or team leader is pivotal, since he or she can have great influence on the learning opportunities shown as D, E and F in the table.

This view of CPD brings almost all teaching staff into the picture, whereas traditional, course based models have great trouble reaching established, mid-career teachers. It is fairly well accepted that late-career people, who dominate the age profile of western universities, can disengage from their

Table 9.1 Forms of professional development

Form of learning	Possible strengths	Possible problems
A. Centrally-provided courses and workshops	a. Allow for expertise to be shared with a wide range of teachers b. Widespread 'default option'	1. Often have low take-up rates 2. Material may be too general for immediate use in department 3. Ideas need to be translated into departmental context – this is a skilled and difficult activity 4. Focuses on individual learning detached from the social context in which change is to happen (Smylie, 1995)
B. Subject and professional associations	c. Source of expert, practitioner-focused advice on curriculum content and on pedagogical content knowledge	5. Not all faculty are participating members in associations' education sections 6. Communication can be mainly in printed form or be web-based 7. Learning tends to be individual, not collective 8. Problem of translating this into curriculum practice
C. Reading	d. Cheap, flexible and academic staff are accustomed to learning by reading	9. See 7 and 8 above 10. Do academic staff read these books, even if they are not full of jargon?
D. Team or departmental professional development sessions	e. High relevance to team or departmental concerns f. Learning takes place with the school (and departmental) context firmly in mind. g. Learning takes place within the social context in which change is to occur	11. Concern that low-level concerns are addressed – sessions are about assimilating problems to nineteenth-century pedagogic models 12. These sessions may constitute 'contrived' rather than 'true' collegiality (Hargreaves, 1992) 13. Lack of outside expertise and perspectives: danger of perpetuating old patterns

Table 9.1   (cont'd)

Form of learning	Possible strengths	Possible problems
E. Team, departmental and other mandated meetings	See e–g above	See 11–13 above. Meetings can be particularly sterile as learning opportunities, especially where the object is to manipulate collective compliance.
F. Daily work practices	h. Learning is a matter of adjusting to and being accommodated within an activity system (Guile and Young, 1998; Wenger, 1998) i. Learning is social (Wertsch, 1985) j. Learning is continuous, not an event k. Most professional learning is 'informal' (Becher, 1996)	14. It is easy for a group, such as a department, to become 'stuck' so that no change takes place, or so that only cosmetic changes take place. In these circumstances, there is no learning 15. People can reinvent the wheel 16. Faulty or inadequate thinking can be perpetuated by norms and routines – no error checking mechanisms in place

work, although others stay full of professional vitality (Karpiak, 2000). Central staff development provision can easily be ignored by the disengaged, even though the accelerating pace of professional obsolescence means that it is bad for HEIs and departments trying to improve the quality of student learning (Knight, 1998). They need to reach all faculty with some form of CPD, especially if they have adopted programme-wide, systemic approaches to curriculum, learning, teaching and assessment. A department based approach to CPD reduces the risk that tenured and greying teachers become curators of tired practices that hold back attempts to meet demanding and broad mandates for higher education.

The community of practice approach to CPD is about trying to distribute expertise among team members. Following Nonaka and Takeuchi (1995) we claim that this learning begins with reflection to make some individual and tacit knowing explicit. The next step is for it to be shared with colleagues, who may adopt this new knowledge and bring it into their practices. Over time it becomes part of subliminal, collectively held, tacit knowledge. Chapter 7 described occasions and routines to encourage this cycle of reflection, sharing and take-up. Any of the following activities can also stimulate and support it: action research (Gibbs, 1995; Checkland and Holwell, 1998); departmental problem-working (Bridges and Hallinger,

1996); curriculum development (Knight, 1998); soft systems thinking (Checkland and Scholes, 1990); continuous quality improvement (Harvey and Knight, 1996); the development of a 'new professionalism' (Nixon *et al.*, 1997); and reflection in general (Day, 1993; Moon, 1998). Just as research into improving schooling indicates that different starting points, or portals to improvement, can all lead to the same place, so departments can use different activities to stimulate continuous learning: learning the lost art of curriculum development can be as good a spur to professional learning as mastering the subtleties of soft systems methodology.

The idea that the department is the hub of professional development work was familiar to some of our informants. A new head of department in the UK said that he used, 'Staff meetings, strategy days, staff working beyond the boundaries of the department e.g. at faculty, university and outside in the profession'. Another leader said:

I carry out annual staff development and career review and set a requirement that staff must attend at least one learning and teaching development workshop/conference during the course of a year. I 'encourage', i.e. they have to do it, all my staff to complete the university's postgraduate certificate in tertiary level teaching methods. The Subject Quality Groups do help to create a 'learning culture' as staff can see what others are doing and are now well aware that they must be able to evidence research and scholarly underpinning for their teaching, particularly at the higher levels. What inhibits me is the (unfortunately) lazy attitudes of a small minority of staff, who are happy to coast on what they have been doing for years. I am about to move from a strategy of 'carrots' to one of 'sticks' for certain individuals.

(Female, experienced leader, Scotland)

Notice that the experienced head of department whose words follow made it a priority to fund professional learning well:

We have put in place an individual led appraisal system. I am also meeting with the senior researchers to assess their work. We have monthly research meetings (of researchers), monthly meetings of all staff to discuss our research. We have biweekly teaching sessions and monthly journal clubs. We spend about 10% of our grant on training and have a T&D (Training and Development) committee with representatives from all staff. We are part of an institute that also has weekly seminars. We arrange other seminars ad hoc as well. I think we are getting there.

(Female, experienced leader, USA)

This department-centred model does not mean that teams should be self-contained entities that create their own strategies to cope with the problems that they identify as significant for them and their distinctive cultures. We have already said that teams and departments are only distinctive within the spaces that are left by wider organization and societal factors.

Furthermore, teams do not always have the expertise they need if they are to work well on the issues they have identified or in order to identify problems that get overlooked in their taken-for-granted practices. Outside help is needed to help identify areas for attention; in order to learn how to do, say, action research, problem-based learning or curriculum development; and to provide information about research findings, policies and practices elsewhere. Elton (1995) has praised a 'feedback model' in which staff developers liaise with departmental semi-specialists who then liaise with staff in their departments. Boud has taken a similar position, commending professional learning that is 'not seen as an activity separate from normal business' (2000: 8). He points to the danger that if departments can be seen as the natural sites for professional learning then central provision could be reduced. This could have unfortunate effects, including: the loss of specialist expertise in instructional and curriculum development; inefficiencies arising from departments separately trying to develop their own responses to institution-wide problems; and a lack of challenge to torpid departments. Hicks (2000) described ways in which Australian HEIs are exploring ways of balancing central CPD provision with departmental development, although his analysis is more of a starting point than a conclusion.

Knight (1998) was less convinced that educational developers have sufficient expertise to be curriculum and programme developers. For example, Checkland and Holwell (1998) give a good summary of the hidden complexities of action research and imply that much that is currently claimed as action research may be 'action' but hardly research. Are educational developers sufficiently distanced from trite versions of action research to be good guides to departments wishing to base professional renewal on action research programmes? This is not to demean what they do but to wonder whether what they have learned to do well is that which is needed to help departments to become the prime sites of their own professional learning: are they skilled enough as change agents to be seminal to the growth of learning communities?

CPD in the department

Smylie (1995) argued that CPD should operate on the same principles as adult learning in general, which is broadly our position. The 12 propositions about learning in Chapter 6 are as applicable to faculty's pedagogical learning as to students' studies. Implicit in that is the idea that although there are some people who appear to be born teachers because they have good presentational and interpersonal skills, anyone can become better as a teacher, particularly if teaching is understood to be more than just bravura classroom performances. In this respect, development as a teacher is understood as something akin to the development of what Resnick (1987) called practical intelligence, which is a socially enhanced achievement, not a genetically fixed gift or handicap. Alternatively, it can be described using

Dweck's (1999) terms: incremental theories, which emphasize the significance of effort and mindfulness are more appropriate to thinking about
teaching development than are entity theories, which assume that people
have or lack indivisible attributes such as intelligence, teaching skill, or
self-esteem.

Resnick and Dweck are not the only ones to have recognized that
although beliefs and thinking are important influences on action, they are
by no means the only ones. Schein (1999) compared organizational learning
and the attendant individual learning in the face of change with 'coercive
persuasion' of civilian prisoners in communist China in the 1950s Korean
conflict. He argued that any learning in an organizational context could
cause pain and raised questions about the ethical and moral implications of
coercive persuasion. Knight and Wilcox (1998) invited staff development
professionals to reflect on these ethical implications of their work with
people's feelings, while Hargreaves (1998) argued that when reform efforts
threaten the intrinsic motivation, psychic rewards and opportunities for
fulfilment that make school-teaching worthwhile, then the reforms threaten
the very educational standards that they were intended to raise. Webb (1996)
and Taylor (1999) have emphasized the importance of CPD being sensitive
to the whole person, to emotional and affective aspects of change. These
writers imply that leaders should aim for CPD processes that will be affirming and contribute to team morale or 'feelgood', even if that means being
less ambitious about the skills or knowledge to be gained. This is consistent
with our preference for 'soft' approaches to leadership over 'hard'. Something of this can be seen in this quotation:

> In addition to dollars, I allocate my time to develop a sense of identity
> for the department. I have made it a priority to have lunch with depart-
> ment members at least twice a week. We meet informally and just eat
> and chat. No formal or hidden agenda. I also make sure to e-mail them
> with the content of any administrative meetings I have so they feel like
> they are part of the community. I plan at least one non school social
> event at my house each year with families invited which helps faculty
> members to see each other in a real life setting.
>
> (Female, experienced leader, USA)

That in turn recalls the earlier theme that the ingredients for change
may be assembled but that complex outcomes can neither be prescribed
nor predicted (Fullan, 1991, 1993, 1999). Staff development events can be
planned, action research projects can be set going and programme development can be initiated, but outcomes will remain to a greater or lesser
extent uncertain. Furthermore, other learning will take place in all sorts of
interchanges; planned and unplanned, wanted and unwanted. This is less
true of single-loop learning, which is mainly a matter of substituting one
fairly clear-cut procedure for another, so leaders who want the securities of
planning get drawn towards single-loop CPD, which can be pretty clearly
defined, delivered and measured. And there are times when every team

needs single-loop learning, which is what keeps an organization running well in its established grooves (Weick and Westley, 1996).

But the more innovation is needed, the more important it is to break with this '"normal science" or single-loop learning. Creativity or original thinking seems to involve exactly the opposite processes... "insight" involves the disruption of these same controlled thinking processes' (Weick and Westley, 1996: 447). For this double- or triple-loop learning, which seems to be very appropriate for professional work in complex, fast-changing settings facing multiple mutating demands, organizations need to be 'disorganized' enough to 'retain an element of slack, redundancy, disorder, and hence of flexibility. Humour is a good example of the creation of disorder from within' (1996: 452). In addition to humour, there could be a tolerance of error, encouragement of exploration and 'a deep appreciation of the aesthetics of imperfection' (1996: 454). In other words, if double- and triple-loop learning are about boundary crossing by going outside cultural norms and rituals of the community of practice or activity system, then there are risks, there will be errors, some disorganization is likely and only then may complex learning be seen to have happened. Indeed, this account of organizational learning takes us so far from rational planning for professional development that it is possible to sympathize with Weick's (1995) view that plans are ways of explaining what has happened and that we walk the talk in the sense that we don't know what the talk is until we've done the walk (beliefs and much thought follow action, rather than precede it).

This resonates with Argyris's work (1990) on organizational defences. He lists seven world-wide errors made by intelligent people who believe that they are committed to changing things in organizations. In practice, planned changes don't happen because these errors and organizational defence routines thwart them. For action to follow on intention, new social virtues are needed that allow people to be clearer and more candid with one another. Unless those values are learnt and adopted, planning will remain an impoverished way of thinking about the advancement of complex learning.

So rather as we argued that it is better to plan curriculum in terms of learning experiences than of learning outcomes (although they have their place), our position on leading for professional learning is that it is about giving permission for there to be collaborative cultures in which people feel pretty good about crossing boundaries, going into zones of proximal development, getting things wrong, laughing and learning. Get the team or department right and learning will follow. An ambitious CPD event would be based on Argyris's *Overcoming Organizational Defenses* (1990), and consider the gaps between what we say and what we think and feel but do not communicate – he illustrates this well – and then explore the possibilities of reflecting on his five new social virtues:

• Articulate fears, assumptions and biases (rather than approving, praising and seeking to avoid discomfort).

- Expect that others can engage in self-examination without undue distress (rather than cosset them by not challenging them).
- Be self-critical, acknowledging that 'feeling vulnerable while encouraging inquiry is a sign of strength' (1990: 107) (rather than 'advocate your position in order to win' (1990: 107)).
- 'Encourage yourself and other people to say what they know yet fear to say' (1990: 107).
- Advocate principles, values and beliefs in ways that hold them open to inquiry.

Institutional responsibility for CPD

There is a considerable amount of research into the conditions that are most conducive to professional learning. Differences in research sites, methods, concepts and ontological assumptions mean that there is a lack of consensus. We offer a résumé of some prominent points in the literature.

An important message for the institution, of which teams and departments are a part, takes us back to the idea that there are senses in which efficiency is an enemy of learning. If efficiency means doing tasks with the minimum of resources, there is nothing available for doing other things, like innovating. Lean organizations may be unchallenged at what they do *and* beyond redemption when they are threatened by competitors offering different and more attractive services. Learning, especially double- and triple-loop learning require '[T]ime set aside for deliberation and review' (Eraut, 1995a: 247). Redundancy, which is where a function can be done by more than one person or group, can also be an asset, not only because it provides fail safes but also because it means that there are colleagues who can be informed contributors to metacognition, reflecting and imagining. Implications for leaders are that: people need to feel that they have space to learn; formal occasions for learning should be provided (see next section); and tasks should be rotated or shared. So looked at from a longer-term point of view, 'inefficiency' is efficient. It may be cheaper to pare an operation to the bone but, quite apart from questions about its feasibility in complex organizations doing professional work, it has no future in an ecosystem where descent with modification is the key to success. The message for HEIs is that environments conducive to adaptive modifications are characterized by:

- spaces and inefficiencies
- redundancy
- tolerance for divergent points of view ...
- tolerance for strategic failure: Valuing failure as a source of learning ...
- speculative thinking (Leithwood *et al.*, 1999: 216).

The work of Wright and O'Neil (1994) gives greater detail about what HEIs can do to support the professional learning that is so important to success in turbulent times. They collected questionnaire responses from 165 faculty with university responsibilities for professional development in HEIs in the USA and a further 51 from their Canadian counterparts. Respondents were asked to rate the significance of 36 teaching improvement practices for professional development purposes. Although the study was carefully done, inherent problems with this method of enquiry mean that the results are best treated as matters for deliberation, especially as there are important differences between the US and Canadian patterns of response. Nevertheless, findings of interest are as follows:

• Educational events, such as workshops, conferences, seminars and speakers on teaching methods and student learning were rated fifth out of nine categories (fourth out of nine in Canada) of teaching improvement practice. (Each of the nine categories comprised 4 of the 36 practices.)
• However, a 'center to promote effective instruction' was very highly rated (fourth out of 36 practices by US respondents, third out of 36 by Canadians). Of course, respondents were people who worked in or who could work in such centres.
• The most important categories of action to improve teaching were 'Leadership: Deans and Heads [of department]' and 'Employment Policies and Practices'. Key actions involved: valuing teaching; recognizing, reviewing and rewarding teaching achievement; and establishing climates of trust in which teaching could be discussed and improvements attempted.
• Spaces in which to undertake teaching development and resources to support it comprised the third most important category of actions for US respondents and the sixth most important for Canadians.
• For Canadians the third most important set of actions were those taken by senior administrators to value, recognize and reward teaching accomplishment (seventh most important in the USA).
• Both groups thought that 'Summative Evaluation of Instruction' was useless for teaching improvement purposes. The four practices in this category were rated 25th, 29th, 32nd and 34th by US respondents and 29th, 32nd, 33rd and 36th by Canadians.

This is broadly consistent with an analysis of recommendations for building faculty vitality programmes made by 141 authors (Bland and Schmitz, 1990). The most frequent recommendations were about clarifying institutional expectations for teaching and aligning recruitment, recognition and reward systems with them. In other words, 'faculty vitality and institutional vitality are the responsibility of faculty and administrators alike' (1990: 48). There is, then, some agreement that if HEIs do not recognize and reward teaching, hire people for teaching accomplishment and make teaching awards, then there are obviously limits to how far team and departmental leaders can make CPD a priority when research and publication have a strong allure (and paperwork and committees call out to those colleagues hoping to make careers as administrators). On the other hand, institutions are not free agents. They do compete on research reputations. They have to be parsimonious because parents baulk at the annual tuition hikes, because of competition from community colleges, in order to invest in high-tech or high prestige areas, or as a result of governments looking for efficiency savings. There are limits to what they can do to make teaching *feel* valued and it is not surprising that symbolic actions in the form of teaching awards are a common way of affirming a commitment to CPD when little else is affordable or politic. This is a constant drag on the efforts of team and department leaders to stimulate professional learning through the lived cultures of practice. However, there are opportunities to act against that drag. The next section describes some of them.

Heads of department and CPD

We echo Chapter 3 by saying that the traditional technical-rational planning approach to change begins with attempts to affect educational beliefs. Work summarized by Prosser and Trigwell (1999) has indicated that the beliefs that teachers have about student learning and their work as teachers are associated with the way they go about their work and with their take-up of new pedagogic practices. Teachers who see the purpose of learning in terms of the banking metaphor of storing up knowledge will find it hard to see the point of a technique such as groupwork, which is a relatively inefficient approach to rote learning. Even if they do adopt the method, they are less likely to be impressed by the outcomes than would be a teacher who believes that the aim of learning is the formulation of personal constructs that can be defended within the communities of practice. Trigwell and Prosser (1997) and Amundsen *et al.* (1998) have described ways of inducing teachers to change those beliefs that have a considerable part to play in shaping the techniques they use and the effectiveness with which they use them. This is a task that may best be left to staff development professionals, since it is no simple matter to work on beliefs that may be simultaneously powerful and subliminal. Assuming that team and departmental leaders have beliefs that are consistent with the propositions about learning outlined in Chapter 7, they can encourage conceptual change by being open about these beliefs and by referring to them when explaining their proposals for curriculum change, CPD activities, assessment practices and such like.

Alternative views of the ways in which people act and make sense of their worlds lead to the proposition that it is equally valid to begin by changing practices. Earlier we referred to Weick's idea that action frequently precedes thinking. This complements postmodern analyses that point to the multiple, shifting and contradictory ways in which the same events can be interpreted, even by the same person. Evans's (1999) exploration of the ways in which people tell changing, incomplete and self-interested stories about their own lives can be set alongside Harré's (1998) discussion of the complexity of selves, to give further support to the view that while beliefs are important contributors to action, they are not invariably consistent, compatible or compelling. So another powerful way of bringing about pedagogical change is establishing educationally fruitful routines that have to be followed but that are not distressing. The assumption is that over time beliefs will tend to shift to become congruent with the new practices. Something of this can be seen with English government interventions in compulsory schooling. It has insisted that a national curriculum be followed and that national standards guide pedagogy. Most teachers who were deeply unhappy with this when it was introduced have come to believe that it has distinct advantages, partly because practice almost always (re)constructs policy as well as implements it, as we suggested in Chapter 3 (McCulloch *et al.*, 2000).

Leaders can do a lot for professional development by intervening in practices but care needs to be taken in this exercise of power. Even when power is used softly, where persuasion and incremental changes are the norm, change can be threatening and the emotional health of the group can be compromised. That said, ways in which leaders can stimulate professional development include: the induction of new colleagues; mentoring; the observation of teaching; professional learning plans; portfolios; and appraisals and 360° evaluations.

The induction of new colleagues

In a series of papers we have suggested that procedures for the induction of new teachers are widely deficient (Knight and Trowler, 1999; Trowler and Knight, 2000). Tierney had reached a similar conclusion, suggesting that for new members of staff, 'Grand markers that conveyed institutional meaning were absent, as were explicit, consistent messages on a more intimate level about what really mattered' (1997: 13). Remedying this is not something that can simply be deputed to a central professional development unit, for induction is so obviously a matter of socialization with an activity system or community of practice that university-level attempts to acclimatize new appointees are patently insufficient. Formal and informal mentoring arrangements are important for induction, as are reduced teaching and administrative loads. We would also suggest that as much engagement as possible with departmental committees, projects and research proposals is valuable as an induction into the system's lived culture. So too is shadowing a colleague doing an administrative task and accompanying people to inter-departmental meetings. This cornucopia of possibilities must be approached with moderation, since there is teaching to prepare and research to do and there are papers to write. Nevertheless, if induction comes from doing, there needs to be enough doing to give a fair picture of what the system is. Less obviously, the more the new member of staff is involved in the team's business the greater the scope he or she has for having an influence on the ways in which things are done, especially if leaders regularly ask the new faculty member for observations, questions and ideas for improvement. In this way induction becomes far more of a two-way and interactive process.

Mentoring

In Chapter 7 we said that mentoring, probably on an informal 'buddy' basis, has potential to help people reflect upon their research activity. The same can be said for all aspects of work as a member of a team or department, as long as all parties are clear about the purposes of the mentoring arrangements. If they are summative, or if the mentor is likely to be called on to make an official judgement about the mentee, then it has to be accepted that mentees will be in the business of image management and that they will seldom feel that they can talk in confidence to someone who might later feel compelled to use disclosures against the mentee's best interests. If the purposes are formative and the aim is to maximize disclosure and learning potential, then, while leaders may encourage mentoring relationships, they need to be voluntary, to involve self-selected pairings or other groupings (people may want more than one mentor or may want to operate in a mentoring or self-support group), and to begin with agreement on the ethical principles that are to underpin the relationship.

In both cases participants can benefit from guidelines. They are necessary in formal, summative relationships and useful in formative ones, where they can act as prompts on how to do it (schedule at least two meetings a semester, before meeting use email to explore what you might begin talking about, etc.) and on what could be explored (views of teaching and learning, efficient grading practices, etc.). Suggestions for mentors include:

- take it seriously – make quality time available;
- listen well and with an open mind, and be careful lest you go into seminar mode and overwhelm the mentee with your talk;
- review what has happened since the last meeting;
- give proper weight to achievements and to problems that have become less worrying;
- try to concentrate on two or three things at a time: help the mentee to select them;
- contributing your ideas, work with the mentee to establish two or three areas for reflection or action over the next few weeks;
- help the mentee to identify things that can – realistically – be done to sustain that reflection or action;
- contact the mentee between meetings – do it lightly and easily;
- stick to the ethical agreement you made.

Suggestions for mentees are the same as for mentors *and*:

- accept that you are responsible for your own growth and development – mentors can help you to take that responsibility;

- reflect on your work, feelings and thoughts but use something like Figure 6.1 to prompt you; the mentoring relationship will have the best chance if you are primed to look quite systematically at your self-theories and explanations;
- expect all growth to instantiate suggestions for further development.

The observation of teaching

This is one of the least reliable, least valid and least useful ways of improving teaching quality (Knight, 1993). However, administrators weaned on inappropriate concepts of quality control often insist that leaders observe teaching. If you have to do it as a part of the job, the only advice is to stick rigorously to the guidelines you are given and try to make it as pleasant a business as possible.

Teaching observation is, however, very useful if it is voluntary, formative in intent, mindful and purposeful, and continues until one participant calls a halt. The underlying assumptions are usually that teaching performance is satisfactory and that observation is about building upon existing competence. In some cases course evaluations will have indicated good starting points but self-diagnosis is an alternative, or the observer(s) may be invited to see a couple of classes and then to suggest things that could be looked at more thoroughly. Observation's potential is related to the skill and knowledge of the observer(s) and to the quality of the emotional relationship between the different players in this observational game. However, although good higher education teachers are clear, enthusiastic and interesting (Perry and Smart, 1997), there is little further agreement on what makes for good higher education teaching. (The same is true of school-teaching, where more and better research has been done.) Since teaching certainly involves good planning, thinking, assessment, feedback and counselling, so it would be perverse to observe classroom performance without also reflecting on these other activities and it would be unscientific to insist that some teaching approaches are invariably superior to others. Judgements need to consider their fitness for purpose in a context.

Professional learning plans

Eraut (1995a) recommends that teachers negotiate professional development plans (PDPs), which could be done within the formal, annual staff appraisal process. This prompts them to think about the directions they want to take and about the support they might need; it reminds the leader that it is valuable to talk with individuals about their teaching and its renewal; and as a conversation, it involves reflecting, and then reconsidering as other possibilities and priorities. When PDPs have some formal place in team or department routines they can help all concerned to establish priorities that reflect individuals' wishes, departments' preferences and resource availability. In some places there may be an inclination to treat PDPs as quasi contracts but it will be evident that we do not think this is very helpful. When someone's pedagogical work demands improvement (unlike the normal situation where the standard of work is fine and PDPs are occasions for thinking about the growth that goes with professional vitality), then more formal agreements may be made within the HEI's agreed procedures for dealing with unsatisfactory performances. Except in those special cases, professional development planning and being called to account do not go together in our thinking.

The format, timing and frequency of professional development planning are less important than its existence as a prompt for thinking purposefully about what could be possible. That will involve looking back to previous plans but there is little point in being savage about the shortfalls. They happen, not least because richer opportunities often emerge. It is important, though, to look realistically at the hopes that did not happen and use that in the conversations that attach to the updated PDP.

Portfolios

It is usual for applicants for appointment, tenure and promotion to establish their competence as a teacher by means of a teaching dossier or portfolio (Seldin and associates, 1993; O'Neil and Wright, 1996). Interest is growing in the idea that all faculty should be encouraged to maintain dossiers, which would go hand-in-glove with professional development planning. The problem is that there is little incentive for established teachers to keep portfolios, apart from the intrinsic interest that some might have in looking systematically at their teaching accomplishments. Where PDPs can be portrayed as brief documents, portfolios cannot. They may be like plans in that they contain directions for development but they are also fuller and more systematic analyses of achievements accompanied by quite a volume of supporting evidence. Creating and maintaining them can seem like a chore. Where there are no formal incentives for keeping a dossier, teaching portfolios may seem like an idea whose time has not come.

Nevertheless, many teachers, particularly part-time colleagues and those on fixed-term contracts, do need to keep convincing portfolios and others would do well to keep a 'dump file' of documents about teaching achievements, because accreditation, inspection and audit processes may mean that evidence of achievement will need to be produced in the future. Leaders, then, might: encourage all colleagues to keep material that illustrates their work as teachers; suggest that this material might be re-read when reflecting on teaching for the preparation of a PDP; and help those who keep portfolios to make them as effective as possible.

Without trying to duplicate the good advice of O'Neil and Wright (1996) and Seldin and associates (1993), we suggest that leaders would do well to think of portfolios in the following terms:

- A teaching portfolio is not a summary of research achievements but it should show how teaching is related to research vitality.
- Evidence of teaching accomplishment should be much more interesting than a set of course evaluation summaries. The nature of the evidence presented does depend on the sort of claims that are being made but it could easily include thank you notes and cards from students; samples of student work; evidence of good planning, perhaps in the form of the course handbook or syllabus; responses to course evaluations showing that actions have been taken; comments from colleagues who have observed teaching in the role of critical friends; examples of feedback on assignments; screen shots, CD-ROMs and references to the course website, video or audio tape.
- The first part of the portfolio, amounting to perhaps 2000 words, is what matters (and in some US HEIs this by itself is known as the dossier or portfolio). It does two jobs. Firstly, it establishes a claim to be a good teacher by identifying characteristics of good teaching and saying how practice matches up to them. Secondly, it tells the reader which pieces of evidence support each aspect of the claim and – importantly – why the piece of evidence should be read as supportive of the claim. For example, it is not very helpful to say, 'Exhibit 3A shows that I give good feedback'. Better to say, 'Exhibit 3A shows that I give good feedback because . . .'
- PDPs should be included because they show growth in recent years and imply a commitment to mindful continuing professional development.
- Mentors and leaders might set an example and make theirs available to their colleagues.

Appraisals and 360° evaluations

Appraisals have been mentioned in Chapter 7. It will be clear that we see them as important occasions for consideration of achievements and developments – as opportunities for reflecting and learning – and are uneasy when they are about being called to account, partly because learning then becomes constrained by the dance of deception and partly because most people are doing perfectly satisfactory jobs and do not need to be called to account; they need to be enthused to keep growing. Of course, HEIs do require formal appraisals and may be quite specific about what has to be done. In those cases it is still open to the head of department or team leader to make it clear that those requirements will be interpreted as formatively as possible. There is something of an exception to this when a leader is 'dealing with deadwood' (Tierney, 2000: 1). That does not mean that the person supposed to be 'deadwood' should be discriminated against but it does mean that the leader needs to ensure that clear expectations are set and that plans for coming up to them are agreed. With other appraisals leaders can live comfortably with more ambiguity and uncertainty.

Whatever the purpose of an appraisal, there is usually benefit to be had by looking at achievements from a 360° perspective. This means getting evidence from: students or other customers; from colleagues and other peers; and from accreditors, auditors, senior staff and external examiners. Appraisals might also be 360° in another sense. McLeod and Jennings described how a professional development course they ran for IBM (UK) included '*gestalt* work, personal construct theory, guided affective imagery, Chinese philosophy, psychosynthesis, and using the right-hand side of the brain' (1990: 69). This principle of considering the whole person – feelings and thinking, being and doing – is as much a part of 360° appraisals as is the principle of hearing multiple voices.

Conclusion

In my discipline, Geography, an awful lot of energy is spent keeping the members who represent sometimes rather disparate areas of the discipline together and co-operating as a team. This isn't easy sometimes. Social functions are far more important than I had at first thought. Drinking coffee together, going for lunch, booze-ups on Fridays, Christmas parties, summer barbecues. This doesn't sound like a 'learning culture' but sometimes I think that without co-operation there isn't much learning. Having an hospitable spouse helps. Having a big deck and a reasonably large house helps. Having some personal funds to buy those extra few beers and wines helps. Being personally aware of academic issues in the discipline is most important. Although I am very specialized in my research, I have a knack of latching onto important issues from browsing journals and dipping into papers at conferences. I take some pride in being able to talk for hours if necessary on something close to their field of expert research. I think it makes them feel 'understood' – 'The Chair's on my side!' It sounds contrived, and I suppose it is. But I do enjoy it and the effect it creates.

Timetables are the most inhibiting factor. Ours is jammed. Even finding a single hour in a week for departmental meetings is difficult: it means when a guest speaker visits, usually only half the department are free to watch the presentation or meet him/her. So the opportunity for a shared experience is lost. As soon as the teaching term is over, field and laboratory work, conferences and holidays mean again that it is hard to get people together to share something, other than a drink in the evening!

(Male, experienced leader, Canada)

This model of professional learning underpins our view, developed in Chapter 10, of how leaders might learn to lead.

10

Learning to Lead

individual and organizational learning embraces both 'tacit' and 'explicit'
dimensions, drawing attention to the fact that we learn through 'feel' and lived
experience, as well as through abstract conceptual processes.

(Morgan, 1997: 396)

There seems to be almost nothing on managing an academic department,
and the 'broad-brush' courses I've attended [e.g. on 'time management' or
'negotiation'] haven't been of much use – not geared to academic settings
and the particular kinds of challenges and problems we have to face.

(Male, experienced leader, Scotland)

I have learned by watching, reading and doing.

(Female, experienced leader, USA)

Preview

If learning is as contexted as we have repeatedly suggested it is, how then
are leaders to prepare for a role that, to some degree at least, will be
learned by doing it? Our suggestions are based on a seven-fold account of
leadership and management knowledge. They, like the quotations above,
take learning to lead to be something that could not be done by course
attendance, even if courses were better than they are. To repeat what one
informant said:

> Leadership is highly contextual, but basic strategies and value systems
> remain the same. Treating others with dignity and respect, honoring
> what they value, providing opportunity for growth and additional re-
> sponsibility as appropriate . . . these translate across contexts. Individual
> tactics change, but strategies and values do not.
>
> (Female, new leader, Canada)

Learning to lead

A list of heads of department's responsibilities shows how much leaders
need to learn in order to lead. A concise list of responsibilities, based on
Lucas (1994) is:

- articulating a shared vision and fostering a problem-solving learning environment compatible with its challenging goals;

- promoting ways of communicating in the department or team that empower people by making knowledge widely available and by encouraging open speech;
- motivating people to learn and achieve more and better;
- motivating teaching staff to teach better;
- motivating staff to sustain and develop their scholarship;
- promoting mentoring and appraisal arrangements and other means of giving feedback in order to energize colleagues' learning;
- encouraging colleagues to make more commitment to being of service to others in the institution;
- managing conflict;
- looking after yourself by having stress- and time-management skills.

'Tucker's 1993 edition of the encyclopaedic *Chairing the Academic Department* catalogues fifty-four separate duties. In a study of heads of department in eight Australian universities, forty functions were identified' (Lucas, 1994: 24). But Lucas also reports that these mid-level managers are largely left to get on with the job, which was a story we heard from some of our informants as well: 'My leadership training can be best defined as "biblical", i.e. seek and ye shall find', said a man who was new to the job of departmental chair in a Canadian university. An experienced English head of department said he learned to lead:

> for the most part . . . [by] being left to one's own devices (including learning from mistakes), with few structured opportunities to share those experiences and reflect on their significance with one's peers. The amateurish manner in which management staff development tends to be handled in higher education could explain why academic staff are not enamoured with the majority of their managers.
>
> (Male, experienced leader, England)

If secondary schools are anything to go by then, as we saw in Chapter 4, any formal preparation for leadership will be too little and too late. The problems with course based CPD provision that were mentioned in Chapter 9 also apply to learning to lead as well. For example, an experienced Canadian chair said that he,

> [H]ad no explicit preparation for the role [of departmental chair]. I have occasionally taken part in workshops and courses for heads (as participant and facilitator) and would say that the main thing they offer is ability to talk over issues with colleagues, learn what is done elsewhere, make useful contacts. I have also found role-playing exercises useful if they are very close to real situations (e.g. simulating a tenure and promotions committee). The masses of information usually given at such events (e.g. about university policies) are usually redundant – largely because such information is only valuable at the time it is going to be used.
>
> (Male, experienced leader, Canada)

There is a surprising shortage of books on learning to lead, although plenty on leadership. For example, a recent and substantial British book in the better developed area of leadership in schools (Law and Glover, 2000): is not sensitive to departmental leadership issues, but just treats leadership as a generic activity; contains plenty of detail, complemented by many bullet-point lists, charts and summaries, of what leaders could do, should do and how they might do it; makes plenty of use of wider management and leadership theories; has virtually nothing to say about how to learn to lead.

Learning to lead involves more than acquiring knowledge. It is likely to disturb some unexamined assumptions, which can cause a lot of difficulty for those whose assumptions had a 'do not disturb' notice nailed to them. Take assumptions about time as an example. The volume of administrative work is likely to be disconcerting, especially for heads of science departments with large amounts of plant and equipment to oversee, health and safety regulations to enforce, and more people to manage than the typical humanities or social science department. Although learning how to administer is obviously important, it is just as important to appreciate that this administrative work is a major reason why time itself is likely to change. According to Hales (1993) management is frenetic: time is fragmented and tasks get compressed into short periods that are liable to be interrupted by other calls. Management is reactive and to a large extent *ad hoc*, a form of thinking-in-action where decisions and plans emerge, or as Weick (1995) suggests, turn out to have been made. Here is a view of management that is quite different from the clean, organized, rational and planful assumptions that many people have about what management *ought* to be. The new head of department who is influenced by the ideal and not by Hales's reality is liable to become frustrated and to feel guilty when time does not turn out to operate the way that the rational concept of management assumes. Even more frustrated will be the new chair who is not aware that leaders are expected to have a public presence in the office throughout the working day and for most of the working year. Time becomes not only fractured, but public. In these two ways it comes to be less like disposable income to be spent (which is how ordinary faculty can often treat it) and more like wages that are largely spoken for before they have even been earned. And leaders' time will be dominated by tasks that are quite different from the interest in research or teaching that vivified their careers to date, which means that a sense of loss may compound a sense of guilt. On this analysis, learning to lead should include appreciating that the job has the potential to erode the self-identity that has brought career success.

There are other potential sources of difficulty. Although prudent leaders delegate areas of responsibility to others, new leaders can be perturbed by the expectation that they understand the full sweep of the department's operations and have views about how they might develop or dwindle. This generalist pull has a counterpart in academic terms, where chairs may be assumed to have interests in the full range of departmental research interests whereas they were, until appointment, specialists in one area only. Chairs are expected to care about things to which they were formerly indifferent. That can also be seen in the institutional expectation that chairs will place the interests of the institution at least as high as those of their department or team. That can be quite unpopular with colleagues who take the more restricted view that the leader's job is to fight their corner, pure and simple. That is one sign of something else that new leaders have to learn, which is that their relationships with colleagues will change. Some faculty will become oppositional, many will become more demanding and most, even long-term friends, will be at least a bit careful about what they say to the team or department leader. Learning to lead means learning to be more isolated, to be criticized and criticized unfairly, and to attract more criticism by taking decisions.

What is emerging is a view of learning to lead that involves general, decontexted learning, for sure, and also a lot of situated learning that is located within and appropriate to a community of practice. This sounds rather unsatisfactory, though, because there are much more obvious risks to having a leader learn on the job than there are having a novice faculty member learn how to become established. New departmental chairs will indeed learn by doing but they are also expected to do things right from the start. Where thought has been given to this an answer has been to provide training for new heads of department, but this is problematic on three grounds. Firstly, it is not compulsory, and secondly, the quality of provision varies considerably. Thirdly, even good quality training is usually skewed to the general side of learning to lead. This leaves a paradox. If contexted learning is so important, and if team and department leaders should be proficient from day one, how are they to learn in context before they have taken up their contexted role? An answer hinges on the claim that those who have been members of learning departments that have been mindful about assessment, learning, teaching and research will be substantially prepared to take on the job of leading. One informant takes a similar line but more purposefully:

> I wasn't offered the opportunity for formal training until I insisted upon it as part of my appointment. Otherwise my leadership skills were developed by trial and error. I am trying to appoint younger staff to positions of responsibility in the Department earlier in their career so that they have a better understanding of the role of leadership before they have it thrust upon them without relevant experience.
>
> (Male, new leader, Canada)

Getting leadership knowledge

Turner and Bolam's (1998) review of the role of heads of department in secondary schools suggests that they need six types of knowledge. Table 10.1

Table 10.1   Developing seven forms of leadership and management knowledge

Forms of knowledge	Ways of developing and sustaining them
1. Control knowledge – self knowledge, including metacognitive knowledge	Reflecting individually and with others. It may entail keeping journals, identifying mentors/ critical friends, 360° appraisals, review of critical incidents, allocating time for reflecting and planning. Reading, workshops, networking.
2. Knowledge of people	The problem is how to refine the tacit knowledge we have. Workshops, reading and *skilled* mentoring can be good ways of disconfirming our working assumptions (prejudices) and extending our understandings.
3. Knowledge of educational practice	In some cases, new leaders bring rich knowledge to the job. Others are strong on research but need courses, reading and continual advice from colleagues to gain, maintain and use educational knowledge appropriately. Chapters 5, 6 and 9 are relevant.
4. Conceptual knowledge, in this case knowing about management and leadership concepts and research	Books on management abound (e.g. Bolton (2000) is good on the process knowledge that academic leaders need). Websites are easily found (e.g. www.thenationalacademy.org/index.html).
5. Process knowledge, in this case to do with the processes of leadership and management	General management courses are plentiful and often expensive. Mid-level leadership courses are fewer. *Skilled* mentors can be especially helpful with process knowledge. See also the fuller discussion below.
6. Situational knowledge – understanding contingencies that have made the department or team what it is and affect what it might be.	Departmental and team documents, conversations with students, support, technical and academic staff, advice from colleagues outside the team or department It is invaluable to have been a member of the department's management team with responsibility for operations in one major area (research, undergraduate programme, professional development). Handbooks (Tucker, 1993; Lucas, 1994) may sensitize new leaders to things to look for and ask about.
7. Tacit knowledge that integrates the other six forms in expert practice	Good experience and reflection.

lists them, adds a seventh and suggests some ways in which leaders might develop them.

The mainstays of management and leadership training are usually the areas numbered 4 and 5 in Table 10.1. Our argument is that important though these areas are, even in conjunction with areas 1–3, more is needed. That extra is the situational knowledge identified as area 6 plus a change of thinking from knowledge to knowing; from thinking of leadership to thinking about the dynamic business of leading. Learning about situationally sensitive leading is the theme of the final section of this chapter. It is, of course, assumed that expertise in leading, like expertise in other fields, comes from a practised integration of the different components of knowledge (e.g. Eraut, 1994). Constructing this seventh form of knowledge is a continuing activity but it is not explored here, where the emphasis is on identifying the six constitutive forms of knowing.

Conceptual and process knowledge

As Table 10.1 indicates, there is no shortage of ways of developing conceptual and process knowledge. What this section offers is a sketch map of the territory and, in so doing, identifies some of the limitations of this sort of knowledge as it is represented in books and articles.

The terrain looks quite different according to the standpoint of the inquirer. A great deal of the literature is about managing essentially stable systems, although there has been a strong interest in the 1990s, especially in the USA, in leading organizations in turbulent times. When talking of leadership it is usual to emphasize a transformational concern, while appreciating that transactional work has to be done (a distinction we noticed in Chapter 2). The emphasis is reversed when talking of management. Some writers attempt to give both points of view, although their stereoscopic vision often seems rather blurred because one side – management and transactional, leadership and transformational – dominates. Others are dissatisfied with two-fold distinctions and show how a range of assumptions about, and metaphors for managing or leading evoke very different ideas about what is involved, with consequent differences in the meanings for leading and managing. For example, Easterby-Smith (1997) has shown that the ways in which organizational learning has been conceptualized and investigated are varied and reflect different disciplinary perspectives, with the result that there is limited overlap between, say, those starting from a psychological base and those with a sociological one. Hunt's (1991) substantial synthesis of research into leadership develops the same theme by arguing that research into leadership operates on a variety of epistemological and ontological assumptions, some of which are entirely at variance with others. One consequence is that findings from one research perspective can hardly be reconciled with those from enquiry based on different core assumptions. Hunt also points out that there are assumptions about human beings involved in research and thinking about leadership and, like Morgan (1997), he explores the ways in which the metaphors and language we use to talk about leadership (or leading!) subtly shape the ideas we can hold and the findings that inquiry yields. This shades into poststructuralist ideas about knowing as something constructed in dynamic and situated discourses (e.g. Putnam, 1995).

An implication of this way of looking at the literature on learning to lead is that there is no simple way into process and conceptual knowledge. It involves appraising one's own metaphysical assumptions and reflecting on the best fit between the different analyses on offer, one's own values and the situation in which leading is to be done. This is a version of learning to lead that is about much more than getting wisdom. The message is 'first, choose the wisdom(s) you want to get'. This is more pronounced when the focus moves from metaphysics to theories of leading and managing. An unsystematic list of influential ideas and theories is:

- re-engineering (lean and mean is best);
- organizational learning;
- knowledge management;
- development of leadership skills and qualities;
- leadership as networking and management by wandering about;
- management as politics (for example *Leadership Secrets of Attila the Hun*, Wess, 1991);
- the leader as change agent;
- leadership as articulating visions and core values;
- leadership as fostering appropriate cultures;
- unpredictability theories, drawing on the sciences of complexity and chaos – 'Form emerges. It cannot be imposed' (Morgan, 1997: 272);
- management as technical skill (budgeting and project management, for example).

Some stances are pretty incompatible (for example re-engineering and organizational learning), while some interpretations of others might be gathered together (organizational learning, vision-development and culture-shaping are frequently conjoined). Here too it is not so much a case of getting knowledge as of choosing from the competing accounts of how leading is done. Nor does a decision on this put an end to the need for choice. For example, it is fashionable to say that leading well means nurturing certain workplace cultures: a key tenet of the 'new leadership approach' discussed in Chapter 2. That is not without its problems: what, exactly, is a 'workplace culture'? Can cultures be formed or do they happen? Are they needed? After all, research reported in Chapter 4 found that some effective departments relied only on shared operational structures. And when does fostering a culture slide into indoctrination or stifle innovation? Reservations apart, Kotter and Heskett say that success cultures have 'values that cynics would liken to motherhood, but that when followed can be very powerful' (1992: 55). The implication is that those wanting to lead through culture-building should be concerned to gain the knowledge needed to foster characteristics such as:

- entrepreneurship (a bias to change);
- prudent risk-taking (writers such as Peters (1994a) have approved of cases where not taking risks is punished and where not making mistakes is seen as evidence of not learning);
- flexibility (as opposed to 'a perspective that values stability and order' (Kotter and Heskett, 1992: 72));
- candour in open communication, which implies participative decision making and collegiality;
- concern for all stakeholders, not just for one group, which means concern for students, teachers, parents and others in the community;
- good leadership. A culture is bedded on vision and shared values (but not on sycophancy and groupthink). Leaders help to shape, articulate and extend these goals. The section below is more detailed.

These ideas are hardly contentious, nor are they hard to grasp. The difficulty is that content and process knowledge like this is inert. 'Flexibility', for example, only has meaning when it can be shown why acting one way would be 'inflexible' while another action would denote 'flexibility' (and not fickleness).

Another illustration of our claim that it is not sufficient to have leadership knowledge in the form of general propositions returns us to the view mentioned in Chapter 9 that leading well means sustaining inefficiencies. It is often assumed that organizations need to be efficient in the sense of being lean. We have argued that this may be largely true in a stable environment where success is bought by turning out a known, well-defined and sought after product. In times of change, when innovation is needed, organizations need to provide a refuge or shelter from market forces within which their employees have the time and space to dream up new products; they need to create space in which people can think about the future. Historically, companies that have prospered have made spaces for thought and innovation. 'Spaces' has two senses. One is in the sense of spare capacity. Creating cultures of success needs the time and resources to think, talk and share, experiment, evaluate and to keep on trying. Action research, reflective practice and organizational learning are neither cost-free, nor, in a sense, efficient. So, 'any system with an ability to self-organize must have a degree of redundancy: a kind of excess capacity that can create room for innovation and development to occur' (Morgan, 1997: 108–10). Then there are spaces that come from freedom. For Morgan a system 'must have a certain degree of "space" or autonomy that allows appropriate innovation to occur . . . in many organizations the reverse happens because management has a tendency to overdefine and overcontrol instead of just focusing on the *critical* variables that need to be specified, leaving others to find their own form' (1997: 114).

The reason for this apparent digression is that the problems with the somewhat counter-intuitive idea that 'inefficiency' is desirable are operational ones, ones that cannot be alleviated by having more of the fourth and fifth forms of leadership knowledge. Leaders have to do more than sign up to the principle that some 'inefficiencies' are valuable. They have to have views about how much inefficiency they can accommodate, of what sorts, in what areas of activity (research, teaching, administration), when and at what cost in terms of lost opportunities to do other things. Workshops, websites and books may help them to appreciate what would count as wise answers to these practical problems but the wisdom to make judgements that suffice in the circumstances comes with experience and understanding of those circumstances. Our reading of research papers in the fields of organizational and management studies is that they frequently provide evidence that disrupts theories and generalizations by showing them to be rather like a smooth line that is used to represent a fractal reality: too neat. Just as school improvement research is practical reasoning that goes beyond the neat lists provided by much school effectiveness research so, to take a famous example, the message of Peters and Waterman's *In Search of Excellence* (1982) has proved too simple a guide to practice. Significantly, what Peters (1994a) developed in its place was an emphasis on vision and culture that empower all members of an organization to create opportunities from contingencies. More recently, Lewin and Regine (1999) have applied complexity theory to leading and Fullan (1999) has made much of it in his analysis of change forces in the school sector. Unpredictability and contingency are prominent in both. We see an expression of that in the words of an experienced, British leader:

> I only have experience of working in one university and one department. What I would say is that leadership behaviour has to be flexible to fit the different personalities in your department. Some might respond to encouragement, or to a 'softly softly' line; others need the facts spelled out to them and a harder line taken. You must be fair to everyone, but the way you react with each individual can vary. In that sense, I am sure it must be true that what works in one place might not work in another.
>
> (Female, experienced leader, UK)

So we have acknowledged that the first five forms of leadership knowledge can all, to some degree, be acquired 'off the job'. However, the sixth (and, indeed, the seventh) has to be learned in situ, and the first five only come to make practical sense in context. When learned off the job they are learned as empty concepts. How, then, is learning for leading to be had?

Situated learning

People who work in departments and teams that operate on the lines we sketched in Chapters 5–9 are best placed to learn what is involved in leading

them. That is all the more so when they serve in a department's or programme's leadership team, especially if their service is sustained enough for
them to come to grips with more than one role. Membership of a leadership
team can be an introduction to leading, while participation in a well-led
department implies: engagement with the range of teaching, development,
service and research issues because these are all issues that are brought
before all members of the community; the development of a habit of reflecting and of discussing the thoughts that are constructed with others;
and the practice of continuous learning, and not just learning more about
one's specialist area of study.

Ideally, people should have good notice that they are going to be leading
departments and teams and, when this does not involve a change of institution, staff development professionals can help them prepare for the job. We
have acknowledged that this will involve exploring general ideas about leading and mean clarifying one's priorities and feelings about the discomforts
of leadership work and expect that these will be themes of any preparation
for leading course. So too with the specifics of the institution's policies,
financial operations and other administrative practices. This is open to our
earlier objection that it is insufficiently context-specific. To some extent this
objection can be met by teaching for transfer, by which we mean that the
emphasis should not so much be on the ideas but on working out what they
might mean. Part of that might be done through case studies and another
part might involve each participant speculating on the potential the literature has for their own practices in leading their department or team. There
is some risk that this speculation might be self-confirming, so we have two
additional recommendations. One is that leaders-to-be learn a discipline to
help them in their learning for transfer. For example, Checkland's soft
systems methodology (Checkland and Scholes, 1990) is a widely used and
powerful way of thinking about issues in organizations and *The Fifth Discipline Fieldbook* (Senge, 1994) is a strong US alternative. What system they use
is less important than having a simple set of principles that can bounce
them out of tramlined thinking about transferring ideas to practice.

One new Canadian chair told us that he regretted that, 'We [Dept Heads]
don't get together and discuss the things that we think we did better or
worse. Learning about leadership is hit and miss'. When heads of department have a semi-formal network that helps them to learn to do the job,
leaders-to-be should benefit from joining it early. A new leader in the USA
told us that he believed that, '[A] structured experience would have been
helpful, not so much with respect to becoming a leader, but with respect to
how to carry out the administrative end of the job'. An experienced British
leader implied that he would have valued, 'structured opportunities to share
those experiences and reflect on their significance with one's peers'.

It also helps to have a leadership mentor, who would be a volunteer with
experience of leading and who is chosen by the leader-to-be. One informant was appreciative that, 'My leadership training involved learning by
experience and that did include being advised or mentored by those who

filled my positions before' (male, new leader, USA). The benefits should be greatest when this mentoring relationship begins before the new leader takes up his or her responsibilities, especially if some element of job shadowing is included. This extends our thinking about the ways in which new members of departments come to be full participants (Trowler and Knight, 1999, 2000) to the special case of learning to lead.

Three other valuable sources of situated learning are: deans; other members of the department's management team; and colleagues in subject associations and networks.

While it is certain that doing the job will involve learning more quickly than did any off-the-job preparation, leaders who have experience of good leaders and who have prepared by thinking systematically about transfer of ideas from the literature to practice are better placed than others. HEIs that recognize the great importance of middle managers – team leaders, chairs and heads of department – will carefully consider how they can be prepared for the job and learn from it. But it is easy for HEIs to give this a low priority because few leaders obviously fail: many cope. Coping is a way of dealing with stress and, while it is sometimes necessary, people who merely cope have lost control of their destinies and often survive by insisting on their positional authority, and by depending on bureaucratic routines, measurement and compliance. They may not be very nice to know and the stance we have taken throughout this book implies that we do not think they will actually be very effective as leaders (they might be tolerable as managers).

For us, learning to lead is successful to the extent that new leaders remain nice to know and do more than cope. HEIs have a responsibility to help that happen. It is a responsibility that calls for a more subtle view of professional learning than is implied by a two-day induction course for new leaders at the beginning of their term of office.

Conclusion

In writing this book our primary aim was to provide theoretical and conceptual resources for the use of higher education professionals in the practice of leadership. We concentrated in particular on:

- alternative perspectives on change processes in organizations and the ways these are influenced by broader environmental change;
- differing perspectives on leading as they apply to higher education contexts;
- ways of thinking about ideas and practices in higher education contexts that take into account social processes oriented around the completion of tasks at the departmental and workgroup level; characteristics of the individual leader; and policy making and implementation at the organizational level.

In each case we wanted to consider the implications of the conceptual approach offered for leadership practice, and to evaluate critically those corollaries. So, for example, in considering change we wanted to consider processes associated with implementation and the management of change in particular. Likewise in looking at leading we explored, in Chapters 4–10, the implications for academic practices that are usually analysed from an institutional or personal standpoint, concerning ourselves instead with understanding practice at the level of the department, teams, activity system or community of practice.

We have tackled this project not only from a neutral 'academic' position but have been concerned to advocate a particular approach. This is not unusual: indeed it is probably the norm in writing about leadership. It is not a difficult task to list the positions advocated by writers over the years: 'educative leadership' (Duignan and Macpherson, 1992); 'transformational leadership' (Bennis, 1984); 'leadership as a moral art' (Hodgkinson, 1991); and so on. A compressed summary of the position we adopt is as follows:

- Leadership in higher education at the departmental level and below is best when it is distributed across the workgroup rather than being located solely in the person of one individual, although final responsibility usually rests with the formal group leader and he or she has a special role. As a consequence the following points ideally relate to the department or workgroup, not just its formal leader.
- Good local leaders are in tune with the sociocultural context in which they operate. The ability to influence and shape cultural characteristics requires this very close familiarity. Much of what usually remains tacit is brought to the surface by these leaders so they are able to address issues in clear, conceptually elaborated terms. Within the 'sociocultural' context we include issues concerning recurrent practices in the department, the mix of professional identities there, sets of taken-for-granted understandings, rules of appropriateness and value positions as well as the educational ideologies involved.
- Tuned-in leaders are able to 'read' the likely ways in which proposals and policies will be received. They can accurately anticipate the consequences of alternative actions and distinguish relatively reliably between good and bad choices. We have described this in terms of reflection-on-action and theories-in-use.
- Some aspects of tacit understandings do not or cannot come to the surface, however. In these cases good leaders are also able to operate well at the level of 'gut feelings': they have internalized the lessons of past instances and apply them in the present.
- Beyond these points, the actions that constitute 'leading well' will vary from context to context. What counts as 'good leadership' in one place may not do so in another. Departmental and workgroup histories and settings will affect what happens next and how it is understood. So will the organizational environment and the particular configuration of cultural flow into the department or workgroup, because these are open systems.

One might describe this as 'distributed conceptual leadership', although we have no wish to add to the plethora of competing names for models of leadership. However we fully acknowledge that this *is* an ideal; something to work towards rather than something that already exists or that can easily be created. Some higher education departments are so deeply fractured ideologically or by personal enmities that their members talk past each other rather than to each other.

Some departments unfortunately also have the problem of containing individuals who are deeply problematic: a significant minority of respondents to our electronic enquiries said that only retirements from the department could solve its most pressing problems. One felt it necessary to say that for good departmental working 'it helps to avoid persons with personality disorders or other severe mental health problems', while another, quoted on page 137, listed in detail the sorts of personality disorders best avoided.

We acknowledge, too, that there are some 'wicked issues' (Rittel and Webber, 1973; Watson, 2000) that simply defy rational, consensual solution and on which there is little or no 'common ground on which to build pragmatic solutions to complex problems' (Duignan and Macpherson, 1992: 46). These issues, as University Director David Watson suggests, tend to generate a considerable amount of heat but very little light. They tend to be defined differently by different participants so that one person's 'solutions' merely represent more problems for another. Curiously, Watson suggests that car-parking, tobacco-smoking and security are important examples of wicked issues in universities. Different contentious areas occupy the minds and energies of local leaders, but they are equally perplexing. Even in collegial departments these are sometimes sparked by the need to respond to government or QAA policy and often relate to notions of professionalism. Should we comply or resist? Should we institute staff appraisal? What form might it take? Should we respond to mechanistic quality assurance processes by introducing equally mechanistic procedures? Another set of issues is pedagogical: how punitive should we be about poor spelling or late submission of assignments? Should peer assessment be used and to what extent should students determine each other's final grades? There is no right answer to these sorts of questions, but the exercise of judgement based on good theory and reflection-on-action can lead to the least 'worst' outcome, and sometimes it is necessary to resort to necessary but undesirable leadership approaches: ones far removed from our ideal. In these circumstances we very much agree with Ramsden that the art of leadership in contemporary higher education is about tensions and balances, about finding a way between conflicting priorities:

> We must trust people; but not everyone can be trusted. We must focus on traditional academic values; but we must also respond to new demands from employers, companies, governments and students. We must look outwards to the strategic advantage of our work unit; but we should never neglect internal processes and relationships. We must listen and consult; but we must have the wisdom to know when the advice we receive is correct. We must walk ahead; we must also serve.
>
> (1998a: 8–9)

One of our respondents noted one of the paradoxes of leadership:

> I sometimes feel as though I fail the department because I am quite easy going and collaborative. I don't see other heads as competitors. I resent the idea of fighting over public funds . . . I'm not sure other heads always see it that way and sometimes the loud and forceful win the day. My staff sometimes accuse me of being naive although they also sometimes say that's what they like about me.
>
> (Male, new leader, Scotland)

Books of 'tips and tricks' for leaders are of little help in balancing conflicting priorities of this sort. Each decision needs appropriate judgement according to the particulars of the situation. *Wisdom* is the key word in the passage from Ramsden above, a kind of shorthand for a combination of emotional intelligence (Goleman, 1998), the application of theories-in-use (Argyris and Schön, 1974) and good organizational sensemaking (Weick, 1995).

We will conclude the book with some comments on this kind of wisdom from our respondents, which, we hope, will resonate with readers. The following quotes were responses to an enquiry about what had contributed to personal successes as a leader in a higher education department:

> The most important factor that helps me to lead is my ability to find and use the passion within individuals based on their value systems. And . . . this is different for every individual. In addition – the communication skills I bring to helping individuals in my team get in touch with what is important to them and helping them to relate it to the work at hand is very important.
>
> (Female, new leader, Canada)

> Thinking together, sharing clarity about goals, developing vibrant investigative relationships. Getting the balance right in developing individual [*sic*] and developing the group, looking ahead to anticipate challenges.
>
> (Female, new leader, England)

> * Clear priorities and associated objectives;
> * Promoting shared understanding of the nature of the changing opportunities and threats in University education;
> * Playing to the different strengths of different staff in the Department ('horses for courses');
> * Public recognition of achievement balanced by honest interaction in individual performance reviews where there are problems to be addressed;
> * Demonstrating therefore that staff other than the Head will attract plaudits for successes;
> * Understanding that, in the final analysis, there are issues to do with cultural change that cannot/should not be avoided;
> * Yet, having some appreciation of the inevitable organizational politics.
>
> (Male, experienced leader, England)

> I think the universals of leadership, across time and space, are a sense of self, a knowledge of the circumstances and a sense of where the leader (and thus the people) need to be to survive, and the capacity to communicate this direction (typically by example).
>
> (Female, experienced leader, USA)

References

Adelman, C. (ed.) (1990) *A College Course Map: Taxonomy and Transcript Data.* Washington, DC: US Government Printing Office.

Adey, K. and Jones, J. (1998) Development needs of middle managers: the views of senior managers, *Journal of In-service Education,* 24(1): 131–44.

Airaison, P. (1988) Symbolic validation: the case of state-mandated high stakes testing, *Educational Evaluation and Policy Analysis,* 10(4): 301–13.

Allix, N.M. (2000) Transformational leadership: democratic or despotic?, *Educational Management and Administration,* 28(1): 7–20.

Alvesson, M. (1990) On the popularity of organizational culture, *Acta Sociologica,* 33(1): 31–49.

Alvesson, M. (1993) *Cultural Perspectives on Organisations.* Cambridge: Cambridge University Press.

Amundsen, C., Saroyan, A. and Frankman, M. (1998) Changing methods and metaphors: a case study of growth in university teaching, *Journal on Excellence in College Teaching,* 7(3): 3–42.

Apple, M. (1982) *Education and Power.* New York: Routledge and Kegan Paul.

Apple, M. (1989) *Teachers and Texts.* London: Routledge.

Apple, M. (1993) *Official Knowledge: Democratic Education in a Conservative Age.* New York: Routledge.

Argyris, C. (1990) *Overcoming Organizational Defenses.* Needham Heights, MA: Allyn and Bacon.

Argyris, C. and Schön, D.A. (1974) *Theory in Practice: Increasing Professional Effectiveness.* San Francisco: Jossey-Bass.

Arnot, M., David, M. and Weiner, G. (1996) *Educational Reforms and Gender Equality in Schools.* Manchester: Equal Opportunities Commission.

Astin, A.W. (1997) *Four Years that Matter: The College Experience Twenty Years on.* San Francisco: Jossey-Bass.

Astin, A.W. (1999) Assessment, student development and public policy, in S. Messick (ed.) *Assessment in Higher Education: Issues of Access, Quality, Student Development and Public Policy.* Mahwah, NJ: Lawrence Erlbaum Associates.

Bacharach, S.B. and Lawler, J.G. (1980) *Power and Politics in Organizations.* San Francisco: Jossey-Bass.

Bachrach, P. and Baratz, M.S. (1962) The two faces of power, *American Political Science Review,* 56: 947–52.

Bailey, J.G. (1999) Academics' motivation and self-efficacy for teaching and research, *Higher Education Research and Development*, 18(3): 343–59.

Bakhtin, M. (1986) The problem of speech genres, in C. Emerson and M. Holquist (eds) *Speech Genres and Other Late Essays*, V.W. McGee (trans.). Austin, TX: University of Texas Press.

Baldridge, J.V. (1971) *Power and Conflict in the University*. New York: John Wiley.

Ball, S. (1987) *The Micropolitics of the School: Towards a Theory of School Organization*. London: Methuen.

Ball, S. (1990) *Politics and Policy Making in Education*. London: Routledge.

Ball, S.J. (1994) *Education Reform: A Critical and Post-structural Approach*. Buckingham: Open University Press.

Barnett, R. (1994) *The Limits of Competence: Knowledge, Higher Education and Society*. Buckingham: SRHE/Open University Press.

Bass, B.M. and Avolio, B.J. (1990) The implications of transactional and transformational leadership for individual, team and organizational development, *Research on Organizational Change and Development*, 4: 231–72.

Bauman, Z. (1995) *Life in Fragments: Essays in Postmodern Morality*. Oxford: Basil Blackwell.

Baumard, P. (1999) *Tacit Knowledge in Organizations*. London: Sage Publications.

Becher, T. (1988) Principles and politics: an interpretative framework for university management, in A. Westoby (ed.) *Culture and Power in Educational Organizations*. Buckingham: SRHE/Open University Press.

Becher, T. (1996) The learning professions, *Studies in Higher Education*, 21(1): 43–55.

Becher, T. and Trowler, P. (2001) *Academic Tribes and Territories: Intellectual Enquiry and the Cultures of Disciplines*, 2nd end. Buckingham: SRHE/Open University Press.

Becker, H. (1986) *Writing for Social Scientists*. Chicago, IL: University of Chicago Press.

Beckhard, R. and Pritchard, W. (1992) *Changing the Essence: The Art of Creating and Leading Fundamental Change in Organisations*. San Francisco: Jossey-Bass.

Bennett, N., Desforges, C.W., Cockburn, A. and Wilkinson, B. (1984) *The Quality of Pupil Learning Experiences*. London: Lawrence Erlbaum Associates.

Bennis, W. (1984) Tranformative power and leadership, in T. Sergiovanni and J. Corbally (eds) *Leadership and Organizational Culture*. Urbana, IL and Chicago, IL: University of Illinois Press.

Bennis, W. and Nanus, B. (1985) *Leaders*. New York: Harper Row.

Berger, P. and Luckmann, T. (1966) *The Social Construction of Reality*. Harmondsworth: Penguin.

Bergquist, W.H. (1993) *The Four Cultures of the Academy*. San Francisco: Jossey-Bass.

Berman, P. (1980) Thinking about programmed and adaptive implementation: matching strategies to situations, in H. Ingram and D. Mann (eds) *Why Policies Succeed or Fail*. Beverly Hills, CA: Sage.

Birnbaum, R. (1988) *How Colleges Work*. San Francisco: Jossey-Bass.

Black, P. (1998) Learning, league tables and national assessment, *Oxford Review of Education*, 24(1): 57–68.

Black, P. and Wiliam, D. (1998) Assessment and classroom learning, *Assessment in Education*, 5(1): 7–74.

Blackburn, R.T. and Lawrence, J.H. (1995) *Faculty at Work*. Baltimore, MD: Johns Hopkins University Press.

Blackler, F. (1993) Knowledge and the theory of organizations: organizations as activity systems and the reframing of management, *Journal of Management Studies*, 30(6): 863–84.

Blackler, F. (1995) Knowledge, knowledge work and organizations: an overview and interpretation, *Organization Studies*, 16(6): 1021–46.

Bland, C. and Schmitz, C. (1990) An overview of research on faculty and institutional vitality, in J. Schuster and D. Wheeler (eds) *Enhancing Faculty Careers: Strategies for Development and Renewal*. San Francisco: Jossey-Bass.

Blase, J. (1988) The teachers' political orientation vis-à-vis the principal: the micropolitics of the school, *Politics of Education Yearbook*, 3(5): 113–26.

Blase, J. and Anderson, G.L. (1995) *The Micropolitics of Educational Leadership; from Control to Empowerment*. London: Cassell.

Blumberg, A. (1992) Foreword, in J. Blase and P. Kirby (eds) *Bringing Out the Best in Teachers: What Effective Principals Do*. Newbury Park, CA: Corwin Press.

Blum-Kulka, S. (1997) Discourse pragmatics, in T. Van Dijk (ed.) *Discourse as Social Interaction*. London: Sage.

Boice, R. (1992) *The New Faculty Member: Supporting and Fostering Professional Development*. San Francisco: Jossey-Bass.

Bolton, A. (2000) *Managing Change in Organizations*. Buckingham: Open University Press.

Boud, D. (1995) Assessment and learning: contradictory or complementary?, in P.T. Knight (ed.) *Assessment for Learning in Higher Education*. London: Kogan Page.

Boud, D. (2000) Situating academic development in professional work, *Journal of Academic Development*, 4(1): 3–10.

Bowe, R., Ball, S.J. and Gewirtz, S. (1994) Captured by the discourse? Issues and concerns in researching parental choice, *British Journal of Sociology of Education*, 15(1): 63–78.

Boyatzis, R.E. and associates (1995) *Innovation in Professional Education*. San Francisco: Jossey-Bass.

Boyer, E.L. (1990) *Scholarship Reconsidered: Priorities of the Professoriate*. Princetown, NJ: Carnegie Foundation for the Advancement of Learning.

Boyer, E., Altbach, P. and Whitelaw, M.J. (1994) *The Academic Profession: An International Perspective*. Princeton, NJ: Carnegie Foundation for the Advancement of Teaching.

Bradley, H., Conner, C. and Southworth, J. (eds) (1994) *Developing Teachers, Developing Schools*. London: David Fulton.

Breland, H.M. (1999) From 2 to 3Rs: the expanding use of writing in admissions, in S.J. Messick (ed.) *Assessment in Higher Education: Issues of Access, Quality, Student Development and Public Policy*. Mahwah, NJ: Lawrence Erlbaum Associates.

Bridges, E. and Hallinger, P. (1996) Problem-based learning, in M. McLaughlin and I. Oberman (eds) *Teacher Learning: New Policies, New Practices*. New York: Teachers' College Press.

Broadfoot, P. (1988) What professional responsibility means to teachers: national contexts and classroom constants, *British Journal of Sociology of Education*, 9(3): 265–87.

Brown, J.S. and Duguid, P. (1991) Organizational learning and communities of practice: toward a unified view of working, learning and innovating, *Organization Science*, 2(1): 40–57.

Brown, J.S. and Duguid, P. (1993) Stolen knowledge, *Educational Technology*, 33(3): 10–15.

Brown, J.S. and Duguid, P. (1996a) Organizational learning and communities of practice, in M.D. Cohen and L.S. Sproull (eds) *Organizational Learning.* London: Sage.

Brown, J.S. and Duguid, P. (1996b) Universities in the digital age, *Change,* 28(4): 11–19.

Brown, M. and Rutherford, D. (1998) Changing roles and raising standards, *School Leadership and Management,* 18(1): 75–88.

Brown, S. and Knight, P. (1994) *Assessing Learners in Higher Education.* London: Kogan Page.

Brown, S.J., Collins, A. and Duguid, P. (1996) Situated cognition and the culture of learning, in H. McLellan (ed.) *Situated Learning Perspectives.* Englewood Cliffs, NJ: Educational Technology Publications (First published as: S.J. Brown, A. Collins and P. Duguid (1989) Situated cognition and the culture of learning, *Educational Researcher,* 18(1): 32–42.)

Bryman, A. (1992) *Charisma and Leadership of Organizations.* London: Sage.

Bryman, A. (1999) Leadership, in S. Clegg, C. Hardy and W. Nord (eds) *Managing Organizations: Current Issues.* London: Sage.

Busher, H. and Harris, A. (1999) Leadership of school subject areas, *School Leadership and Management,* 19(3): 305–17.

Buswell, C. (1980) Pedagogic change and social change, *British Journal of Sociology of Education,* 1(3): 293–306.

Cameron, K. and Tschirhart, M. (1992) Postindustrial environments and organizational effectiveness in colleges and universities, *Journal of Higher Education,* 63(1): 87–108.

Cameron, K.S. and Ettington, D.R. (1988) The conceptual foundations of organisational culture, in J.C. Smart (ed.) *Higher Education: Handbook of Theory and Research Vol 4.* New York: Agathon.

Case, R. (1985) *Intellectual Development.* New York: Academic Press.

Cerych, L. and Sabatier, P. (1986) *Great Expectations and Mixed Performance.* London: Trentham.

Chambers, E. (1992) Work load and the quality of student learning, *Studies in Higher Education,* 17(2): 141–53.

Checkland, P. and Holwell, S. (1998) Action research: its nature and validity, *Systemic Practice and Action,* 11(1): 9–21.

Checkland, P. and Scholes, J. (1990) *Soft Systems Methodology in Action.* Chichester: John Wiley.

Chi, M. and Koeske, R.D. (1983) Network representations of a child's dinosaur knowledge, *Developmental Psychology,* 19(1): 29–39.

Chickering, A. (1999) Personal qualities and human development in higher education, in S.J. Messick (ed.) *Assessment in Higher Education: Issues of Access, Quality, Student Development and Public Policy.* Mahwah, NJ: Lawrence Erlbaum Associates.

Chickering, A. and Ehrmann, S. (1997) *Implementing the Seven Principles: Technology as a Lever.* Washington, DC: American Association for Higher Education.

Chickering, A.W. and Gamson, Z.F. (1991) *Applying the Seven Principles to Good Practice in Undergraduate Education.* San Francisco: Jossey-Bass.

Clark, B. (1972) The organisational saga in higher education, *Administrative Science Quarterly,* 17: 178–83.

Clark, B. (1983) *The Higher Education System.* Berkeley, CA: University of California Press.

Clark, B. (1998) *Creating Entrepreneurial Universities: Organizational Pathways of Transformation*. London: Pergamon.

Clegg, S., Hardy, C. and Nord, W. (1999) Introduction: organizational issues, in S. Clegg, C. Hardy and W. Nord (eds) *Managing Organizations: Current Issues*. London: Sage.

Coe, J. and Fitzgibbon, C. (1998) School effectiveness research: criticism and recommendations, *Oxford Review of Education*, 24(4): 421–38.

Cohen, M.D. and March, J.G. (1974) *Leadership and Ambiguity: The American College President*. New York: McGraw-Hill.

Covey, S.R. (1992) *The Seven Habits of Highly Effective People*. London: Simon and Schuster.

Covey, S., Merrill, A. and Merrill, R. (1994) *First Things First*. New York: Fireside.

Cowan, J. (1998) *On Becoming an Innovative University Teacher*. Buckingham: Open University Press.

Csikszentmihalyi, M. (1990) *Flow: The Psychology of Optimal Experience*. New York: Harper and Row.

Cuming, J. and Maxwell, G. (1999) Contextualising authentic assessment, *Assessment in Higher Education* 6(2): 177–94.

Currie, J. (1996) The effects of globalization on 1990s academics in greedy institutions, *Melbourne Studies in Education*, 37(2): 101–28.

CVCP/HEFCE (Committee of Vice-chancellors and College Principals/Higher Education Funding Council (England)) (2000) *The Business of Borderless Education: UK Perspectives*. HEFCE/CVCP.

Cyert, R.M. and March, J.G. (1963) *A Behavioural Theory of the Firm*. Englewood Cliffs, NJ: Prentice Hall.

Dalziel, J. (1998) Using marks to assess student performance, *Assessment and Evaluation in Higher Education*, 23(4): 351–66.

Daniel, J.S. (1996) *Mega-Universities and Knowledge Media: Technology Strategies for Higher Education*. London: Kogan Page.

Davenport, J. (1993) Is there any way out of the andragogy morass?, in M. Thorpe R. Edwards and A. Hanson (eds) *Culture and Process of Adult Learning*. Buckingham: Open University Press.

Davenport, T.H. and Prusak, L. (1998) *Working Knowledge*. Boston, MA: Harvard University Press.

Day, C. (1993) Reflection: a necessary but not sufficient condition for professional development, *British Education Research Journal*, 19(1): 83–93.

De Miguel, M., Escudero, T. and Rodriguez, S. (1998) Spanish universities' quality: the incentive of external evaluation, *Quality in Higher Education*, 4(2): 199–206.

Deal, T.E. and Kennedy, A.A. (1982) *Corporate Cultures*. Reading, MA: Addison-Wesley.

Dearing, R. (1997) *Higher Education in the Learning Society* (The NCIH Report). London: HMSO.

De Corte, E. (1996) Learning theory and instructional science: introduction, in P. Reimenn and H. Spada (eds) *Learning in Humans and Machines: Towards an Interdisciplinary Learning Science*. London: Pergamon.

Deem, R. (1996) Border territories: a journey through sociology, education and women's studies, *British Journal of Sociology of Education*, 17(1): 5–19.

Denzin, N. (1992) Whose Cornerville is it anyway?, *Journal of Contemporary Ethnography*, 21(1): 120–32.

The Department Chair (2000) How Professors spend their time, *The Department Chair*, 10(3): 17.

DfEE (Department for Education and Employment) (1997) *Excellence in Schools.* London: HMSO.

DfEE (Department for Education and Employment) (1999) *Learning to Succeed.* London: The Stationery Office.

DES (Department of Education and Science) (1987) *Higher Education: Facing the Challenge.* London: HMSO.

Dill, D. and Sporn, B. (eds) (1995) *Emerging Patterns of Social Demand and University Reform: Through a Glass Darkly.* Oxford: IAU Press/Elsevier.

DiMaggio, P. and Powell, W. (1991) Introduction, in W. Powell and P. DiMaggio (eds) *The New Institutionalism in Organizational Analysis.* Chicago, IL: University of Chicago Press.

Downs, A. (1966) *Inside Bureaucracy.* Boston: Little, Brown.

Dretske, F. (1981) *Knowledge and the Flow of Information.* Oxford: Blackwell.

Duignan, P.A. and Macpherson, R.J.S. (1992) Educational leadership and curriculum development: a synthesis and commentary, in P.A. Duignan, and R.J.S. Macpherson (eds) *Educative Leadership: A Practical Theory for New Administrators and Managers.* London: Falmer Press.

Dukes, W.F. (1970) N=1, in P. Badia, A. Huber and R. Runyon (eds) *Research Problems in Psychology.* Reading, MA: Addison-Wesley.

Dweck, C. (1999) *Self-theories: Their Role in Motivation, Personality and Development.* Philadelphia, PA: Psychology Press.

Dyer, C. (1999) Researching the implementation of educational policy: a backward mapping approach, *Comparative Education,* 35(1): 45–61.

Earley, P. and Fletcher-Campbell, F. (1989) *The Time to Manage? Department and Faculty Heads at Work.* Windsor: NFER-Nelson.

Easterby-Smith, M. (1997) Disciplines of organizational learning: contributions and critiques, *Human Relations,* 50(9): 1085–113.

Edmundstone, J. (1990) What price the learning organization in the public sector?, in M. Pedler, J. Burgoyne, T. Boydell and G. Welshman (eds) *Self Development in Organizations.* London: McGraw-Hill.

Edwards, A. and Knight, P. (1995) *Effective Early Years Education.* Buckingham: Open University Press.

Eisenberg, E.M. and Goodall, H.L. (1993) *Organizational Communication: Balancing Creativity and Constraint.* New York: St. Martin's Press.

El-Hage, N. (1997) Evaluation of higher education in Germany, *Quality in Higher Education,* 3(3): 225–34.

Ellington, H. (1999) Generic level learning outcome templates: a tool for benchmarking student achievement levels throughout a university, *Quality Assurance in Education,* 7(1): 47–58.

Elmore, R. (1978) Organizational models of social program implementation, *Public Policy,* 28: 185–228.

Elmore, R.F. (1982) Backward mapping: implementation research and policy, in W. Williams (ed.) *Studying Implementation.* London: Chatham House.

Elton, L. (1995) An institutional framework, in A. Brew (ed.) *Directions in Staff Development.* Buckingham: SRHE/Open University Press.

Elton, L. (1998) Are degree standards going up, down or sideways?, *Studies in Higher Education,* 23(1): 35–42.

Engestrom, Y. (1990) *Learning, Working and Imagining: Twelve Studies in Activity Theory.* Helsinki: Orienta-Konsutit Oy.

Entwistle, N. and Ramsden, P. (1983) *Understanding Student Learning.* London: Croom Helm.

Eraut, M. (1993) The characterisation and development of professional expertise, *Educational Management and Administration*, 21(4): 224–32.

Eraut, M. (1994) *Developing Professional Knowledge and Competence.* London: Falmer Press.

Eraut, M. (1995a) Developing professional knowledge within a client-centred orientation, in T.R. Guskey and M. Huberman (eds) *Professional Development in Education.* New York: Teachers' College Press.

Eraut, M. (1995b) Schön shock: a case for reframing reflection in action?, *Teachers and Teaching: Theory and Practice*, 1(1): 9–22.

Eraut, M. (1997) Perspectives on defining 'the learning society', *Journal of Education Policy*, 12(6): 551–8.

Erwin, T.D. (1995) Attending to assessment: a process for faculty, in P. Knight (ed.) *Assessment for Learning in Higher Education.* London: Kogan Page.

Evans, M. (1999) *Missing Persons: The Impossibility of Auto/biography.* London: Routledge.

Fairclough, N. (1992) *Discourse and Social Change.* Cambridge: Polity Press.

Fiedler, F.E. (1967) *A Theory of Leadership Effectiveness.* New York: McGraw-Hill.

Fiedler, F.E. and Chemers, M.M. with Mahar, L. (1976) *Improving Leadership Effectiveness: The Leader Match Concept.* New York: Wiley.

Flavell, J.H., Miller, P.H. and Miller, S.A. (1993) *Cognitive Development*, 3rd edn. Engelwood Cliffs, NJ: Prentice-Hall.

Fleming, N. (1999) Biases in marking students' written work, in S. Brown and A. Glasner (eds) *Assessment Matters in Higher Education.* Buckingham: SRHE/Open University Press.

Foucault, M. (1975) *Discipline and Punish.* Harmondsworth: Penguin.

Foucault, M. (1977) *The Archaeology of Knowledge.* London: Tavistock.

Fox, A. (1974) *Beyond Contract: Work, Power and Trust Relations.* London: Faber.

Fullan, M. (1989) Planning, doing, and coping with change, in B. Moon, P. Murphy and J. Raynor (eds) *Policies for the Curriculum.* London: Hodder and Stoughton.

Fullan, M. (1991) *The New Meaning of Educational Change.* London: Cassell.

Fullan, M. (1993) *Change Forces.* London: Falmer.

Fullan, M. (1999) *Change Forces: The Sequel.* London: Falmer.

Fullan, M. and Miles, M. (1992) Getting reform right: what works and what doesn't, *Phi Delta Kappan*, 73(10): 744–52.

Gee, J. and Lankshear, C. (1995) The new work order: critical language awareness and 'fast capitalism' texts, *Discourse: Studies in the Cultural Politics of Education*, 16(1): 5–20.

Gee, P.J., Hull, G. and Lankshear, C. (1996) *The New Work Order: Behind the Language of New Capitalism.* London: Allen & Unwin.

Gerth, H.H. and Mills, C.W. (1970) *From Max Weber: Essays in Sociology.* London: Routledge (first published 1948).

Gewirtz, S. (1998) Can all schools be successful? An exploration of the determinants of school success, *Oxford Review of Education*, 24(4): 439–58.

Gewirtz, S., Ball, S. and Bowe, R. (1995) *Markets, Choice and Equity in Education.* Buckingham: Open University Press.

Gherardi, S., Nicolini, D. and Odella, F. (1998) Towards a social understanding of how people learn in organizations: the notion of situated curriculum, *Management Learning Journal*, 29(3): 273–97.

Gibbons, M. (1997) Development of science and basic research: the implications of mode 2 science, in H. Etzkowitz and L. Leydesdorff (eds) *Universities and the Global Knowledge Economy: A Triple Helix of University–Industry–Government Relations*. London: Pinter.

Gibbons, M., Limoges, C., Nowotry, H. *et al.* (1994) *The New Production of Knowledge: The Dynamics of Science and Research in Contemporary Societies*. London: Sage.

Gibbs, G. (1995) Changing lecturer's conceptions of teaching and learning through action research, in A. Brew (ed.) *Directions in Staff Development*. Buckingham: SRHE/Open University Press.

Giddens, A. (1983) Comments on the theory of structuration, *Journal for the Theory of Social Behaviour*, 13: 75–80.

Glassick, C.E., Huber, M.T. and Maeroff, G.I. (1997) *Scholarship Assessed: Evaluation of the Professoriate*. San Francisco: Jossey-Bass.

Glover, D. and Miller, D. (1999) As others see us . . . perception of the work effectiveness of subject leaders, *School Leadership and Management*, 19(3): 331–44.

Gold, A. (1998) *Head of Department: Principles in Practice*. London: Cassell.

Goleman, D. (1996) *Emotional Intelligence*. London: Bloomsbury.

Goleman, D. (1998) *Working with Emotional Intelligence*. New York: Bantam Books.

Goodman, P. (1962) *The Community of Scholars*. New York: Random House.

Goodyear, P. (1995) Situated action and distributed knowledge: A JITOL perspective on EPSS, *Innovations in Education and Training International*, 32(1): 45–55.

Gray, J., Hopkins, D., Reynolds, D. *et al.* (1999) *Improving Schools: Performance and Potential*. Buckingham: Open University Press.

Grbich, C. (1998) The academic researcher: socialisation in settings previously dominated by teaching, *Higher Education*, 36: 67–85.

Greatorex, J. (1999) Generic descriptors: a health check, *Quality in Higher Education*, 5(2): 155–66.

Greenfield, T. and Ribbins, P. (eds) (1993) *Greenfield on Educational Administration: Towards a Humane Science*. London: Routledge.

Griffith, B.C. and Mullins, N.C. (1972) Coherent social groups in scientific change, *Science*, 177(4053): 956–64.

Grunert, J. (1997) *The College Syllabus*. Bolton, MA: Anker.

Guile, D. and Young, M. (1998) Apprenticeship as a conceptual basis for a social theory of learning, *Journal of Vocational Education and Training*, 50(2): 173–92.

Hackman, J.R. and Walton, R.E. (1986) Leading groups in organizations, in P.S. Goodman (ed.) *Designing Effective Workgroups*. San Francisco: Jossey-Bass.

Hales, C. (1993) *Managing through Organisation*. London: Routledge.

Halsey, A.H. (1992) *Decline of Donnish Dominion: The British Academic Professions in the Twentieth Century*. Oxford: Oxford University Press.

Handy, C. (1992) The language of leadership, in M.S. Syrett and C. Hogg (eds) *Frontiers of Leadership*. Oxford: Blackwell.

Hannan, A. (1980) Problems, conflicts and school policy: a case study of an innovative comprehensive school, *Collected Original Resources in Education*, 4(1).

Hargreaves, A. (1992) Contrived collegiality: the micropolitics of teacher collaboration, in N. Bennett, M. Crawford and C. Riches (eds) *Managing Change in Education: Individual and Organizational Perspectives*. London: Paul Chapman Publishers/Open University Press.

Hargreaves, A. (1998) The emotional practice of teaching, *Teaching and Teacher Education*, 14(8): 835–54.

Harré, R. (1998) *The Singular Self*. London: Sage.

Harris, A., Bennett, N. and Preedy, M. (eds) (1997) *Organizational Effectiveness and Improvement in Education*. Buckingham: Open University Press.

Hart-Landsberg, S., Braunger, J., Reder, S. and Cross, M. (1992) Learning the ropes: the social construction of work-based learning, *ERIC*, accession number 363726.

Harvey, L. and Knight, P.T. (1996) *Transforming Higher Education*. Buckingham: SRHE/Open University Press.

Heaney, S. (trans.) (1999) *Beowulf: A New Translation*. London: Faber and Faber.

Hecht, I.D., Higgerson, M.L., Gmelch, W.H. and Tucker, A. (1999) *The Department Chair as Academic Leader*. Phoenix, AZ: American Council on Education/Oryx Press.

HESA (Higher Education Statistics Agency) (1999) *Students in Higher Education Institutions*. Cheltenham: HESA.

Hicks, O. (2000) Integration of central and departmental development – reflections from Australian universities, *Journal of Academic Development*, 4(1): 43–51.

Higher Education Quality Council (HEQC) (1997) *Graduate Standards Programme: Final Report*. London: HEQC.

Hill, M. and Bramley, G. (1986) *Analysing Social Policy*. London: Blackwell.

Hodgkinson, C. (1991) *Educational Leadership: The Moral Art*. Albany, NY: State University of New York Press.

Hopkins, D. (1992) Changing school culture through development planning, in S. Riddell and S. Brown (eds) *School Effectiveness Research: Its Messages for School Improvement*. Edinburgh: HMSO.

Hounsell, D., McCulloch, M., Scott, M. *et al.* (1996) *The ASSHE Inventory*. Sheffield: Universities and Colleges Staff Development Agency.

Huber, R.M. (1992) *How Professors Play the Cat Guarding the Cream*. Fairfax, VA: George Mason University Press.

Huberman, M. (1993) *The Lives of Teachers*. London: Cassell.

Hudson, B. (1993) Michael Lipsky and street level bureaucracy: a neglected perspective, in M. Hill (ed.) *The Policy Process: A Reader*. London: Harvester Wheatsheaf.

Hunt, J.G. (1991) *Leadership: A New Synthesis*. Newbury Park, CA: Sage.

James, M. and Gipps, C. (1998) Broadening the basis for assessment to prevent the narrowing of curriculum, *Curriculum Journal*, 9(3): 285–98.

Jessop, B. (1989) Conservative regimes and the transition to post-Fordism: the cases of Britain and West Germany, in M. Gottdeiner and N. Komninos (eds) *Capitalist Development and Crisis Theory: Accumulation, Regulation and Spatial Restructuring*. London: Macmillan.

Joint Task Force on Student Learning (1998) *Powerful Partnerships: A Shared Responsibility for Learning*. Washington, DC: American Association for Higher Education, American College Personnel Association & National Association of Student Personnel Administrators.

Karpiak, I. (2000) The 'second call': faculty renewal and recommitment at midlife, *Quality in Higher Education*, 6(2): 125–34.

Katzenbach, R.R. and Smith, D.K. (1993) *The Wisdom of Teams: Creating the High Performance Organization*. Boston, MA: Harvard Business School.

Kennedy, D. (1997) *Academic Duty*. Cambridge, MA: Harvard University Press.

Kenny, S.S. (1998) *The Boyer Commission on Education. Reinventing Undergraduate Education: A Blueprint for America's Research Universities*. New York: State University of New York at Stony Brook.

Kickert, W. (1991) Steering at a distance: a new paradigm in public governance in Dutch higher education. Paper presented to the European Consortium for Political Research, March, University of Essex, Colchester.

Knight, P.T. (ed.) (1993) *The Audit and Appraisal of Teaching Quality in Higher Education.* Birmingham: SRHE and the Standing Conference on Educational Development.

Knight, P.T. (1995) *Records of Achievement in Higher and Further Education.* Lancaster: the Framework Press.

Knight, P.T. (1998) Professional obsolescence and continuing professional development in higher education, *Innovation in Education and Training International,* 35(3): 241–8.

Knight, P.T. (1999) Get the assessment right and everything else will follow?, *Quality in Higher Education,* 5(2): 101–5.

Knight, P.T. (2001) *Small-scale Research.* London: Sage.

Knight, P.T. and Trowler, P.R. (1999) It takes a village to raise a child, *Mentoring and Tutoring* 7(1): 23–34.

Knight, P.T. and Trowler, P.R. (2000a) Editorial, *Quality in Higher Education,* 6(2): 109–14.

Knight, P. and Trowler, P.R. (2000b) Department-level cultures and the improvement of learning and teaching, *Studies in Higher Education,* 25(1): 70–83.

Knight, P.T. and Wilcox, S. (1998) The ethics of staff and educational development, *International Journal of Academic Development,* 3(2): 97–106.

Knight, P.T., Aitken, N. and Rogerson, R. (2000) *Forever Better: Fine-tuning your Teaching Practices.* Oakland, OK: New Forums Press.

Knight, S. (1999) *Making Sense of NLP.* London: Institute of Personnel and Development.

Knowles, M. (1990) *The Adult Learner: A Neglected Species.* Houston, TX: Gulf.

Kosko, B. (1994) *Fuzzy Thinking.* London: HarperCollins.

Kotter, J.P. and Heskett, J.L. (1992) *Corporate Culture and Performance.* New York: The Free Press.

Kouzes, J.M. and Posner, B.Z. (1993) *Credibility: How Leaders Gain and Lose It, Why People Demand It.* San Francisco: Jossey-Bass.

Latham, G., Daghighi, S. and Locke, E. (1997) Implications of goal-setting theory for faculty motivation, in J. Bess (ed.) *Teaching Well and Liking It.* San Francisco: Jossey-Bass.

Laurillard, D. (1993) *Rethinking University Teaching.* London: Routledge.

Lave, J. (1988) *Cognition in Practice: Mind, Mathematics and Culture in Everyday Life.* Cambridge: Cambridge University Press.

Lave, J. (1993) The practice of learning, in S. Chaiklin and J. Lave (eds) *Understanding Practice.* Cambridge: Cambridge University Press.

Lave, J. and Wenger, E. (1991) *Situated Learning: Legitimate Peripheral Participation.* Cambridge: Cambridge University Press.

Law, S. and Glover, D. (2000) *Educational Leadership and Learning.* Buckingham: Open University Press.

Leithwood, K., Jantzi, D. and Steinbach, R. (1999) *Changing Leadership for Changing Times.* Buckingham: Open University Press.

Leslie, D.W. (ed.) (1999) The growing use of part-time faculty, *New Directions for Higher Education,* 44.

Letherby, G. (1996) Roles and relationships: issues of self and identity at home and at work. Paper presented at the Dilemmas of Mass Higher Education conference, April 10–12, Staffordshire University.

Levine, A. (1980) *Why Innovation Fails.* New York: State University of New York Press.

Lewin, R. and Regine, B. (1999) *The Soul at Work: Unleashing the Power of Complexity Science for Business Success.* London: Orion Business Books.

Lieberman, A. and McLaughlin, M. (1996) Networks for educational change, in M. McLaughlin and I. Oberman (eds) *Teacher Learning: New Policies, New Practices.* New York: Teachers' College Press.

Lindblom, C.E. (1959) The science of 'muddling through', *Public Administration,* 19: 79–99.

Lindquist, J. (1978) *Strategies for Change.* Berkeley, CA: Pacific Surroundings Press.

Lipsky, M. (1980) *Street Level Bureaucracy: Dilemmas of the Individual in Public Services.* Beverley Hills, CA: Sage.

Lucas, A.F. (1994) *Strengthening Departmental Leadership.* San Francisco: Jossey-Bass.

Lukes, S. (1974) *Power: A Radical View.* London: Macmillan.

Lukes, S. (1979) Power and authority, in T. Bottomore and R. Nisbet (eds) *A History of Sociological Analysis.* London: Heinemann.

Machiavelli, N. (1961) *The Prince,* G. Bull (trans.). Harmondsworth: Penguin (originally published 1514).

Maclean, D. (1996) Quick! Hide! Constructing a playground identity in the early weeks of school, *Language in Education,* 10(2&3): 171–86.

MacLeod, D. (2000) You've been warned, *Guardian Higher Education,* 25 January: 1.

Manz, C.C. and Sims, H.P. (1991) SuperLeadership: beyond the myth of heroic leadership, *Organizational Dynamics,* 19: 18–35.

March, J.G. and Olsen, J.P. (1975) Choice situations in loosely coupled worlds. Unpublished manuscript, Stanford University.

Martin, B. and Irvine, J. (1992) Government spending: trends in government spending on academic and related research. An international comparison, *Science and Public Policy,* 19: 211–219.

Marx, K. (1950) The eighteenth brumaire of Louis Bonaparte, in *Karl Marx and Frederick Engels: Selected Works in Two Volumes, Volume 1.* Moscow: Foreign Languages Publishing House.

Masland, A.T. (1985) Organisational culture in the study of higher education, *Review of Higher Education,* 8(2): 157–68.

Massy, W. (1997) Teaching and learning quality-process review: the Hong Kong programme, *Quality in Higher Education,* 3(3): 249–62.

McCulloch, G., Helsby, G. and Knight, P.T. (2000) *The Politics of Professionalism.* London: Cassell.

McGuinness, A.C. (1995) The changing relationships between the states and universities in the United States, *Higher Education Management,* 7(3): 263–79.

McInnis, C. (1996) Change and diversity in the work patterns of Australian academics, *Higher Education Management,* 8(2): 105–17.

McInnis, C. (2000) Changing academic work roles: the everyday realities challenging quality in teaching, *Quality in Higher Education,* 6(2): 115–24.

McLeod, S. and Jennings, J. (1990) Fit for the future, in M. Pedler, J. Burgoyne, T. Boydell and G. Welshman (eds) (1990) *Self Development in Organizations.* London: McGraw-Hill.

McNay, I. (1995) From collegial academy to corporate enterprise: the changing cultures of universities, in T. Schuller (ed.) *The Changing University?* Buckingham: SRHE/Open University Press.

McPherson, A. and Raab, C. (1988) *Governing Education: A Sociology of Policy since 1945.* Edinburgh: Edinburgh University Press.

Mead, G.H. (1913) The social self, *Journal of Philosophy, Psychology and Scientific Methods,* 10: 374–80.

Mead, G.H. (1934) *Mind, Self and Society.* Chicago: University of Chicago Press.

Menges, R. and associates (1999) *Faculty in New Jobs*. San Francisco: Jossey-Bass.

Mentowski, M., Astin, A., Ewell, P. and Moran, E.T. (1991) *Catching Theory up with Practice: Conceptual Frameworks for Assessment*. Washington, DC: AAHE Assessment Forum.

Metz, M.H. (1986) Sources of workers' subcultures in organizations: a case study of a public school faculty. Paper presented to the Annual Meeting of the American Sociological Association, Washington, DC, August.

Millett, J. (1962) *The Academic Community*. New York: McGraw-Hill.

Mitchell, J. (1997) Quantitative science and the definition of measurement in psychology, *British Journal of Psychology*, 88: 355–83.

Moon, J. (1998) *Reflection in Learning and Professional Development*. London: Kogan Page.

Morgan, G. (1997) *Images of Organization*, 2nd edn. Thousand Oaks, CA: Sage.

Mortimore, P., Sammons, P., Stoll, L., Lewis, D. and Ecob, R. (1988) *School Matters*. Wells: Open Books.

Munasinghe, L. and Jayawardena, P. (1999) Continuous quality improvement in higher education: a model for Sri Lanka, *Quality in Higher Education*, 5(1): 69–80.

Murphy, J. (1994) Transformational change and the evolving role of the principal, in J. Murphy and K. Seashore Louis (eds) *Reshaping the Principalship: Insights from Transformational Reform Efforts*. Newbury Park: Corwin Press.

National Committee of Inquiry into Higher Education (1997) *Higher Education in the Learning Society*. London: HMSO.

NCES (National Center for Education Statistics) (2000) The condition of education, http://nces.ed.gov/pubs99/condition99/indicator-49.html (accessed 16 November 2000).

Neave, G. (1997) The stirring of the prince and the silence of the lambs, in H. Etzkowitz and L. Leydersdorff (eds) *Universities and the Global Knowledge Economy: A Triple Helix of University–Industry–Government Relations*. London: Pinter.

Neave, G. (1998) The evaluative state revisited, *European Journal of Education*, 33(3): 265–84.

Nias, J., Southworth, G. and Yeomans, K. (1992) *Whole School Curriculum Development in the Primary School*. London: Routledge.

Nieva, V.F. and Gutek, B.A. (1981) *Women and Work: A Psychological Perspective*. New York: Praeger.

Nixon, J., Martin, J., McKeown, P. and Ranson, S. (1997) Towards a learning profession: changing codes of occupational practice within the new management of education, *British Journal of Sociology of Education*, 18(1): 5–28.

Nonaka, L. and Takeuchi, H. (1995) *The Knowledge-creating Company*. Oxford: Oxford University Press.

Northouse, P.G. (1997) *Leadership Theory and Practice*. London: Sage.

Nunes, T. and Bryant, P. (1996) *Children Doing Mathematics*. Oxford: Blackwell.

Ohlsson, S. (1996) Learning to do and learning to understand, in P. Reimenn and H. Spada (eds) *Learning in Humans and Machines*. London: Pergamon.

O'Neil, M.C. and Wright, A.W. (1996) *Recording Teaching Accomplishment: A Dalhousie Guide to the Teaching Dossier*, 5th edn. Halifax, Canada: Dalhousie University.

Ozga, J. (1999) *Policy Research in Educational Settings: Contested Terrain*. Buckingham: Open University Press.

Palincsar, A.S. (1989) Less charted waters, *Educational Researcher*, 18(4): 5–7.

Palomba, C.A. and Banta, T.W. (1999) *Assessment Essentials: Planning, Implementing and Improving Assessment in Higher Education*. San Francisco: Jossey-Bass.

Perkins, D. (1996) Minds in the 'hood, in B. Wilson (ed.) *Constructivist Learning Environments*. Englewood Cliffs, NJ: Educational Technology Press.

Perry, R. and Smart, J.C. (eds) (1997) *Effective Teaching in Higher Education*. New York: Agathon Press.

Perry, W.G. (1970) *Forms of Intellectual and Ethical Development*. New York: Holt, Rinehart and Winston.

Peters, T. (1994a) *In Pursuit of WOW!* London: Pan.

Peters, T. (1994b) *The Tom Peters Seminar: Crazy Times Call for Crazy Organizations*. New York: Vintage Books.

Peters, T. and Waterman, R. (1982) *In Search of Excellence*. New York: Harper and Row.

Peterson, C., Maier, S. and Seligman, M. (1993) *Learned Helplessness: A Theory for an Age of Personal Control*. New York: Oxford University Press.

Peterson, P.L. (1979) Direct instruction reconsidered, in P.L. Peterson and H.J. Wahlberg (eds) *Research on Teaching*. Berkeley, CA: McCutcheon.

Pintrich, P.R. and Schunk, D.H. (1996) *Motivation in Education*. Englewood Cliffs, NJ: Prentice-Hall.

Polanyi, M. (1983) *The Tacit Dimension*. Gloucester, MA: Peter Smith.

Popper, K.R. (1945) *The Open Society and its Enemies*. London: Routledge.

Powell, W. and DiMaggio, P.J. (1991) *The New Institutionalism in Organizational Analysis*. Chicago, IL: University of Chicago Press.

Price, M. and Rust, C. (1999) The experience of introducing a common criteria assessment grid across an academic department, *Quality in Higher Education*, 5(2): 133–44.

Prichard, C. (1999) Identity work – moving the 'theory of the subject' from 'division' to 'depth' in critical organizational analysis. Paper presented to the Critical Management Studies Conference, July, UMIST, Manchester.

Prosser, M. and Trigwell, K. (1999) *Understanding Learning and Teaching*. Buckingham: SRHE/Open University Press.

Putnam, H. (1995) *Pragmatism: An Open Question*. Oxford: Blackwell.

QAA (Quality Assurance Agency) (1998) *Quality Assurance in UK Higher Education: A Brief Guide*. Gloucester: QAA.

QAA (Quality Assurance Agency) Institutional Review Directorate (1998) Special Review of Thames Valley University: Conclusions and Recommendations. http://www.qaa.ac.uk/TVU/Conclusions.htm (accessed 24 January 2000).

Ramsden, P. (1998a) *Learning to Lead in Higher Education*. London: Routledge.

Ramsden, P. (1998b) Managing the effective university, *Higher Education Research and Development*, 17(3): 347–70.

Ramsden, P. and Moses, I. (1992) Association between research and teaching in Australian higher education, *Higher Education*, 23: 273–95.

Rein, M. (1983) *From Policy To Practice*. London: Macmillan.

Resnick, L.B. (1987) *Education and Learning to Think*. Washington, DC: National Academy Press.

Resnick, L.B. (1999) From aptitude to effort: a new foundation for our schools, *American Educator*, 23(1): 14–18.

Reynolds, J. and Saunders, M. (1987) Teacher responses to curriculum policy: beyond the 'delivery' metaphor, in J. Calderhead (ed.) *Exploring Teachers' Thinking*. London: Cassell.

Rhoades, G. (1997) *Managed Professionals: Restructuring Academic Labor in Unionized Institutions*. Albany, NY: State University of New York Press.

Rice, R.E. (1996) Making a place for the new American scholar, paper presented to AAHE Conference 'Faculty Roles and Rewards', 20 January 1996, Atlanta, GA.

Rittel, H. and Webber, M. (1973) Dilemmas in General Theory of Planning, *Policy Sciences*, 4: 155–69.

Robertson, D. (1994) *Choosing to Change*. London: Higher Education Quality Council.

Rosenholtz, S. (1989) *Teachers' Workplace*. New York: Macmillan.

Rudduck, J. (1991) *Innovation and Change*. Buckingham: Open University Press.

Sadler, D.R. (1989) Formative assessment and the design of instructional systems, *Instructional Science*, 18(2): 119–44.

Sambell, K. and McDowell, L. (1998) The construction of the hidden curriculum, *Assessment and Evaluation in Higher Education*, 23(4): 391–402.

Sammons, P., Hillman, J. and Mortimore, P. (1995) *Key Characteristics of Effective Schools: A Review of School Effectiveness Research*. London: Ofsted/Institute of Education.

Sammons, P., Thomas, S. and Mortimore, P. (1997) *Forging Links: Effective Schools and Effective Departments*. London: Paul Chapman.

Sammons, P., Thomas, S., Mortimore, P. and Walker, A. (1998) Practitioner views of effectiveness, *Improving Schools*, 1(1): 33–40.

Sarason, S. (1982) *The Culture of the School and the Problem of Change*. Boston, MA: Allyn and Bacon.

Sarros, J.C., Gmelch, W.H. and Tanewski, G.A. (1997) The role of the department head in Australian universities, *Higher Education Research and Development*, 16(3): 283–92.

Sarros, J.C., Gmelch, W.H. and Tanewski, G.A. (1998) The academic dean, *Higher Education Research and Development*, 17(1): 65–88.

Sayer, A. (1992) *Method in Social Science: A Realist Approach*, 2nd edn. London: Routledge.

Scardamalia, M. (2000) A design experiment for democratizing knowledge. Paper presented at The Open University, 12 January, Milton Keynes.

Schein, E.H. (1985) *Leadership and Organizational Culture*. San Francisco: Jossey-Bass.

Schein, E.H. (1999) Empowerment, coercive persuasion and organizational learning: do they connect? *The Learning Organization*, 6(4): 17–23.

Schön, D. (1971) *Beyond the Stable State*. New York: Norton.

Schön, D.A. (1987) *Educating the Reflective Practitioner*. San Francisco: Jossey-Bass.

Schuster, J. (1990) The need for fresh approaches to faculty renewal, in J. Schuster and D. Wheeler (eds) *Enhancing Faculty Careers: Strategies for Development and Renewal*. San Francisco: Jossey-Bass.

SCANS (Secretary of Labor's Commission on Achieving Necessary Skills) (1991) *What Work Requires of Schools: A SCANS Report for America 2000*. Washington, DC: US Department of Labor.

Seldin, P. and associates (1993) *Successful Use of Teaching Portfolios*. Bolton, MA: Anker Publishing.

Seligman, M. (1998) *Learned Optimism*. New York: Pocket Books.

Senge, P. (1990) *The Fifth Discipline*. New York: Doubleday.

Senge, P. (1994) *The Fifth Discipline Fieldbook*. London: Nicholas Brearley.

Sennett, R. (1999) *The Corrosion of Character*. New York: Norton.

Sims, H.P. and Lorenzi, P. (1992) *The New Leadership Paradigm*. Newbury Park, CA: Sage.

Siskin, L. (1994) *Realms of Knowledge*. London: Falmer Press.

Slaughter, S. and Leslie, L.L. (1997) *Academic Capitalism: Politics, Policies and the Entrepreneurial University*. Baltimore, MD: Johns Hopkins University Press.

Slowey, M. (1995) *Implementing Change from Within Universities and Colleges.* London: Kogan Page.

Smart, J.C. and Hamm, R.E. (1993) Organisational culture and effectiveness in two year colleges, *Research in Higher Education,* 34(1): 95–106.

Smircich, L. and Morgan, G. (1982) Leadership: the management of meaning, *Journal of Applied Behavioral Science,* 18: 257–73.

Smith, A. and Webster, F. (1997) *The Postmodern University?* Buckingham: SRHE/ Open University Press.

Smith, N. (ed.) (1982) *Mutual Knowledge.* New York/London: Academic Press.

Smylie, M. (1995) Teacher learning in the workplace, in T.R. Guskey and M. Huberman (eds) *Professional Development in Education.* New York: Teachers' College Press.

Smyth, J., Dow, A., Hattam, R., Reid, A. and Shacklock, G. (2000) *Teachers' Work in a Globalizing Economy.* London: Falmer.

Snell, R. and Chak, A. (1998) The learning organization: learning and empowerment for whom?, *Management Learning,* 29(3): 337–64.

Somekh, B. and Thaler, M. (1997) Contradictions of management theory, organisational cultures and the self, *Educational Action Research,* 5(1): 141–60.

Southworth, G. (1995) *Looking into Primary Headship.* Lewes: Falmer.

Southworth, G. (1999) Primary school leadership in England: policy, practice and theory, *School Leadership and Management,* 19(1): 49–65.

Spencer, L.M. and Spencer, S.M. (1993) *Competence at Work: Models for Superior Performance.* New York: Wiley.

Sproull, L. and Kiesler, S. (1991) A two-level perspective on electronic mail in organizations, *Journal of Organizational Computing,* 1(2): 125–34.

Stacey, R.D. (1996) *Complexity and Creativity in Organizations.* San Francisco: Bennett-Koehler Publishers.

Stenhouse, L. (1975) *An Introduction to Curriculum Research and Development.* London: Heinemann.

Stephenson, J. (1998) The concept of capability and its importance in higher education, in J. Stephenson and M. Yorke (eds) *Capability and Quality in Higher Education.* London: Kogan Page.

Sternberg, R.J. (1997) *Successful Intelligence.* New York: Plume.

Strauss, A. (1978) *Negotiations: Varieties, Contexts, Processes and Social Order.* San Francisco: Jossey-Bass.

Stroup, H.H. (1966) *Bureaucracy in Higher Education.* New York: Free Press.

Strydom, A. and Lategan, L. (1998) State of the art of quality assurance in South African Higher Education, *Quality in Higher Education,* 4(1): 73–84.

Svinicki, M.D., Hagen, A.S. and Meyer, D.K. (1996) How research on learning strengthens instruction, in R.J. Menges and M. Weimer (eds) *Teaching on Solid Ground.* San Francisco: Jossey-Bass.

Sykes, C.L. (1988) *Profscam: Professors and the Demise of Higher Education.* Washington, DC: Regnery Gateway.

Tait, H. and Godfrey, H. (1999) Defining and assessing competence in generic skills, *Quality in Higher Education,* 5(3): 243–54.

Taylor, P.G. (1999) *Making Sense of Academic Life: Academics, Universities and Change.* Buckingham: SRHE/Open University Press.

Teddie, C. and Reynolds, D. (2000) School effectiveness research and the social and behavioural sciences, in C. Teddie and D. Reynolds (eds) *The International Handbook of School Effectiveness Research.* London: Falmer Press.

Terenzini, P.T. (1998) Research and practice in undergraduate education. Paper presented at Kansas State University, Manhattan, KS.

Tierney, W. (1987) The semiotic aspects of leadership: an ethnographic perspective, *American Journal of Semiotics*, 5: 233–50.

Tierney, W. (1989) Symbolism and presidential perceptions, *The Review of Higher Education*, 12(2): 153–66.

Tierney, W. (1997) Organizational socialization in higher education, *Journal of Higher Education*, 68(1): 1–16.

Tierney, W. (2000) Dealing with deadwood, *The Department Chair*, 10(3): 1–3.

Tomlinson, P. (1999) Conscious reflection and implicit learning in teacher preparation. Part I: recent light on an old issue, *Oxford Review of Education*, 25(3): 405–20.

Tompkins, J. (1992) The way we live now, *Change*, 24(6): 12–19.

Toohey, S. (1999) *Designing Courses for Higher Education*. Buckingham: Open University Press.

Torrance, H. and Pryor, J. (1998) *Investigative Formative Assessment: Teaching, Learning and Assessment in the Classroom*. Buckingham: Open University Press.

Training Zone (2000) Embrace ignorance and incompetence argues Peter Senge as he kicks off HRD 2000, *The Learning Wire*, 96, 10 April http://www.trainingzone.co.uk/cgi-bin/item.cgi?id=14912&d=1 (accessed 1 August 2000).

Trigwell, K. and Prosser, M. (1997) Changing approaches to teaching: a relational perspective, *Studies in Higher Education*, 21(3): 275–84.

Tripp, S. (1996) Theories, traditions and situated learning, in H. McLellan (ed.) *Situated Learning Perspectives*. Englewood Cliffs, NJ: Educational Technology Publications.

Trotter, A. and Ellison, L. (1997) Understanding competence and competency, in B. Davies and L. Ellison (eds) *School Leadership for the 21st Century: A Competency and Knowledge-based Approach*. London: Routledge.

Trow, M. (1970) Reflections on the transition from mass to universal higher education, *Daedalus*, 90: 1–42.

Trow, M. (1972) *The Expansion and Transformation of Higher Education*. Berkeley, CA: General Learning Corporation.

Trowler, P.R. (1996) Angels in marble? Accrediting prior experiential learning in higher education, *Studies in Higher Education*, 21(1): 17–30.

Trowler, P.R. (1998) *Academics Responding to Change: New Higher Education Frameworks and Academic Cultures*. Buckingham: SRHE/Open University Press.

Trowler, P.R. (1999) Captured by the discourse? The socially constitutive power of new higher education discourse in the UK. Paper presented to Re-organizing Knowledge/Transforming Institutions conference, September 17–19, Amherst, Massachusetts.

Trowler, P.R. and Hinett, K. (1994) Implementing the recording of achievement in higher education, *Capability*, 1(1): 53–61.

Trowler, P.R. and Knight, P.T. (1999) Organizational socialization and induction in universities: reconceptualizing theory and practice, *Higher Education*, 37: 177–95.

Trowler, P.R. and Knight, P.T. (2000) Coming to know in higher education: theorising faculty entry to new work contexts, *Higher Education Research and Development*, 19(1): 27–42.

Trowler, P.R., Corker, M. and Turner, G. (1999) Exploring the hermeneutic foundations of university life: deaf academics in a hybrid community of practice. Paper presented to the SRHE annual conference, December, Manchester.

TTA (Teacher Training Agency) (1998) *National Standards for Headteachers.* London: TTA.

Tucker, A. (1993) *Chairing the Academic Department.* Phoenix, AZ: American Council on Education/Oryx Press.

Turner, C. and Bolam, R. (1998) Analysing the role of the subject head of department in secondary schools in England and Wales, *School Leadership and Management,* 18(3): 373–88.

Turpin, T. and Garrett-Jones, S. (1997) Innovation networks in Australia and China, in H. Etzkowitz and L. Leydesdorff (eds) *Universities and the Global Knowledge Economy: A Triple Helix of University–Industry–Government Relations.* London: Pinter.

Van Maanen, J. and Kunda, G. (eds) (1989) Real feelings: emotional expression and organizational culture, in B. Straw and L. Cummings (eds) *Research in Organizational Behaviour.* London: JAI Press.

Van Maanen, J. and Schein, E.H. (1979) Toward a theory of organizational socialization, in B.M. Straw (ed.) *Research in Organizational Behaviour, Vol. 1.* Greenwich, CT: JAI Press.

Vanderslice, V.J. (1988) Separating leadership from leaders: an assessment of the effect of leader and follower roles in organizations, *Human Relations,* 41(9): 677–96.

Vaughan, D. (1996) *The Challenger Launch Decision: Risky Technology, Culture and Deviance at NASA.* Chicago, IL: University of Chicago Press.

Walker, C.J. and Quinn, J.W. (1996) Fostering instructional vitality and motivation, in R.J. Menges and M. Weimer (eds) *Teaching on Solid Ground.* San Francisco: Jossey-Bass.

Walvoord, B.E. and Anderson, V.J. (1998) *Effective Grading: A Tool for Learning and Assessment.* San Francisco: Jossey-Bass.

Warren, B. (1998) On the curious notion of 'academic leadership': some philosophical considerations, *Higher Education Review,* 30(2): 50–69.

Watson, D. (2000) Managing in higher education: the 'wicked' issues, *Higher Education Quarterly,* 54(1): 5–21.

Webb, G. (1996) *Understanding Staff Development.* Buckingham: SRHE/Open University Press.

Weick, K. (1995) *Sensemaking in Organizations.* Thousand Oaks, CA: Sage.

Weick, K.E. and Westley, F. (1996) Organizational learning: affirming an oxymoron, in S. Clegg, C. Hardy and W.R. Nord (eds) *Handbook of Organizational Studies.* London: Sage.

Weil, S. (1994) *Introducing Change From the Top: 10 Personal Accounts.* London: Kogan Page.

Weimer, M. and Lenze, L.F. (1991) Instructional interventions: a review of the literature on efforts to improve instruction, in J.C. Smart (ed.) *Higher Education: A Handbook of Theory and Practice,* vol. 3. New York: Agathon.

Wenger, E. (1998) *Communities of Practice: Learning, Meaning and Identity.* Cambridge: Cambridge University Press.

Wertsch, J.V. (1985) *Vygotsky and the Social Formation of Mind.* Cambridge, MA: Harvard University Press.

Wess, R. (1991) *Leadership Secrets of Attila the Hun.* New York: Warner Books.

West, M. (2000) Supporting school improvement, *School Leadership and Management,* 20(1): 43–60.

Whitaker, P. (1993) *Managing Change in Schools.* Buckingham: Open University Press.

White, J. (1997) Philosophical perspectives on school effectiveness, *Curriculum Journal,* 8(1): 29–44.

Williams, G.L. (1995) The marketization of HE: reforms and potential reforms in HE finance, in D. Dill and B. Sporn (eds) *Emerging Patterns of Social Demand and University Reform: Through a Glass Darkly*. Oxford: IAU Press/Elsevier.

Willmott, H. (1993) Strength is ignorance; slavery is freedom: managing culture in modern organizations, *Journal of Management Studies*, 30(4): 515–52.

Wolcott, H. (1977) *Teachers Versus Technocrats: An Educational Innovation in Anthropological Perspective*. Oregon City, OR: University of Oregon Press.

Wolf, A., Harrison, A., Jones, P., Sylva, K. and Wakeford, R. (1997) *Assessment in Higher Education and the Role of 'Graduateness'*. London: HEQC.

Woods, P. (1995) *Creative Teachers in Primary Schools*. Buckingham: Open University Press.

Woods, P., Bagley, C. and Glatter, R. (1996) Dynamics of competition, in C. Pole and R. Chawla-Duggan (eds) *Reshaping Education in the 1990's: Perspectives on Secondary Schooling*. London: Falmer Press.

Woolf, H. and Cooper, A. with others (1999) Benchmarking academic standards in history: an empirical exercise, *Quality in Higher Education*, 5(2): 145–54.

Wright, W.A. and O'Neil, C. (1994) Teaching improvement practices: new perspectives, *To Improve the Academy*, 13: 5–36.

Wright, W.A. and Knight, P.T. with Pomerleau, N. (1999) Portfolio people: teaching and learning dossiers and the future of higher education, *Innovative Higher Education*, 24(2): 89–102.

Zaleznik, A. (1977) Managers and leaders: are they different?, *Harvard Business Review*, 55: 67–78.

Index

The Society for Research into Higher Education

The Society for Research into Higher Education (SRHE) exists to stimulate and coordinate research into all aspects of higher education. It aims to improve the quality of higher education through the encouragement of debate and publication on issues of policy, on the organization and management of higher education institutions, and on the curriculum, teaching and learning methods.

The Society is entirely independent and receives no subsidies, although individual events often receive sponsorship from business or industry. The Society is financed through corporate and individual subscriptions and has members from many parts of the world.

Under the imprint *SRHE & Open University Press*, the Society is a specialist publisher of research, having over 80 titles in print. In addition to *SRHE News*, the Society's newsletter, the Society publishes three journals: *Studies in Higher Education* (three issues a year), *Higher Education Quarterly* and *Research into Higher Education Abstracts* (three issues a year).

The Society runs frequent conferences, consultations, seminars and other events. The annual conference in December is organized at and with a higher education institution. There are a growing number of networks which focus on particular areas of interest, including:

Access	Learning Environment
Assessment	Legal Education
Consultants	Managing Innovation
Curriculum Development	New Technology for Learning
Eastern European	Postgraduate Issues
Educational Development Research	Quantitative Studies
FE/HE	Student Development
Funding	Vocation at Qualifications
Graduate Employment	

Benefits to members

Individual

• The opportunity to participate in the Society's networks

- Reduced rates for the annual conferences
- Free copies of *Research into Higher Education Abstracts*
- Reduced rates for *Studies in Higher Education*
- Reduced rates for *Higher Education Quarterly*
- Free copy of *Register of Members' Research Interests* – includes valuable reference material on research being pursued by the Society's members
- Free copy of occasional in-house publications, e.g. *The Thirtieth Anniversary Seminars Presented by the Vice-Presidents*
- Free copies of *SRHE News* which informs members of the Society's activities and provides a calendar of events, with additional material provided in regular mailings
- A 35 per cent discount on all SRHE/Open University Press books
- Access to HESA statistics for student members
- The opportunity for you to apply for the annual research grants
- Inclusion of your research in the *Register of Members' Research Interests*

Corporate

- Reduced rates for the annual conferences
- The opportunity for members of the Institution to attend SRHE's network events at reduced rates
- Free copies of *Research into Higher Education Abstracts*
- Free copies of *Studies in Higher Education*
- Free copies of *Register of Members' Research Interests* – includes valuable reference material on research being pursued by the Society's members
- Free copy of occasional in-house publications
- Free copies of *SRHE News*
- A 35 per cent discount on all SRHE/Open University Press books
- Access to HESA statistics for research for students of the Institution
- The opportunity for members of the Institution to submit applications for the Society's research grants
- The opportunity to work with the Society and co-host conferences
- The opportunity to include in the *Register of Members' Research Interests* your Institution's research into aspects of higher education

Membership details: SRHE, 3 Devonshire Street, London W1N 2BA, UK Tel: 020 7637 2766. Fax: 020 7637 2781. email: srhe@mailbox.ulcc.ac.uk world wide web: http://www.srhe.ac.uk./srhe/ *Catalogue*: SRHE & Open University Press, Celtic Court, 22 Ballmoor, Buckingham MK18 1XW. Tel: 01280 823388. Fax: 01280 823233. email: enquiries@openup.co.uk

ACADEMICS RESPONDING TO CHANGE
NEW HIGHER EDUCATION FRAMEWORKS AND ACADEMIC CULTURES

Paul R. Trowler

Paul R. Trowler takes a close look inside one British university to explore how academic staff at the ground level respond to changes in higher education. During the period of this study there was a remarkably rapid expansion in student numbers and, at the same time, a shrinking unit of resource. Meanwhile new systems and structures were being put in place, particularly those associated with the 'credit framework': the constellation of features associated with the assignment of credit value to assessed learning, including modularity, franchising and the accreditation of prior learning. The book explores the nature and effects of academics' responses to these changes and develops a framework for explaining these responses. It offers a valuable insight into change in higher education and highlights some of the processes which lead to policy outcomes being rather different from the intentions of policy-makers.

Contents
Introduction – Contexts – The credit framework – Responding to change – Policy and practice at the ground level – Reconceptualizing academic responses to change – New light on old issues – Conclusions and implications – Appendix: research issues – Glossary – Bibliography – Index.

208pp   0 335 19934 8 (Paperback)   0 335 19935 6 (Hardback)

TRANSFORMING HIGHER EDUCATION
Lee Harvey and Peter T. Knight

Several apparently contradictory forces have been at work on higher education in the last decade. The pressure to cut unit costs forces institutions to look at ways of teaching more students with the same or fewer resources and staff. Yet, at the same time, governments have launched a plethora of quality assurance measures, intended to ensure that cost-cutting does not compromise quality but, ideally, is accompanied by enhanced quality. These issues are not confined to the British higher education system: declining unit of resource, more accountable universities and massification of higher education are issues being faced by higher education systems across the world.

Transforming Higher Education asks:
• How should quality in higher education be conceptualized?
• How should quality be promoted?
• How can higher education be transformed so that student learning may also be transformed?

The theme of the book is that the drive for quality in Britain and elsewhere, and the reform of teaching and learning processes have not been connected, organizationally or in practice: change has been driven by the search for efficiency and by a quest for greater bureaucratic accountability. Harvey and Knight argue that, whatever the merits of these developments, they have not been directly concerned to improve the quality of student learning. They argue not just that student learning ought to be at the centre of discussions about quality enhancement, but that the goal ought to be transformation: transformation of universities with a view to transforming learners.

Contents
Quality and learning – Students and staff – Employers – Policy and accountability – External quality monitoring – Quality as transformation – A view of learning – Assessment for learning – Teaching – Professional development for transformative learning – Conclusions – References – Index.

224pp   0 335 19589 X (Paperback)   0 335 19590 3 (Hardback)

MANAGING THE ACADEMIC UNIT

Allan Bolton

As universities and colleges undergo significant change, then so do academic units (whether faculties, schools or departments) and the roles of their managers. *Managing the Academic Unit* explores these changes and tackles key issues such as devolution of responsibility, methods of decision making and formation of strategy. It is full of case study material which provides insider experience of, and practical advice for, running an academic unit. Allan Bolton gives guidance on key departmental concerns such as resource allocation, personnel, marketing, student recruitment, facilities and quality. He covers the varying needs of different academic units, from relatively well-developed and large schools to small departments and start-up operations. He also examines the qualities required of key players such as directors, deans, heads of department and faculty administrators, and presents ideas for improved induction and development opportunities for academic leaders.

Managing the Academic Unit is a key resource for actual and aspiring academic leaders. It provides both an overview and 'hands on' help for unit managers, and invites the 'head offices' of universities and colleges to reconsider ways to release the energy available in its academic units.

Contents

A world of change – Decision making – Allocating resources – Setting strategy – Staff roles – Business issues – Building a support team – Representing the unit – Benchmarking – Preparing to lead, manage and depart – Bibliography – Index.

176p   0 335 20404 X (Hardback)   0 335 20403 1 (Paperback)